THE WALL
ROME'S GREATEST FRONTIER

ALISTAIR
MOFFAT

BIRLINN

This edition first published in 2017 by
Birlinn Limited
West Newington House
10 Newington Road
Edinburgh
EH9 1QS

www.birlinn.co.uk

Reprinted in 2021

Originally published in hardback by Birlinn Ltd in 2008.

Copyright © Alistair Moffat 2008

ISBN: 978 1 78027 455 3

British Library Cataloguing-in-Publication Data
A catalogue record for this book is available from the British Library

Typeset by Hewer Text UK Ltd, Edinburgh

Printed and bound in Great Britain by Clays Ltd, Elcograf S.p.A.

Alistair Moffat was born and bred in the Scottish Borders and studied at the universities of St Andrews, Edinburgh and London. A former Director of the Edinburgh Festival Fringe, Director of Programmes at Scottish Television and founder of the Borders Book Festival, he is also the author of a number of highly acclaimed books. From 2011 to 2014 he was Rector of the University of St Andrews.

In memory of
Malcolm Thomas

Contents

Acknowledgements

Sandy Mackie – sorry, that's Mr Mackie – taught me history at Kelso High School, and he certainly made an impression. This is the fourteenth history book I have written. Perhaps at last he should be seen to shoulder some of the responsibility. I gladly accept all of the blame.

Hugh Andrew and his superb team at Birlinn are blameless, of course. Excellent publishers, with great enthusiasms, thorough professionalism and always up for a laugh; they have had a great deal to put up with. Thanks to all.

My agent, David Godwin, also puts up with me and as ever I am grateful for his sage advice. Thanks to him.

Liz Hanson has once again adorned a book with her perceptive photographs. I am glad to have supplied an extended caption. Many thanks.

Paddy Merrall and Graeme Thompson of ITV Border and ITV Tyne Tees respectively and jointly commissioned a TV series based on this book. I am grateful for their faith and confidence. Valerie Lyon directed the series with aplomb – and tact. It gave me the chance to make a journey along the Wall with my co-presenter, Tanni Grey Thompson, and with Paul Dobson, Allan Tarn, Paul Caddick, and Beth Moffat. It was great fun, and very informative. Thanks to all.

Robin, Patricia, Andrew and Tony Birley are simply an adornment to the Wall and its history. Robin, Pat and Andrew's stewardship of Vindolanda is inspirational and Tony Birley's scholarship exceptional. I am very grateful to all of them for their patience and kindness.

And to everyone who listened to my incessant moaning as I wrote this book, I apologise. I enjoyed the journey very much. This never became *that damned book* at any time in its writing. Hadrian's Wall is a fascinating subject, and I remain fascinated.

Alistair Moffat
Selkirk

List of Illustrations

The rubble core of the Wall at Walltown

The early turret at Walltown Crags

Milecastle, near Birdoswald

An impressive run of wall east of Birdoswald

Birdoswald Fort

Turret at Birdoswald

Poltross Burn milecastle, near Birdoswald

The garrison city of Dura Europos

Gonio, on the Black Sea coast in Georgia

Massive frontier defences along the Euphrates frontier at Halabiya, Syria

The superbly built stone *praetorium* at Halabiya

The frontier forts at Hallabat, Jordan

The Hunting Baths at Leptis Magna in Libya

The immense cistern at Rasafa

A magnificent stretch of Roman road behind Tarsus, Turkey

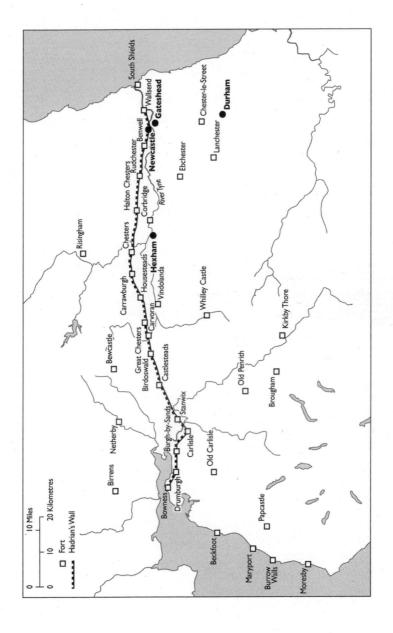

South Shields
Wallsend
Gateshead
Benwell
Rudchester
Newcastle
Halton Chesters
Corbridge
River Tyne
Ebchester
Chester-le-Street
Durham
Lanchester
Chesters
Risingham
Carrawburgh
Housesteads
Hexham
Carvoran
Vindolanda
Whilley Castle
Great Chesters
Birdoswald
Castlesteads
Kirkby Thore
Bewcastle
Stanwix
Burgh-by-Sands
Old Penrith
Brougham
Netherby
Carlisle
Old Carlisle
Birrens
Bowness
Drumburgh
Papcastle
Beckfoot
Maryport
Burrow Walls
Moresby

10 Miles
20 Kilometres

☐ Fort
▬▬ Hadrian's Wall

0   10
0   10   20

Preface

There is something about barricades, high ramparts overlooking long vistas, crenellated walkways patrolled by watchful soldiers, strong towers, formidable castles. Perhaps the attraction comes from years of television and film: American Indians charging across the plains, whooping and yelling, hurtling towards camera, loosing off arrows at the good guys safe behind the stockade; or baddies assaulting the walls of mighty castles while desperate defenders hurl everything and anything that comes to hand. Feeling safe inside from danger outside – probably a primitive instinct lurking in the shadows of many a subconscious.

Ramparts are attractive – and surely none more than Hadrian's Wall. There is nothing else remotely like it west of China, nothing bigger, grander, more masterful and more impressive. Standing on the Whin Sill at Housesteads Fort, looking over the northern moorland, perhaps scanning the horizon for a flicker of movement, or up at Walltown Crags, where the Wall glowers over grey Thirlwall Common, there is a sense of borrowed authority, of *let them come* or, to paraphrase a little, *let them gaze upon my works and despair*.

Even though it nowhere rises to its original height, and long stretches of it have disappeared, power pulses from Hadrian's Wall. Built by a culture galvanised by the will of one man, it is a miracle of self-aggrandisement and ancient disregard for practicalities. A mighty Wall which divides our island, devised by conquerors to limit their empire, it somehow still manages to play to the little boy and his toy soldiers in an imagined landscape.

Although it never marked a cultural frontier, or the line along which the border between England and Scotland would eventually run, Hadrian's Wall nevertheless had an important early role in creating an idea of the north of Britain. For almost three centuries, savagery and danger lay beyond it. The north was threatening while the south was sunlit, civilised, sophisticated. It is impossible to say when or how these notions came into play, but they are there, as surely as the Wall. And its story is fascinating.

Very little in what follows is original and much depends on the superb corpus of research and archaeology produced in the last sixty years. But there are differences of emphasis. The native British story of Hadrian's Wall cannot be easily told: neither the archaeology nor written sources exist in any quantity. Such records as do are gossamer scant, mostly allusory or opaque. But an attempt must be made. How the native peoples treated the Wall and its builders and garrison is a vitally important component too often relegated to the background, only faintly heard as mood music behind the onward march of the legions. After all, the native kings and their warriors had a motive role in persuading Hadrian to build a wall, and not just any barrier but a truly monumental solution to a serious military problem. The following pages attempt to find more of a role for the British, the ancestors of many of most of us.

Another difference in emphasis is prompted by the remarkable letters and lists found at the fort at Vindolanda which lies a kilometre or so to the south of the central sector of the Wall. These unique records predate the arrival of Hadrian and his builders in AD 122 by twenty years but they shine a brilliant light on the everyday lives of the Roman garrison in the north – and even occasionally have something to say about the natives. The Vindolanda letters and lists insist on a central place in any understanding of Hadrian's Wall.

Roman actions and attitudes are comparatively well documented and are rehearsed at some length at the beginning of the book. The where and the why of Hadrian's Wall is much better understood by building a detailed context, and a long preamble attempts that, beginning with the first contacts through Julius Caesar and his expeditions of 55 BC and 54 BC, and leading up to the invasion of the north under Agricola more than a century later. Caesar is the most famous Roman of them all, and even over two millennia his dash and bravery is unmistakable; he begins the story of the Wall.

Along the way the text contains many boxed items of information which seemed interesting, even important, in themselves but did not necessarily fit into the narrative. They can be read as asides, skipped and read later, or ignored. The last chapter is also not part of the narrative. Having spent a lot of time on Hadrian's Wall during the writing and research for this book, and knowing it reasonably well, it occurred to me that an itinerary taking in the places I enjoyed most might be more helpful than an exhaustive list of internet addresses and opening times. Others will have different views, but I found the visits to the places set out in the last chapter very pleasurable.

As I was finishing this book, in December 2007, my father-in-law, Malcolm Thomas, died. He had been a regular soldier, a man with many old-fashioned virtues and few old-fashioned opinions. Cawfields milecastle would have made him smile with recognition of its daftness, and the whole enterprise of building and garrisoning the Wall would have prompted perceptive and informed comments. I am sorry not to have them, and out of the greatest respect and affection, this book is dedicated to his memory.

1

Caesar, Claudius and the Elephants

It was midnight before the wind turned. All day the soldiers of the VII and the X Legions had been embarking onto the transport ships. Only eighty were assembled in the harbour at Boulogne, and more than 100 men in full armour, carrying all their weapons and kit, had been crammed onto the decks of each ship. Legionaries were much happier tramping the metalled roads of the fast-expanding Roman Empire and may well have been apprehensive as their heavily laden ships bobbed at anchor, waiting for the entire expedition to be ready to sail. They faced a journey into the unknown, a voyage across the Ocean, a real danger of being swept out into the vastness of the open sea.

As evening approached and a waxing moon rose in the sky, the sea-captains at last made ready and hoisted sails to catch the freshening wind. It would, it should, blow the invasion fleet on a north-westerly course across the Channel. In the moonshine, lookouts hoped soon to make out the white cliffs of Britannia, luminous in the summer dark, and use them as a sea-mark to guide their steersmen. The late August of 55 BC, the 25th, was indeed late to be mounting such an audacious expedition, but Julius Caesar was indeed an audacious general.

Most of the staff officers and their daring commander sailed on warships, and they led the fleet out of the safety of Boulogne and the calm estuary of the River Liane. Powered by banks of oars, they depended a little less on the vagaries of the elements than the eighteen transports which had been allocated the more awkward business of taking a force of 500 cavalrymen across the Channel. Their embarkation had been delayed and, in order to catch up, the troopers rode north, up the coast road to Ambleteuse where they again failed to embark and join the main fleet. The wind and the tide had turned against them.

Caesar pressed on and, by dawn, his lookouts will have seen the ghostly shapes of the white cliffs looming out of the grey light. From East Wear Bay and around the blunt headland at South Foreland, the high chalk cliffs were often sailors' first sight of Britain. By mid morning the little harbour at Dover had come into view. But there was no possibility of a landing. Strung out along the cliffs overlooking the harbour were thousands of British warriors. Battle-horns blaring, weapons rattling against their shields, chariots drawn up, the war-bands of the southern kings had come to defend their island, roaring defiance across the waves.

LANDS LOST AND FOUND

Climate change in ancient times is difficult to discern but sea-levels appear to have fluctuated a good deal. Calais and its harbour are much nearer the Kentish coast than Boulogne, and on a clear day the white cliffs can often be made out. So why did the Romans prefer to sail from Boulogne? Because in 55 BC and AD 43 Calais and the area around it was under the sea. Now 40 kilometres inland, St Omer was then on the coast of Gaul. The English coastline also looked very different. Romney Marshes was probably under water in the winter and a waterlogged, impenetrable waste in the summer. East of Beachy Head a shallow bay cut inland where the town of Pevensey now stands. The Thames estuary had many more large islands, including Thanet, and further up the North Sea coast, the Wash reached down to Cambridge – and the Isle of Ely really was an island.

If Dover had indeed been his preferred destination, then Caesar will have been unpleasantly surprised. The massing of two legions and the gathering of an invasion fleet at Boulogne could have been no secret. When Caesar's plans had first become known in Britain, some native kings had sent ambassadors across the Channel. They pledged obedience to Rome and promised hostages to guarantee it. Commius, a king with some authority and influence in both Britain and northern Gaul, was despatched back to Britain with the ambassadors and a brief to negotiate on Caesar's behalf. Peaceful submission was always preferable, cheaper, and almost as glorious as victory in war. It may have been Caesar's objective to visit Britain with an appropriate show of strength, accept promises of loyalty, and then leave without a blow being struck. But on arrival Commius was immediately arrested and the detail of Rome's plans presumably extracted. When he saw the British kings and their warriors in battle order, arrayed along the ramparts of the white cliffs, Caesar may well have had to change those plans.

Riding at anchor in the roadsteads off Dover, the Roman warships waited until the whole fleet had come together. The heavily laden transports had made slower headway. On board his flagship Caesar held a council of war, some time in the early afternoon. In the weeks before the expedition sailed, he had sent Caius Volusenus on a reconnaissance, his warship nosing along the Kentish coast looking for good landing sites. It seems that the Romans knew that the white cliffs gave way to beaches north-east of Dover, in Sandwich Bay. As the fleet weighed anchor and made for the new landing sites, the British army shadowed it up the coast.

Somewhere near Deal, Caesar signalled his captains to steer straight and fast for the shore and run their warships up onto the beaches. They carried artillery, and arrows, slingshot and crossbow bolts could be brought to bear on the British. When the troop transports attempted to rasp up onto the shore, their weight and deep draught prevented them from getting close enough. The sea-bed shelved away steeply into the Channel, and fully armed legionaries were reluctant to jump into deep water. Their kit weighed them down and they were forced to wade a long way before they could defend themselves from British missiles. Men who did risk the deep water were fighting their way ashore in small groups only, failing to form up into the disciplined close order which could be so effective on the battlefield.

Humiliation stared hard at Caesar and his legions. And then, as sometimes happened in battle, an example of extraordinary individual bravery proved decisive. Here is Caesar's own account:

And then, when our soldiers were still hanging back, mainly because of the depth of the water, the standard-bearer of the Tenth offered up a quick prayer and then shouted out, 'Jump down, soldiers, unless you want to give up your eagle to the enemy; everyone will know that I at least did my duty to the Republic and my commander!' After saying this in a loud voice he jumped off the ship and began carrying the eagle standard towards the enemy. Then our soldiers called out to each other not to allow so terrible a disgrace [as to lose the standard] and leapt down from the transport. When those on the nearby ships saw them, they followed and began to close with the enemy.

In the long and narrow confines of the beach, the legionaries gradually formed a line and pushed forward. Behind the battle, watching from his warship, Caesar could see where his men needed reinforcements. Using rowing boats, he sent small detachments to wherever weak points threatened. Closing into a tight line, protected by their long, curved shields, thrusting with their short swords, the VII and X Legions gained control.

Chasing the Roman fleet up the Channel coast to the beach landing had meant that most of the British infantry had been left behind, and their cavalry and charioteers were finding it difficult to match the well-armoured and disciplined ranks of the invaders. As the battle wore on, more and more men landed safely and the British kings signalled a retreat.

Not for the first time in this short campaign, Caesar was lucky. Although his attempts at preparatory diplomacy had failed badly and Volusenus' reconnaissance seems to have been sadly deficient, Caesar's famous luck had held. But it was seen as more than luck by his soldiers: it was a sign of the gods' favour. *Well-omened* is a clumsy alternative meaning for the Latin *felix*, or lucky, but it conveys something of how it was understood. Luck did not come from nowhere.

Once the beach had been cleared, Caesar's tactical instinct would have been to pursue the British inland and inflict as heavy a defeat as possible. Most casualties in battle came in the aftermath when men were cut down as they fled. But the cavalry had still not arrived, and so Caesar was forced to secure only the immediate hinterland. Having fought long and hard, probably into the evening, the legionaries were forced to set to and build a marching camp on the beachhead to protect their position.

Beyond the freshly dug ditches and ramparts an unknown land stretched far to the north. From the Greek traveller Pytheas of Massilia, and other writers, the Romans knew that Britain was a large and long island. But it lay on the far side of the dangerous Ocean and, as the legionaries lay down exhausted in their leather tents, they will have wondered what the morning would hold.

TOUGH LOVE

A legionary's training, experience, uniform and kit combined into a valuable investment, which Rome took care of. When her armies took the field, doctors and first-aid orderlies were right behind them. *Medici*, legionary doctors, carried a bag full of evil-looking instruments: fierce forceps, razor-sharp scalpels, hooks and clamps were all designed to deal with puncture wounds (and the removal of foreign bodies such as arrowheads), severe cuts and bone breaks. The doctors knew that the minutes immediately following a bad wound were critical, and their orderlies, *capsarii*, carried bandages to staunch heavy bleeding on the battlefield so that injured men could be safely removed behind the lines, where the *medici* set to work with their toolkit of alarming instruments. There was no anaesthetic, but more importantly no antibiotic. What the *medici* feared most was the onset of infection and, unlike modern doctors – and patients – they did not care at all if they inflicted pain as they cut away damaged tissue or cleaned out bad wounds. In fact, it would help if the agony caused a man to faint.

In the ranks of Celtic armies, medical help is not recorded, and no recognisable surgical instruments have yet been found. But the principles and practices of Celtic medicine have survived. Although the witch hunts of the sixteenth and seventeenth centuries had the effect of wiping out much of Britain's so-called 'folk medicine' – the herbal and traditional cures passed down through uncounted generations – in the Highlands of Scotland the Gaelic language protected the knowledge. The Celtic *materia medica* was used in very sophisticated ways: for example, decoctions and infusions of herbal drinks were given as anaesthetics; instead of injections, poultices were made up and applied where the skin is thinnest, under the armpits and in the groin. (St Columba famously applied a soothing poultice to a young monk by placing it in his armpit.) But, despite the medical care, Roman and Celtic soldiers fought in the knowledge that even the slightest wound could kill and that most men did not die outright in battle but in a lingering agony hours, days or weeks afterwards.

In the middle of the first century BC Britain was a shifting patch-work of small kingdoms, each with its own political interests and priorities. Rome seemed a colossus by comparison, a juggernaut which had rolled over the vast territory of Gaul. Some Britons had crossed the Ocean to fight against Caesar's legions alongside their Gallic neighbours, many knew that Rome was a world power, capable of any action, no matter how merciless, in pursuit of its aims. Still more will have seen the Empire as a golden opportunity. The trickle of luxury goods which had come into Britain from the Mediterranean spoke of wealth and glamour, and a much wider world.

For whatever reason the British kings did not attack again. Instead their envoys sought peace, promising hostages and freeing Commius, possibly in the hope that he might mediate. The British army, mostly levied from farms and settlements, melted back into the countryside leaving the native kings with only their warbands and charioteers.

BATTLELINES

Roman infantry training was tough. Those who failed to follow commands properly or show sufficient stamina were punished by being put on poor rations, which seemed to consist of a foul-smelling barley porridge. But it was vital that soldiers reacted instantly to commands in the heat and noise of battle. Roman legionaries had five basic formations. A single battleline was most common and, through its shield-wall, spears and short swords bristled. A double line was sometimes called to withstand the weight of a charge. There was also a square, not unlike that used by British armies in the eighteenth and early nineteenth centuries. The flying wedge was used in attack. Probably led by a centurion, a wedge charged at an enemy line and tried to smash through it, widening the breaking point as the wedge went in. Most famous was the *testudo*, the tortoise, with shields held overhead and to the sides. It was said that its strength was tested by having carts driven over it.

Four days after the battle on the beach, lookouts at last sighted the cavalry transports. Five hundred troopers would transform Caesar's options. But a storm blew down the Channel and prevented the transports from landing, and a high tide had an even more devastating impact. It refloated the beached transports: some smashed into each other and onto the shore, others were swept out to sea. Suddenly Caesar's expedition found itself dangerously exposed. The legionaries had brought little in the way of supplies, and food was fast running out. They were stranded, unable to get off the island and back to the sanctuary of Gaul. Seeing at first hand all that happened, the British envoys in the Romans' camp stole away quietly to inform their kings that the gods were smiling.

Forced to send out forage parties into the Kent countryside to find food, Caesar was in a very precarious position. But once again luck and good soldiering came to the rescue. As the VII Legion was harvesting fields of ripe wheat, a British ambush erupted out of nearby woods. The Romans, many of them armed only with sickles, were quickly surrounded by charioteers and cavalry. Very fortunately a sharp-eyed lookout at a forward watchtower saw a cloud of dust rise in the distance, in the direction the VII Legion had gone. It was too much dust for marching men to make and Caesar quickly realised what had happened. With a small troop of riders brought by Commius, and his own men, he dashed to the rescue. With only a thousand men, a potentially disastrous outcome was averted. But more trouble was coming.

The British kings massed their host again and attacked the beach-head camp. The legions had time to form up in battle order outside the rampart and, in the close-quarter fighting which followed, the British were driven back and defeated. This time Caesar did not delay. Most of the transports had been repaired and the legions squeezed onto them and sailed back to Gaul. Hostages had been demanded but Caesar did not wait for them to be delivered. September often saw bad weather in the Channel – and enough risks had already been taken to stretch the favour of the gods beyond breaking point.

News of Caesar's expedition electrified public opinion in Rome. What had in reality been a lucky escape from near disaster became a propaganda triumph. Rome had reached out to the very ends of the Earth. Her armies had crossed the dangers and mysteries of the Ocean and subdued the savage primitives who lived at the edge of the world. The Senate rejoiced and voted twenty days of public thanksgiving, five more than for the much more significant conquest of Gaul. Caesar's many enemies were silenced. Marcus Porcius Cato embodied all of the stern old Republican virtues of honour and fairness, while attacking what he saw as Caesar's wild ambition – a man who would be king! – and his disregard for the law. He probably spoke against him in the same Senate meeting which voted for the thanksgiving, and was probably drowned out by catcalls and insults. Pompey and Crassus, both rivals and immensely powerful and wealthy, had been elected consuls, the leading political offices in the Roman constitution, in 55 BC. But Caesar's coup in reaching Britain, as far from Rome as it seemed possible to be, eclipsed them. How they must have seethed amid the celebrations.

CAMPS AND FORTS

Roman camps were usually temporary defended bivouacs thrown up by a detachment of soldiers at the end of a day's march. A Roman fort was more permanent and the Latin word for it, *castellum*, is the root of our 'castle'. Both camps and forts were laid out on a standard grid pattern on a reasonably flat site near a water source. Milecastles were small forts positioned at intervals of exactly one mile along a Roman wall. On Hadrian's Wall, Cawfields milecastle is a monument to Roman uniformity and obstinacy. The site slopes steeply and must have been very rocky, but it was exactly one Roman mile from its neighbours on either side. Cawfield's nothern gateway opens onto a sheer drop. There is a much better and flatter site 30 metres further to the west. But no, if it had to be a mile, exactly a mile from the next one, well, that was were it had to go.

The reaction to the expedition has much to say about the political atmosphere of the times. Britain began to occupy a special place in the collective imagination of Rome. Roman legions could march around the shores of the Mediterranean, to the deserts of the east, and north into the dark forests of Germany. But to reach across the Ocean at the edge of the world, to land and defeat the warriors of Britain, showed Rome at her very boldest and mightiest. Nowhere and nothing was beyond her power.

By the early years of the reign of Augustus, the first emperor and Julius Caesar's heir, the expansion of the Empire had found divine support. The poet Virgil put these words in the mouth of Jupiter, Rome's supreme god:

I set upon the Romans bounds neither of space nor of time: I have
bestowed upon them empire without limit . . . to impose the ways of
peace, to spare the defeated, and to crush those proud men who will
not submit.

TOFFS AND PLEBS

The Roman constitution evolved over an immense period and was
very complex. It is the most likely extended explanation of why it
was that Rome, an otherwise inconsequential central Italian settlement, came to be the pre-eminent European power for five hundred
years, whose influence lasted long after its decline. Originally the
city was governed by kings. Their tyrannical behaviour prompted a
coup d'état, and from around 500 BC they were replaced by two
elected magistrates known as consuls. Roman society remained
rigidly hierarchical, and the consulship was at first the exclusive
preserve of the patrician families, an aristocracy which had retained
power despite the demise of the kings. They made up the member-
ship of the Senate, originally an advisory council of elders (the name
derives from *senex*, Latin for 'an old man'). Other magistracies
developed. Praetors were one step down from consuls, and below
them aediles had legal power inside the city of Rome. The most
junior magistrates were quaestors. As Rome grew, its patricians
were forced to cede some power to the poorer citizens, the plebs.
They could turn to a Tribune of the Plebs, who had the right to veto
legislation. In times of emergency, one man could be appointed
dictator, with absolute power for a term of six months. Religious
affairs were in the care of the Pontifex Maximus, and below him
and the others a forest of minor offices grew. The lawyer and orator
Cicero developed the idea of the *cursus honorum*, a career path for
ambitious men. But by then it was a bit too late. Once Augustus had
established the power of the emperors, all of these magistracies
became more or less honorific. The years were still named after the
consuls who held office and, as with the modern honours system in
Britain, people enjoyed fancy titles. Augustus obliged by having
consuls elected for only a part of the year so that more men could
hold the largely meaningless office.

All of this boundless, supposedly god-given ambition was founded on a remarkable phenomenon – the Roman army. One historian has characterised the history of the Republic and the Empire as the long, drawn-out and ultimately unsuccessful process of political institutions attempting to keep pace with the extraordinary and continuing string of victories won by Rome's soldiers.

They won because they were different. Every army that Rome faced in western Europe and around the Mediterranean was largely re-cruited from amateurs, part-time soldiers with an obligation to fight when their aristocracy called upon them. Great hosts were mustered against the legions, often out-numbering them by many times, but they were comparatively poorly equipped, untrained, frightened farmers doing their duty. Rome's army was professional. Killing was its business. Its soldiers were well paid, well trained, well armed and very experienced. When the VII and X Legions faced the warhorns, the hail of insults and the massed ranks of the British army in Kent in 55 BC, they will not have blinked. In Gaul and elsewhere the legionaries had seen it all before. If they kept their discipline, remembered their training and fought as a unit, they would cut these hollering savages to pieces. And, almost always, they did.

It was the long drive for empire which forged the Roman army into a highly professional and deadly force. After Africa, Spain, Greece and Asia Minor had been conquered, the urgent need for an efficient, and permanent, military capability was recognised by the great general Gaius Marius. In 107 BC he was elected consul and immediately abolished the outdated property qualification needed to fight in the army. From landless men and his own supporters, Marius began recruiting full-time soldiers. Many signed up for sixteen years, an unheard-of commitment, and in that time grew experienced and hardy. Training became mandatory, equipment better and standar-dised, and clear organisation was imposed.

Like all talented tacticians, Marius saw mobility as a key to victorious campaigning. From the moment they joined their units, Roman soldiers were trained to march. For four months centurions put them through intensive square-bashing so that they instinctively marched in step and reacted instantly to commands. In battle this sort of collective con-ditioning could be crucial. To arrive at the battlefield quickly and in good order, recruits were put through a punishing schedule of route marching. Once trainee legionaries could march 30 kilometres in five hours, they were appalled to discover that they needed to maintain the same speed – but in full armour and carrying all their kit and equipment. On average this weighed about 50 kilograms. Before Marius' reforms, the Roman army had been followed – and slowed down – by a baggage train of mules. After 107 BC the legionaries carried everything and began to call themselves Marius' Mules.

CARRY ON, SERGEANT

Roman soldiers spent most of their time not fighting. Many were skilled tradesmen able to apply themselves to a wide variety of tasks. The most hated peace-time job was road-building. And in the early years of the province of Britain there was a great deal of that to do. Many men got out of breaking roadstone, digging ditches and laying paving by developing other skills and no doubt sucking up to officers. For example, if they found an inside job as a clerk, they moved from being a mere *miles*, or soldier, to becoming an *immunis*. The next step up the ladder was to the rank of *principales*, the lance-corporals of the Roman army. That meant one and a half times the pay of, say, an orderly in a century. Standard-bearers and *optiones* (second-in-command of a century – roughly equivalent to a sergeant) were on double pay and centurions got even more. In a legion of roughly 4,800 men there were ten cohorts. The first contained five double centuries and the remaining nine had six centuries each. The best that a common soldier could do in his legion was to rise to the rank of *primus pilus*, literally, the first spear, and in reality the senior centurion. Aristocrats held a mono- poly on high command. The legate who led a legion was usually a senator, and his six staff officers were men from patrician families setting out on a career.

Weaponry evolved and adapted at the same time. Most conscript armies, especially those raised amongst the Celtic peoples of Europe, used their large numbers in a simple but effective tactic – the furious charge. It worked for millennia, even after the introduction of muskets and cannons, and was last seen on British soil as late as 1746 at Culloden Moor. The Roman response was the javelin. Carried by each legionary, it had a long, slim and very sharp point attached to a wooden haft. As the enemy ran within range, a dense volley was thrown. Javelins broke up a charge but were not accurate enough to halt it. By the time survivors reached Roman battlelines, shields had locked together and the short sword known as the *gladius* was drawn. No more than 60 centimetres long, it was much more effective in close-quarter fighting than the long, slashing sword used by Celtic warriors. Thrusting, stabbing, pushing and staying together in a tight formation, the legions literally rolled over their enemies. Winning again and again, marching long distances quickly, Roman armies dominated western European warfare for 500 years.

As professional soldiers who trained, lived, fought and died together, the legionaries developed a tremendously powerful *esprit de corps*. The sort of bravery shown by the standard-bearer of the X Legion on the Kentish beaches was by no means unusual. Three years later, Caesar's men led an abortive attack in the Gaulish rebellion led by Vercingetorix. At Gergovia they were forced to retreat downhill and could have suffered terrible casualties. But the centurions of the VII and X Legions made a line and fought a brave rearguard action to allow their men down the slopes to safety. Forty-six centurions fell, but they prevented a disaster. Almost always the toughest soldiers in a legion and used to leading from the front, these men stood fast on the slopes at Gergovia, prepared to buy the safety of their comrades with their lives.

After the Marian reforms, loyalty became an immensely powerful bond, but it was loyalty to their generals which mattered to soldiers, far more than any loyalty to Rome itself. The state paid and equipped their legionaries but crucially, and catastrophically, refused to make any provision for their discharge or retirement. Instead commanders like Marius, Caesar, Pompey and Crassus bound their soldiers to themselves personally by promising to provide for each one of them when their army service was over. This was always expensive, and the need for cash to pay for veterans' retirement, land for them to settle on and booty to help them enrich themselves was one of the most important motives behind continuing conquest.

Roman law was surprisingly inexact when it came to be applied to what the historian Tacitus called the *pretium victoriae*, the wages of victory. This vagueness allowed Caesar and others to become fabulously wealthy as they, nominally at least, acted in the interests of the state. When Gaul was overrun, fortunes were made and as the legions advanced they knew that military success would bring them booty now and a guaranteed retirement later. Their success bound them ever more closely to the likes of Caesar and also gave them powerful incentives to fight hard and earn the wages of victory.

TALKING MACHINES

The unseen, unheard and rarely recorded hands, muscles and brains which underpinned Roman society belonged to the vast number of slaves who lived all over the Empire. In Italy alone in the first century AD, it is thought that there were more than three million. With no rights of any kind, they were treated as objects, an *instrumentum vocale*, a talking tool, or, more brutally, a *res*, a thing. On Greek pottery, their distinctive shaved heads contrast with the aristocrats they are serving. A slave collar found around the neck of a skeleton carried the message 'If captured return me to Apronianus, minister in the imperial palace . . . for I am a runaway slave.' The Roman legal system only allowed slaves to give evidence if they had first been tortured. Otherwise what they said was thought to be inherently unreliable. Roman soldiers had slaves, and Britain was seen as an excellent source. A beautifully made iron chain with collars attached was found at Llyn Cerrig Bach on Anglesey. It had been designed to restrain a chain gang of five and it shows that native British aristocrats also had slaves.

Momentum developed naturally. It is difficult to discern much in the way of coherent policy from the Senate in Rome. The Empire expanded through accident and opportunism, but also because great men wished to become even greater. In Rome there was no meaningful distinction between soldiers and politicians. Senators led legions, generals were senators. Military and political success were largely the same thing. Julius Caesar needed to turn his attention to Britain because he had conquered Gaul. Like a shark he had constantly to move forward.

The reaction in Rome to what amounted to little more than an armed reconnaissance in 55 BC, and the loose ends left when the legions departed quickly, meant that Caesar had to return to Britain. A year was a very long time in politics, and a fresh expedition, perhaps a sustained conquest of the fabled island, would keep his name in the limelight. And, to feed Caesar's coffers, there might be more tangible rewards. The imperial economy had an insatiable appetite for slaves, and war always produced plenty. Britain had mineral wealth: tin certainly, lead, and perhaps gold and silver. Corn was less shiny but always welcome to the quartermasters of the huge army in Gaul and the Rhine basin. But in truth it was prestige, the promise of glory, which drew Caesar back to the shores of the Channel.

During the winter some tactical lessons were learned. Transports were designed differently. More than 600 were built with a shallow draught to allow them to be beached more easily. To augment their sails and make them more manoeuvrable, banks of oars were added on each side. These modifications were important because the new expedition was planned on an altogether different scale. Five legions and 2,000 cavalry troopers would cross the Ocean in the summer of 54 BC. And Britain's defenders could not hope to match such a force once they had gained the safety of the shore. But they had to gain it without all the problems of the previous year. Significantly several private vessels were to accompany the fleet. Merchants perhaps, people who hoped to profit from an assured success.

Archaeologists have not yet found the site of Caesar's second landing, but it is likely to have been close to the first, on the beaches near Deal. Once ashore, Caesar attacked immediately. Having learned that the British had retreated inland, probably at the approach of such a large invasion force, he pursued them hard. With four legions, including the VII and the X, more than 20,000 men and 1,700 cavalry, Caesar at last found part of the British army drawn up behind a river. It was probably the Stour near modern Canterbury. The bulk of the native forces had taken up a defensive position behind the ramparts of a hillfort, almost certainly at Bigbury.

After his cavalry had scattered the skirmishers along the riverbank, Caesar launched the VII Legion in an assault on the fort. Under the protection of the testudo formation, where the legionaries locked their shields over their heads and sides to form a protective shell, the VII built a ramp up to the walls. After a sharp attack, the British fled. Sending his cavalry in only a brief pursuit, Caesar had his men build a marching camp. From there they began the business of subduing the countryside.

So far, so good. But familiar problems surfaced back at the base-camp on the Kentish coast. Despite the redesign of the transports and all the hard-learned lessons of the previous expedition, the same mistakes were made. Left riding at anchor out in the Channel road-steads, the transport fleet was badly damaged in a storm. Belatedly, a huge ship-camp was dug and the fleet beached well above the high tideline. The new fort took ten days to raise.

Meanwhile the British kings had held a council and managed to suppress their differences in the face of the Roman threat. Cassivellaunus was appointed war-leader. The conflict quickly intensified and, as Caesar advanced through Kent towards the Thames, the British attacked at every opportunity, but were not tempted into pitched battle. When the Roman army halted at the end of a day's march, Cassivellaunus saw his chance.

The digging of a temporary marching camp in hostile countryside was absolutely essential, but it presented a short period of dangerous exposure – despite elaborate precautions. As evening approached and the army halted, most of the legionaries deployed in battle order, facing the most likely direction of threat. Behind this protective screen, others dug a deep ditch (three and a half metres wide and two and a half deep) and built a rampart from the upcast. Each man carried two stakes sharpened at either end and with a narrow waist which allowed them to be easily tied together. Made from hard-wearing oak, the stakes might have been lashed in threes and set on top of the rampart like large caltrops. If each were tied to its neighbours, these spikey clusters would have made a very formidable obstacle to an enemy charge. Once one side of the camp was complete, the legionaries in battle order moved behind it, and more men could be released to complete the remaining three as quickly as possible.

Cassivellaunus' soldiers attacked at that moment. And it was only with the aid of reinforcements that they were beaten back. But it was a hard fight, and one of Caesar's senior officers, a tribune, was killed. Pressing on almost immediately through northern Kent, the Roman army arrived on the banks of the River Thames, their first really formidable natural obstacle. It is likely that Cassivellaunus was king of the Catuvellauni, and the river flowed through the heart of his territory. No doubt with local help, Caesar's scouts found a ford, possibly a place now in the centre of modern London. When the Romans waded across the Thames, swept resistance aside and advanced northwards, the British commander changed tactics. Wisely refusing a set-piece battle (and disbanding the bulk of his army – it was harvest-time), he used chariots to skirmish and drove flocks and herds out of the line of march and beyond the reach of legionary foragers.

At this moment, when a long process of attrition threatened and lines of communication with base-camp seemed set to stretch to breaking point, Caesar brought domestic British politics into play. Some time before the invasion, Cassivellaunus had had the king of the Trinovantes killed. Their territory neighboured his own, and the removal of their ruler probably expanded his kingdom into East Anglia. The heir to the Trinovantian throne, Mandubracius, had fled to Gaul to seek Caesar's support, and appears to have accompanied the Roman army in 54 BC. Once across the Thames, it seemed the right time to play this political card. With an agreement to restore Mandubracius, and presumably throw off Catuvellaunian control, the Trinovantes surrendered to Caesar, supplying hostages and much needed food and supplies.

Cassivellaunus countered with an audacious move. Showing that he had both good communications and a long military reach, he ordered four Kentish kings to combine forces and attack the Roman base-camp on the Channel shore. But they failed. Left to guard the precious transports, Quintus Arius and his men defended the ship-camp successfully and inflicted many casualties on the British.

INFANTS

In Western Europe a tradition of hierarchy in battle has grown up and it places the infantry, the foot soldiers, the squaddies, in a lowly position. This is almost entirely a consequence of the rise in the importance of cavalry, especially the heavy cavalry of the Middle Ages. It continued into the Victorian period, and even when the Light Brigade charged into the wrong valley it was considered somehow glorious. If the infantry had marched on the Russian guns, it would just have been thought daft. This pecking order is summed up by the word 'infantry'. It is cognate to *enfant* in French, *infante* in Italian and in essence was a term for the boys, too young or too poor to afford a horse. This attitude would have made tough old centurions smile. For Rome the infantry were the elite, the core of the army, and flapping around the wings were the horse-boys, the cavalry.

Meanwhile Rome's new Trinovantian allies had betrayed the location of Cassivelluanus' headquarters to Caesar. Once they had broken through the defences – which appear to have been long and difficult to man – his soldiers were no doubt delighted to find herds of cattle.

It was enough. Cassivellaunus sued for peace, and once again Commius mediated. Time was pressing hard on Caesar: it was late September, and his commanders in Gaul had sent word that rebellion was in the air. Punitive terms would take too long and might be difficult to enforce. Hostages, an annual tribute and the security of the Trinovantes were quickly agreed, and the Roman army embarked once more to brave the dangers of the Ocean.

This time there were no celebrations in Rome, no vote of public thanksgiving from the Senate. Caesar's political enemies had regrouped. The great orator and lawyer Cicero had been in favour of the expedition to Britain but was becoming increasingly uneasy about Caesar's ambitions. By a stroke of good fortune, Cicero's brother, Quintus, had been a staff officer in 54 BC and he wrote letters home full of disappointment at the lack of booty. In the Senate Cicero could report that there was no silver to be had, no cartloads of loot, only slaves, hostages and a vague promise of tribute. The pyrotechnics of 55 BC and the daring crossing of the Ocean had turned out to be a damp squib. Added to these disappointments was a sense of non-fulfilment. Some of Caesar's actions in Britain hinted that he had planned a thorough conquest (of the south, at least) and was in the early stages of establishing a new province. The whispers of insurrection in Gaul which took him back across the Channel seem to have been an unwelcome interruption.

It would be almost a century before a Roman legionary would again set foot on British soil. Between 54 BC and 50 BC there was almost continuous war in Gaul as Caesar's army criss-crossed the centre of the province suppressing opposition. After the murder of the great man in 44 BC, civil war turned Rome in on itself, and even when Augustus had established himself as the first emperor, it was to Germany that he directed his legions.

Propagandists and apologists nevertheless wrote of Britain as though it was a semi-detached satellite, not a formal part of the Empire but certainly within its control. Rome had only to reach out and take the island if the need arose. As a facet of his self-appointed role as Caesar's heir, Augustus felt that he should complete what his uncle had started. Three expeditions were planned. But in 34 BC, 28 BC and 27 BC other priorities prevented the legions embarking at Boulogne.

While British kings will not have recognised it, the Greek geographer and historian Strabo's view was that there was no need for the Romans to cross the Channel and conquer: Britain was too weak to pose any military threat in Europe (perhaps implying that that had not been true in the past), and in any case the tax yielded by trade was already substantial and cost little effort to collect. So why bother?

Despite this patent political spin, Strabo's observations had some substance. British kings showed themselves acutely sensitive to events inside the Empire. The Catuvellaunians had ultimately ignored Caesar's insistence on the independence of the Trinovantes and overrun the kingdom. But when Augustus was in northern Gaul in 16 BC, the Catuvellaunian king, Tasciovanus, thought it prudent to withdraw. And, as disaster struck Rome in AD 9, when three legions were ambushed and annihilated in the German forests, the Catuvellaunians promptly retreated.

The British economy also saw some profound shifts as it reacted to Roman imperial policy. After the expeditions of 55 BC and 54 BC, the major points of contact with continental commerce moved eastwards. Much evidence of a busy trade in Roman and European goods had been found at Hengistbury Head, near modern Bournemouth, and in the kingdom of the Durotriges. Business appears to have dried up there and the points of entry shift to the Kent and especially the Essex coasts. Around AD 14 Strabo reported that British farmers were producing and exporting a grain surplus, and their customers were almost certainly the Roman legions who had been campaigning in the Rhine basin for more than twenty years. It was much easier to handle bulk commodities like grain by sea and river than overland, and the Essex coast probably thrived as business boomed. British coins minted during this period sometimes have an ear of corn stamped on one side.

On the other side of the coin the name of a substantial British king occasionally appears, someone whose name was remembered long enough to gain him literary immortality. Shakespeare called him Cymbeline, but the mintmasters spelled his name as Cunobelin. The name means 'the Hound of Belenos', a Celtic fire god whose presence flickers in the bonfires of the Beltane celebrations on May Day. King of the Catuvellauni, Cunobelin had extended his grip over the East

Midlands and most of the south-east of Britain, and had probably become wealthy through control of the corn trade. He reigned for a long time, probably from AD 5 to AD 41, and appears to have ruled with caution and determination. After the final takeover of the kingdom of the Trinovantes, he moved his capital place from St Albans to Colchester, perhaps to be closer to the source of his wealth. Suetonius, the historian and former Director of Chancery for the Emperor Hadrian, hailed Cunobelin as *Britannorum Rex*, King of the British, and it may be that his writ ran further than his formal rule.

In his superb account of the campaigns in Gaul and Britain, Caesar characterised Cunobelin's kingdom as the richest part of the island. Its people were like the Gauls he knew so well. And indeed there is evidence that recent migrations had crossed from the continent. From the modern country which bears their name, the Belgae settled in the south of Britain, and some historians believe that they supplanted the aristocracies and royal families of several native kingdoms. In eastern Yorkshire a people known as the Parisii came and their burials strongly suggest a recent European origin. The first century BC coinage issued by British kings certainly shows continental influence, although it is uncertain that a money economy operated in any meaningful sense.

TEN BASE

On memorials and inscriptions on stately buildings the date is often expressed in Roman numerals. It takes time to work out the bits of subtraction and addition, but the basis of ancient arithmetic is very simple. It relates to our hands. Ten fingers (OK, eight fingers and two thumbs) contain most of the basic Roman numbers. I is one finger held up, II is two and so on. V is five and represents the nick between the thumb and index finger. X is ten and is both index fingers crossed. The English counting system is also based on ten but the Celts had a twenty-base system. They used their toes as well. *Fichead*, in Scots Gaelic, is twenty. *Dha fhichead* is two twenties or forty (four tens), and *ceithir fhichead* is four twenties or eighty (eight tens). Simple.

Of those living beyond the fertile cornlands of the southern lowlands, Caesar has been dismissive: *The people of the interior for the
most part do not sow corn but live on milk and meat and dress in
skins.* The impression of a more primitive society, one which had had
much less contact with Roman Europe and the civilising south, is
reinforced by the fact that the peoples of the north were mostly
pastoralists. They walked the ancient paths of transhumance, moving
their flocks and herds up the hill trails and onto the summer pasture,
and then back down to the wintertowns in late autumn. To the city-
dwelling Romans, they will have seemed like semi-nomads: primitives
who wore skins and lived out on the windy hills. Certainly their
summer shielings will have seemed little more than shacks and their
more permanent settlements unimpressive.

Such attitudes were engrained in an Italian aristocrat like Julius
Caesar. The ploughman always had a greater status than the herds-
man. These farmers had formed the backbone of Rome's old citizen
armies, and a heroic figure of the past, the dictator Cincinnatus, had
twice laid down his plough to lead campaigns against the enemies of
the city, and then returned to his farm once the battles were won. By
contrast, tending to flocks and herds was the work of slaves. But to
move from Caesar's cultural biases and simple observations to the
assumption of a lesser, unsophisticated society would be a mistake.
The kingdoms of the north were powerful, they held territory which
the Romans had great difficulty in subduing, and they outlasted them.

When Cunobelin died in AD 41 (or perhaps AD 42), the political
balance tilted. The emperor Gaius, known as Caligula, had followed
Tiberius onto the throne. But his short reign was disfigured by crazy,
impulsive acts. Not the least of these was a planned invasion of
Britain. When Adminius, an exiled son of Cunobelin, arrived at
Caligula's court in AD 39, he persuaded the Emperor that Britain
could be easily conquered – and he himself could of course be made
king of the Catuvellauni. But as the invasion force mustered at
Boulogne a year later, the legionaries refused to embark and mutinied.
Caligula's reaction was bizarre. Here is Suetonius' account:

> Finally, as if he was about to embark on a war, he drew up his
> battlelines and set out his catapults and other artillery on the Ocean
> shore. When no one had the least idea of what he intended, he
> suddenly gave the order that they were to gather sea-shells, filling

their helmets and the folds of their tunics. These were what he termed spoils owed by the Ocean to the Capitol and Palatine. And, as a monument to his victory, he had a very high tower constructed, which would, like the Pharos, send out beams of light to guide the course of ships by night. As if he had exceeded all previous models of generosity in announcing a donative for the troops of a hundred denarii per man, he told them, 'Depart in happiness, depart in wealth.'

It is not difficult to imagine what the soldiers said to each other as they departed with all that wealth and their sea-shells. Despite the charades, it is likely that much of the preparatory work for an invasion had been done. The Roman fondness for organisation will have meant that the legions would not have reached the harbour without all being in readiness – transports, military intelligence and supplies. After Caligula's inevitable assassination, his successor determined to follow through the aborted plan. In AD 42 Claudius had been seriously threatened by a coup which had only fizzled out at the last minute, and to bolster his authority, he needed a military success. And quickly. A triumph to rival those of his glorious predecessors? Britain fitted the bill. Claudius could complete what had been begun by the deified Julius. Glory waited on the shores of the Channel. And the political weather was favourable.

With the death of Cunobelin, his sons, Togidumnus and Caratacus, had divided the Catuvellaunian kingdom between them. The crack Roman legions stationed on the Rhine were a formidable concentration of power which needed to be broken up before another ambitious soldier could organise a coup – and an expedition to Britain would do just that. And another dispossessed British king, Verica, gave Claudius a convenient excuse for intervention, a *casus belli*. In the summer of AD 43, all seemed set fair.

Four legions had marched to Boulogne, the II Augusta, the IX Hispana, the XIV Gemina and the XX Valeria. They were under the command of a notable general, the former govenor of Pannonia (most of modern Hungary), Aulus Plautius, and he had laid meticulous plans. And then, on the shore at Boulogne, everything unravelled. The legions mutinied again, refusing to board the transports, seemingly terrified of the ancient dangers of crossing the Ocean and passing over the edges of the world. They would not shift.

All the efforts of Aulus Plautius were in vain. No inducement or threat would move the obdurate legionaries off dry land and onto the transports waiting in the estuary at Boulogne. When news of the mutiny reached Rome, Claudius himself did not take the risk of being humiliated by his own soldiers. Instead he sent a freed slave, Narcissus, who had risen very high in the new imperial civil service. The sheer weight and complexity needed to run Rome's vast empire demanded the creation of a substantial bureaucracy to deal with it. At first this resembled a vast household department more than an apparatus of state. Freed slaves or freedmen were often appointed by aristocratic families to run their estates and business affairs, and Narcissus' rise seems to have been very much in that tradition. In any case Claudius could trust men who owed him their position entirely rather than rely on aristocrats who had their own independent means, power base and ambitions.

When Narcissus arrived at Boulogne, he insisted to Aulus Plautius that he be allowed to address the legions directly. When Roman commanders spoke to their armies, they climbed onto a platform known as a tribunal so that all could see them. Twenty thousand legionaries and perhaps a further 20,000 auxiliaries made up the invasion force of AD 43. So that commanders could be heard by such a huge assembly, they used professional heralds to repeat their words. With specially trained voices, their words could carry far enough. But when Narcissus, a freed slave and not a soldier, appeared on the tribunal usually occupied by aristocratic generals, the soldiers grew angry and the mood darkened. Then someone made a joke. They shouted *Io Saturnalia!*, a reference to the annual winter festival when slaves exchanged roles with their masters for a day. The affront of being lectured on loyalty by a former slave turned into a piece of daftness, and the atmosphere of tension broke. Amidst the laughter, Narcissus no doubt announced more inducements and made more appeals to nobler instincts, promising glory as the men walked in Caesar's footprints. Whatever the mixture of motives and circumstances, the embarkation of the invasion fleet began almost at once.

Its destination was not to be the beaches near Deal used in 55 BC and 54 BC. Much had been learned about Britain's geography in the intervening century, and Aulus Plautius' sea-captains sailed further north, to what is now Richborough in north-east Kent. It looked different 2,000 years ago. The Isle of Thanet was a genuine island, cut off from the mainland by the Wantsum Channel. Richborough was probably also an island, and the fleet entered the eastern end of the narrow channel and made for the island. Again learning from history, once the transports had disembarked, they were moored in the sheltered anchorage. Traces of the ditching dug around the temporary ship-camp have been found. These now lie about a mile inland from the Channel coast.

ROSTRA

In Latin a *rostrum* was the beak or prow of a warship. Its English meaning of 'platform' developed because of what happened to the beaks of warships captured by the Romans. They set them up as trophies in the Forum and speakers got into the habit of standing on the rostra so that a listening crowd could see them. News was disseminated from these platforms by orators who were often in the service of different generals and senators. Political spin is nothing new.

Perhaps misled by the news of a mutiny at Boulogne, perhaps awed by the scale of the army wading ashore in the Kentish marshlands, perhaps expecting another fiasco, the British kings at first kept their distance. Here is part of the classical historian Dio Cassius's excellent account of the invasion of AD 43:

> . . . they melted into the marshes and forests, hoping that they would wear them down in fruitless effort, so that they would sail back after an abortive mission, as had happened in the case of Julius Caesar.
>
> Plautius experienced a deal of trouble in searching out their forces, but when he did find them, he defeated first Caratacus, and then Togidumnus.

Advancing further into Kent, probably to the line of the River Medway:

> . . . which the barbarians thought the Romans would not be able to cross without a bridge, and consequently they were encamped on its

bank opposite in a rather careless fashion. Plautius sent across the German auxiliaries, who were quite used to swimming easily even in full armour across the swiftest currents. These fell upon the enemy unexpectedly, but they did not shoot mainly at the men: rather they set about wounding the horses which drew the chariots and, when these were thrown into confusion, the mounted warriors were endangered too. Plautius then sent across Flavius Vespasianus (the man who later gained the imperial power), with his brother, Sabinus, who had a subordinate commission on his staff. They too got across the river somehow and killed many of the barbarians who were not expecting them. The rest, however, did not take to flight, but on the next day they joined issue with them again. The battle was indecisive, until Hosidius Geta, who had just missed being taken prisoner, defeated them so soundly that he exceptionally was granted triumphal ornaments, though he had not been consul.

From there the Britons retreated to the River Thames in the area where it empties into the Ocean and at flood-tide forms a lake.

In the first century AD great rivers like the Thames had not been channelled between built-up banks, and their courses were often very wide and changeable. At Southwark, for example, opposite St Paul's Cathedral, the river flowed in a series of channels at least 700 metres further south, creating several river-islands. At high tide the Thames could be as much as a kilometre wide, presenting a real obstacle to an advancing army.

Aulus Plautius relied on his *German* auxiliaries. They were Batavian cavalry originating from the Rhine delta, soldiers well used to crossing rivers. These regiments were recruited from recently conquered provinces and were often led by their own chieftains. Roman policy tried to remove fighting men from an area of potential unrest and post them well out of the way elsewhere in the Empire. When the Batavians attacked the British encampment on the far bank of the Medway, they will have shown skills which seem acrobatic to us now. Throwing javelins and probably firing arrows from the backs of their small ponies, they were able to steer them with their legs and stay wedged into the saddle. Stirrups would gallop into European history much later, with the arrival of the Huns in the fourth century. Roman cavalry troopers did expect to fall off or be knocked off because remounting was an essential – and spectacular – part of cavalry training. It is the origin of that well-worn piece of school gymnastic equipment, the vaulting horse. Roman cavalrymen used it to practise remounting both from the back, in classic manner, and also from the sides at various angles. But, unlike vaulting horses, real ones were usually moving in battle, often very quickly. The writer Arrian claimed that well-trained cavalrymen could vault onto their ponies in full armour, while they were cantering – slowly presumably.

THE REAL BARBARIANS

The application of modern ethical standards to history is inevitable. Even though historians go to some trouble to avoid value judgements, few fail to characterise Roman culture as sophisticated or civilised, particularly while contrasting it with the more primitive people that the Romans conquered, like the native British who were, well, uncivilised. It is a distinction which does not bear examination. The Romans were utterly barbaric in their ruthlessness, slaughtering hundreds of thousands as a matter of imperial policy. They even took some trouble to make a show out of all that appalling slaughter. When he defeated Decebalus, the Dacian/Romanian king, in AD 105, the Emperor Trajan sent 50,000 captives back to Rome to be butchered by gladiators in the circuses for the amusement of spectators. Other massacres routinely took place all over the Empire, especially when new provinces were incorporated. And the Romans did not hesitate when it came to each other. In the civil wars between Marius and Sulla rival factions murdered many thousands. When the Senate met in 82 BC they could barely hear themselves speak because 'the clatter of arms and the groans of the dying were distinctly heard in the Temple of Bellona where Sulla was holding a meeting'. Augustus was a famously cold and ruthless killer. When he, Mark Anthony and Lepidus held power as the Second Triumvirate in 43 BC, more than 300 senators and 2,000 other aristocrats were slaughtered. One of them was Cicero and it was ordered that his head and hands be cut off and spitted on spikes displayed on the rostra in the Forum. Very civilised.

While the Batavians and their ponies were swimming the Thames, another part of the army marched upriver and was able to cross *by a bridge*, perhaps a pontoon bridge anchored at a narrow stretch of the river. At this point in the campaign, Aulus Plautius appears to have got into some difficulty. In pursuits across what sounds like the Essex marshes, *he lost a large number of men* and was forced to retreat behind the line of the Thames.

His prudence was also political. So that the Emperor could take an active part in the conquest of Britain and claim a share – the lion's share – of the glory, Claudius had instructed his commander to pause and send for him before the decisive assault. Sailing from Rome to Marseilles and then travelling overland to either the Biscay or Channel coasts, Claudius arrived on the banks of the Thames to lead his legions into history.

It was mid August AD 43, high summer in the south of England. The Roman invasion army of four legions and many regiments of auxiliaries was encamped at a place now buried by the buildings of central London. It is very likely that Aulus Plautius had halted at a crossing of the Thames, a vital strategic location which he could secure and protect. When Claudius and the imperial retinue arrived at the gates of the camp, British spies will have been amazed. Not at the detachments of the Praetorian Guard led by their commander, Rufrius Pollio, not at the endless number of clerks, their records and the household servants, not even at the splendour of the imperial court. Those watching the coming of the Emperor will have been amazed at the huge grey creatures plodding up the road from Kent. For Claudius had brought elephants.

From the time of the Punic Wars and the spectacular campaigns of Hannibal in Italy, war-elephants had been terrifyingly familiar to Roman armies. First used in India and then by Alexander the Great, they had a simple tactical value: fear. Trumpeting, thundering so that the earth shook, elephants could be made to charge – or stampede. It appears that these normally placid great animals were prone to panic. Either way, they could devastate an enemy battleline. Standing at least 3.5 metres at the shoulder, carrying a howdah, directed by a mahout, their mere presence on a battlefield loosened the resolve of the men facing them. But if elephants could be manoeuvred, their charge could be decisive. Hannibal had a favourite, Sarus, meaning 'the Syrian', and he was evidently huge and fearless. Charging into enemy lines, he could scatter hundreds of men at a time and, where he led, his herd no doubt thundered after him. The British had seen nothing like Claudius' elephants.

WHAT'S IN A NAME?

No Roman ever said 'Hail Caesar!'. Despite the instincts of scriptwriters of Hollywood 'sword and sandal' epics, Gaius Julius Caesar's friends and colleagues would have called him Gaius. Or sir. Free Roman citizens usually had three names, known as a 'praenomen', a 'nomen' and a 'cognomen'. The first was chosen from a traditional list of about twelve possibilities such as Marcus, Lucius, Servius, Gnaeus or Publius. The emperor who built the Wall was Publius Aelius Hadrianus and, before he became too grand, he was called Publius. The nomen was the surname or family name. The dynasty of emperors who followed Caesar was known as the Julians and then the Julio-Claudians. If Hadrian had had children, his dynasty would have been the Aelians. The cognomen was used of people when they were not present and often derived from a nickname. Caesar originally meant 'hairy', which was ironic since Julius was bald. Hadrianus might have meant 'dark one', or more prosaically that the family originated from Hadria in northern Italy.

Once across the Thames, it is not clear where Aulus Plautius and his emperor led their soldiers. But whatever was done was done quickly – and decisively. Claudius needed to recross the Channel to Gaul before the bad weather of mid to late September. The gaggle of senators who accompanied him to Britain to witness the military success of their great army and its elephants will not have wished to linger in these chilly northern latitudes. The invasion force advanced into Essex.

This was significant in itself. They had gone further than Caesar – and perhaps they would do better. In the century between the first expeditions and the Claudian invasions, the army had changed and become even more professional. In 55 BC most of the legionaries were Italians but, as the Empire expanded, the legionaries grew more cosmopolitan. And soldiering became more attractive. Binding the army ever closer to his family – what would become the Julio-Claudian dynasty – Augustus improved pay and conditions of service, committing especially to a comfortable retirement. The auxiliary regiments became integral, and the Praetorians were formally established as the imperial guard. One of their prime responsibilities was to police the city of Rome. In the provinces, particular legions and auxiliaries were posted as garrisons on a semi-permanent basis. Of the legions camped on the banks of the Thames in AD 43, the II Augusta, the IX Hispana and the XX Valeria were to remain in Britain for many generations.

Aulus Plautius and Claudius appear to have run into hard fighting in Essex, although no single pitched, set-piece battle is mentioned in any detail by Dio Cassius: . . . *engaging the enemy who had gathered together to block his* [Claudius'] *advance, he defeated them in battle and captured Camulodunum, which had been the capital of Cuno-belin.* Now modern Colchester, the city's ancient name gives a hint of its status as the prime target of the Roman campaign north of the Thames. Camulodunum means 'the Fortress of the War-God'. Unlike most British Celtic deities, Camulos appears to have been widely worshipped, with dedications as far north as the Clyde. Archaeologists have confirmed that Cunobelin's capital was a powerful sacred centre dedicated to the war-god worshipped by British warriors, who will have prayed hard for victory. Its fall would have been a catastrophe. Bounded by long runs of ditching which enclosed a sanctuary and a royal enclosure, the compound had an intense, even magical importance. The fires of Celtic festivals will have burned there in the winter's dark at the turning points of the year. Sacrifices of propitiation will have been offered and all the drama of royal and priestly ritual will have focused behind the ramparts of the Fortress of the War-God.

The Romans desecrated it immediately. A fort was built by the gates, and inside the sanctuary, the holy of holies, a temple to the cult of the imperial family was ultimately erected. After the shock of defeat, this terrible affront left deep resentments which would continue to simmer.

Camulodunum was equally attractive for more everyday reasons. What had brought Cunobelin and his court to the Essex coast was the corn trade. From Camulodunum he could control it more readily and reap the harvest of the tax revenues as shiploads left to cross the North Sea and feed the legions on the Rhine. Now Claudius and Aulus Plautius had taken over this vital hub and no doubt the corn grew cheaper. Some of the legions of the Rhine had come to consume it *in situ*.

TRIUMPHANT

The greatest honour on offer to a victorious Roman general was a triumph, a huge procession through the streets of Rome. After Claudius enjoyed his in AD 44, there were fewer and fewer. An 'ovation' was a lesser award and, on his return from Britain, Aulus Plautius was granted one – the last, as it happened. But triumphal ornaments appear to have continued. These were insignia given to soldiers involved in a great military success. They could also be awarded medals, called 'phalerae', which took the form of metal discs displayed on the chest. A crescent-shaped neckpiece, a residual item of Roman armour, was copied by German armies of the modern era, and soldiers in Hitler's Wehrmacht wore them as they went into battle.

There followed a revealing sequence of events. On the triumphal arch erected in Rome in AD 51 to advertise and glorify Claudius' personal achievement in conquering Britain, the submission of eleven kings is recorded. It is almost certain that this ceremony of subjugation took place after the capture of Colchester. One of these kings had travelled a long way. A later historian sheds a little light: *Claudius*, wrote Eutropius, *added to the Empire some islands lying in the Ocean beyond Britain, which are called the Orkneys.* This remarkable reference has been thought to be the result of confusion, probably a scribal error. The Emperor was in Britain for only sixteen days. How could news of Roman victories reach Orkney, and its king travel south to submit to Claudius, inside such a tight timetable?

Archaeologists have discovered that there was no mistake. Sherds from a Roman amphora have been found at the impressive broch-village of Gurness on the Orkney mainland – and not just any old amphora but a type which had become obsolete by AD 60. These particular containers had been used to transport a special liqueur probably only consumed by aristocrats – and kings. The nearest example of the same type of amphora was found at Colchester, or Camulodunum.

An Orkney king did come south in AD 43, and his presence at Claudius' moment of triumph had been planned, even stage-managed. Roman diplomacy had reached far to the north and supplied a grateful emperor with a valuable piece of propaganda, something people would remember. Not only had he exceeded the deeds of the deified Julius in actually conquering the island, Claudius' power stretched even beyond the Ocean beyond Britain! Right to the very edge of the world. The Orkney submission had no other possible meaning or value, and no doubt rewards far greater than amphorae of fancy liqueur were handed over.

As Claudius crossed the Channel again and hurried south through Gaul with all the senators who had witnessed the Orkney king bowing before the might of Rome, he will have been savouring the prospect of his triumph. Through the streets of the city and the cheering crowds it would glitter and shimmer in the sunshine. On a chariot the victorious emperor would stand, a laurel wreath held over his head by a man who whispered *Remember! Thou art mortal.* Claudius took the title *Britannicus* and settled down to govern his vast territories with far more authority than he could have imagined when the Praetorian Guard dragged him onto the throne two years before. News of the conquest of Britain and the islands beyond it crackled through the length and breadth of the Empire, triumphal arches being erected as far east as Asia Minor. A letter, written in Greek, from Claudius survives. It thanks a troupe of travelling acrobats for a golden crown they sent him.

Britain had become Britannia, part of the Empire, its symbolic importance great, and its place in imperial history a turning point – for Claudius at least. The new province would last almost four hundred years, but not before a struggle.

2

Britannia Barbarica

Great events not only make history, they make historians. When the Persian Empire overran the Greek towns of what is now Turkey's Aegean coastlands, it looked certain that the swarming armies of Darius and Xerxes would overwhelm Athens, Thebes, Corinth and Sparta. And yet, at the beginning of the fifth century BC, these small states combined to turn back the mighty tide of Persia. At Marathon in 490 BC the infantry of Athens and Plataea astonished the Great King – and themselves – when they stopped the eastern juggernaut in its tracks. Ten years later the heroic delay won by the Spartans at Thermopylae allowed the Greek navy, led by the Athenian admiral, Themistocles, to obliterate the Persian triremes in the narrow waters of the Bay of Salamis. And finally at Plataea a huge Greek army, perhaps 60,000 heavily armoured warriors, annihilated the invaders in 479 BC.

A turning point in world history, the outcome of the Persian Wars was remarkable. Apparently insurmountable odds were overcome by the determination of Greek infantry and sailors drawn from an alliance of small towns and by the brilliance of their generals and admirals. It was a story full of heroes and heroics – and it needed telling and explaining.

The original meaning of the Greek word *histor* was something like 'eye-witness', and *historie* were 'enquiries'. When Herodotus of Halicarnassus (now the city of Bodrum on the Turkish coast) began to write down his *Histories*, his Enquiries, he was moved to do it by the enormity of the world-changing events which swirled around the Aegean in his own lifetime. Taking testimony from many eye-witnesses and ranging widely over the eastern Mediterranean, he compiled the first coherent, and highly idiosyncratic, narrative of real events: what came to be recognised as the first history book.

In the eighth century BC Homer had composed his immense epic poems on the war between the Greeks and the Trojans. Both the *Iliad* and the *Odyssey* are founded on myth-history. Gods, heroes and mere mortals constantly interact, and events are often governed by the supernatural. Although it turned out that Homer's blood-soaked epics were at least sparked by real events, they were not historical. There are no datable events, there is very little sense of the passage of time (when Odysseus returns to Ithaca after a twenty-year absence, it appears that neither he nor his wife, Penelope, are a day older than when they parted) and cause and effect almost always have a divine hand somewhere in the process. But Homer's epics do have much to say about the atmosphere of the Aegean in the eighth century BC. As battle rumbles below the topmost towers of Troy, human relationships are well and sometimes convincingly realised. Homer tells his listeners what the society of the day admired and what it despised. Courage and manly honour were the virtues of a heroic age. Ingenuity and resourcefulness were also pre-miated, and the power of these ancient narratives is so enduring that the *Iliad* and the *Odyssey* are still regularly converted into films and novels. Not historical documents – but the stuff of history nevertheless.

THE HISTORY MEN

Gaius Suetonius Tranquillus kept busy. In addition to writing a defining history, *The Caesars*, he was also a civil servant. Under the Emperor Trajan he held the first of three important posts, Secretary in charge of literary matters. Then he took over responsibility for libraries and, under Hadrian, he was Secretary for correspondence. Usually known as *The Twelve Caesars*, his history of the early Empire was by turns informative, critical and partial. He praised Augustus, and damned Nero and Domitian. The book is dedicated to his friend, the Commander of the Praetorian Guard, Gaius Septicius Clarus. When Hadrian dismissed them both, they were almost certainly close friends and perhaps allies. Suetonius also knew other historians, Pliny the Younger and Tacitus. Rome may have ruled the Mediterranean and western Europe, but its governing caste was small and, as often, everyone of substance knew everyone else. The difference was the power of the pen, or stylus, and despite being sacked or sent into disfavour, Suetonius had, literally, the last word.

The *Iliad* runs to 15,000 lines and the *Odyssey* to 12,000 but, despite this, the poems were almost certainly recited entirely from memory. Professional reciters, known as *rhapsodes*, performed them with music and probably some dramatic accompaniment. With the steady beat of its metre, the use of alliteration, repetition and rhyme, poetry is designed to be remembered, each line suggesting and retrieving the next. Choruses were a device to involve the listeners but also to allow time for the *rhapsodes* to summon up the next verse or passage.

The art of memory is mostly lost now. We admire people who are able to speak in public without notes or a prepared text. We are astonished when someone can recall details of a story such as numbers, dates and quantities without reference to any written data. The ancients would have thought nothing of that. In the long past, very little was written down and almost everything of importance (genealogy, possessions, the cycle of the agricultural year) was held securely in memory. And that is what made Herodotus exceptional. He wrote down his enquiries, what his eye-witnesses could remember. The *Histories* were almost certainly performed at public readings. It is thought that no more than 20 per cent of Greeks were literate. In fact, some time around 443 BC Herodotus himself arrived in Athens, and it seems that he was paid handsomely in silver for giving readings of his work. But, because they were not structured like poetry, not meant to be committed to memory, the *Histories* had a written form from the very beginning. This made for a different sort of transmission. Many texts of Herodotus were copied onto papyrus rolls. The story of the extraordinary victory of the Greeks over the tyrannical Persians must have been very popular – and very lucrative for the author. As the texts multiplied so did their chances of survival. By contrast, memory changes, dilutes and is adapted to changing circumstance, but Herodotus' writings were fixed in time, more or less at the moment when he dipped a stylus in a pot of ink. And so what has come down to us now, whispering across twenty-five centuries, is a largely authentic voice, a collector of *historie*, of enquiries.

Across the rest of Europe in the fifth century BC important events also unfolded. Decisive battles were fought by mighty armies, and against the odds unexpected victories were gained. Strategists as astute as Themistocles succeeded in out-thinking adversaries and warriors as heroic as the Spartans who fought similarly selfless rearguard actions at Thermopylae. But we know little or nothing of them. No Herodotus wrote of their mighty deeds. No one did. But because no epic tales of great generals and their armies survive from fifth-century Spain, France, Germany and Britain, that does not mean that western European societies were somehow backward, or less sophisticated – only that they were different. And that their history was held in memory, not written down, and that it did not survive.

The Persian Wars had another determinant consequence for the history of western Europe. In the summer of 490 BC the great Athenian dramatist Aeschylus put on his body armour, took up his weapons and marched to fight at Marathon, and probably at Salamis and Plataea ten years later. Not surprisingly these battles influenced his plays profoundly. In *The Persians* Aeschylus makes a new and sharp distinction. On one side stand the brave, freedom-loving and civilised Greeks. Opposing them are the seething masses of cruel, cringing, slant-eyed, alien Persians. Forced to fight, whipped into battle by their captains, they were ultimately shown to be cowardly, lesser beings. These were people not even in possession of a proper language, muttering an incomprehensible *bar-bar-bar*. These were barbarians.

Before the Persian Wars, Marathon and Aeschylus' play, the Greeks had seen foreigners as exotic, even supernatural outsiders, like the Titans or the Amazons. Homer composed verses about the Trojans without denigrating them. But after the first battles of the 490s a chasm cracked open and quickly began to widen between the Greeks and the rest, the barbarians. It was a set of attitudes eagerly adopted by the Romans in their turn. And when the Emperor Hadrian came north to Britain and decided to build a wall, its stated purpose sprang straight out of that way of thinking. The Wall ran across the middle of Britain *qui barbaros Romanosque divideret*, to separate the barbarians from the Romans.

The ability to write down history, or at least a version of it, and the invention of the idea of barbarians have been enormously influential. Because written records survive, historians have naturally concentrated on the role of the Roman invaders in British history between 55 BC and AD 410. Less easy to understand is the readiness of many to adopt quasi-Roman attitudes to the natives, the barbarians, our ancestors, their own ancestors. Characterised as primitive, war-painted, wild and hollering, even gormless, governed in tribes by bickering chieftains, the British are often cast as little more than background. Taking centre-stage, the red-cloaked legionaries in disciplined ranks march north with their glittering eagles held high, sweeping all before them. Road-building, town-dwelling, they bring Mediterranean civilisation to a drab, rain-sodden straggle of shepherds cowering in muddy hovels. Perhaps an exaggeration, but not a wild one.

The historical reality must be different. The truth is that the Romans found Britain impossible to conquer entirely. What they did hold was held with some considerable initial difficulty, and when Hadrian's Wall was built its primary military meaning must have been as a huge reaction to real and persistent problems in northern Britannia. For most of the 350-year life of the province, a tenth of the whole Roman imperial army was stationed in that part of the island they were able to control. First-rate generals were usually appointed as governors. Such close policing by very large numbers of expensive legionaries and their commanders would not have been required for 'gormless' drabs. Determined, independent-minded, well organised and consistently courageous are much more apt adjectives. The difficulty is, however, glaringly obvious. Only Roman reactions to British actions survive in the historical record. The British barbarians have left little or no sense of what life was like under Roman rule, or of their successful resistance to it in the north. The impact of Hadrian's Wall can only be surmised. Memory turns out to be much more fragile even than flaking, crumbling papyrus.

Occasionally Roman sources do offer some inklings – but before these are considered, there exists one prime echo of what British society was like in the first century BC, a vivid sense of its atmosphere. At the same time as Julius Caesar was campaigning in Gaul, the four kingdoms of Iron Age Ireland were also at war. Ulster was defended against the armies of Connaught by one man, a champion, the boy-hero, Cuchulainn. Here he is inciting himself to battle:

The rage-fit was upon him. He shook like a bullrush in the stream. His sinews stretched and bunched, and every huge, immeasurable, vast ball of them was as big as the head of a month-old child. His face as a red bowl, fearsomely distorted, one eye sucked in so far that the beak of a wild crane could scarcely reach it, the other eye bulged out of his cheek. Teeth and jawbone strained through peeled-back lips. Lungs and liver pulsed in his throat. Flecks of fire streamed from his mouth. The booming of his heart was like the deep baying of bloodhounds, or the growl of lions attacking bears.

In virulent clouds, sparks blazed, lit by the torches of the war-goddess Badb. The sky was slashed as a mark of his fury. His hair stood about his head like the twisted branches of red hawthorn. A stream of dark blood, as tall as the mast of a ship, rose out of the top of his head, then dispersed into dark mist, like the smoke of winter fires.

This passage comes from an epic poem know as the *Tain Bo Cuailnge*, the Great Cattle Raid of Cooley. Composed in Irish Gaelic, it sings of a pre-Christian society, of heroes and blood-spattered wars, of kings and scheming queens, of covetousness and the wealth in teeming herds of cattle, of gods, greed and revenge: themes equally vividly drawn by Homer in the *Iliad* and the *Odyssey*. The *Tain Bo* is a splash of brilliant colour which scatters the grey mists of early Irish history and which describes a thoroughly Celtic culture. And across the North Channel a similar culture bloomed, perhaps even mediated in the same language along the Argyll and Galloway coasts. The rest of the peoples of Britain certainly spoke a cousin-language and they shared much with the warriors of the *Tain Bo* and the other poems in what is known as the Ulster Cycle. Cuchulainn and his comrades spoke Q-Celtic, what became Manx, Irish and Scots Gaelic, while the British described their islands in dialects of P-Celtic, the ancestors of Pictish, Old Cumbrian, Welsh and Cornish. Much of the evidence for the existence and use of these languages is, paradoxically, supplied by the Greeks and Romans.

Herodotus had heard whispers of a remote island called Britain. The Kassiterides, the Tin Islands, lay somewhere amidst the storms and monsters of the Northern Ocean, but, said the cautious and scrupulous historian, *I cannot speak with any certainty*. Herodotus' work must have been well known in the Greek colony of Marseilles, then called Massalia. Tin was much prized and much needed in the manufacture of bronze. Cornwall was a prime source. Greek merchants trading out of Massalia needed more precision than the hesitant Herodotus could supply (and they probably also wanted to cut out as many middle-men as possible), and around 320 BC one of their citizens, Pytheas, made the first recorded journey to Britain.

Pytheas was intrepid. Arriving on the southern coast of the English Channel, he met sailors who had been to Britain, and he asked them what the inhabitants were called. *Pretannikai* is how he wrote down the reply. And the whole island? That was known as Pretannike. The Celtic-language version is Pretani and it means something very intriguing. The Pretannikai were the 'People of the Tattoos'. It is the derivation of the Roman name *Britannia*, and it changed only a little into *Britain*.

THE PERIPLUS

Pytheas' main aim appears to have been the creation of a *periplus*, a route-guide for those wishing to travel to the Kassiterides and beyond. His original manuscript is now lost and known only in fragments quoted by later authors. In addition to visiting Belerion (Cornwall) and circumnavigating Britain, he also went on to Thule (Iceland or Norway), reported finding precious amber on the coasts of Holland and Germany, and on an island which may have been Heligoland. Some classical historians cast severe doubt on the reliability of Pytheas' discoveries, but the citizens of modern Marseilles had no such difficulty. On the facade of the city's stock exchange, there stands an impressive statue of the great explorer.

It may not have been a name the British themselves recognised, at least until the time of the Roman invasions. They knew the largest island by a very different name. Here is the Roman historian Pliny the Elder, writing in the first century AD:

Across from this location Britannia Island, famed in Greek and in our own records, lies off to the north west, separated from Germany, Gaul, Spain and the greatest portion of Europe by a large interval. Albion was its own name when all were called the Britannias.

Alba is the Gaelic name for Scotland, and Yr Alban is the Welsh version. But its wider application as the native name for the whole island has persisted here and there. When Sir Francis Drake attempted to colonise California in 1579, he planned to name it New Albion, and in 1809 Napoleon's propaganda was directed at Perfidious Albion.

Modern football fans still chant the name Albion at West Bromwich, Brighton and Hove, Stirling and at Albion Rovers' ground in Coatbridge. The name probably means 'White Land' and may be a reference to the rampart of chalky cliffs visible on much of the coastline between South Foreland in Kent to the Isle of Wight. This is the first sight of Britain for travellers crossing the Channel at its narrower points.

When Julius Caesar and his commanders sat down to plan the invasion of 55 BC, they talked of Britannia, but their enemies waiting on the white cliffs probably called it Alba and themselves Albans (perhaps in conjunction with their own tribal names). This is not a petty or perverse point to labour, but an attempt to resist accepting a purely Roman perspective and assert that there was a native point of view – even if it is very difficult to reconstruct.

Nevertheless, the Greek and Roman habit of making a sufficient quantity of written records so that many have survived is useful. It has given us the names of British kingdoms, kings and place-names. Taken together with archaeology and helpful analogy from elsewhere, it makes possible some broad statements about Britain and the British, or Alba and the Albans, on the eve of the Roman invasion.

As Caesar's conquest of Gaul swept northwards, his military intelligence about Britain naturally multiplied. There were clearly connections. Diviciacus was not only a king in northern Gaul, but he also ruled part of Britain. The native merchants of Brittany traded in volume with the southern coast of Britain (Cornish tin being a key commodity) and, when that part of Gaul rebelled against Caesar in 56 BC, help came south across the Channel. A generation before, there had been a substantial migration to the area around the Solent from Belgic Gaul and contacts remained close. The southern British had much in common with the northern Gauls. Language may have been one of the most enduring links. Modern Breton is now thought to be a descendant of Gaulish and it has many points of similarity with Cornish, still stubbornly spoken by a thousand or so people.

In an island as large as Britain, split into several highland and lowland zones and having many clearly distinct geographical regions within those, there will have been local variations of all sorts, most especially linguistic. The names of the small kingdoms which patterned first century BC Britain hint at that. Probably first gleaned by passages of diplomacy and reconnaissance, many of these were plotted on a map made in the second century AD by the Greek cartographer Ptolemy. At first glance it looks wildly distorted. North of the line of the Tay, Ptolemy has bent Scotland through 90 degrees so that Caithness appears to extend east into the North Sea. In fact it was no mad mistake but the solution to a problem. In common with other Greek geographers (who lived far away on the shores of the Mediterranean, and had never travelled to northern Europe), Ptolemy did not believe that human beings could survive in the extreme weather conditions to be found in latitudes beyond 63 degrees. So, instead of extending Britain northwards to a clearly impossible 66 degrees, he bent it east to fall below the limits of survival.

South of this extravagant convulsion the map shows the names of several kingdoms in the area around what was to become Hadrian's Wall. A few of them have a literal meaning and they offer some sense of how the native peoples saw themselves.

PS AND QS

Much of northern and western Europe spoke dialects of Celtic languages in the latter half of the first millennium BC. In Spain and Portugal, Celtiberian was heard for many centuries, and until recent times a remnant clung on in the north-west. Galician has the root 'Gael' as its first syllable. Lepontic was spoken both north and south of the Alps, and across France and Belgium, dialects of Gaulish were used. Only Breton survives, again in the north-west. Modern Celtic languages are almost all found in the west of Britain and Ireland and they divide into two groups. Irish, Scots and Manx Gaelic are all Q-Celtic, while Welsh, Cornish and Breton are P-Celtic. The three languages in each group are just about mutually intelligible but P-Celts cannot understand Q-Celts.

The Wall cut through the wide territories of the Brigantes. Probably a federation of smaller clans, the kingdom straddled the Pennines, perhaps reaching down to both the North Sea and Irish Sea coasts. The Roman historian Tacitus reckoned the Brigantes territory to be the largest British kingdom, perhaps in area, certainly in population. In the years following the invasion of AD 43, their queen, Cartimandua, was a Roman ally, betraying the British rebel leader Caratacus.

Cartimandua's name means 'Sleek Pony'. Perhaps Caratacus called her something else. The name of her kingdom is harder to parse. The *Brig* element may mean 'Honoured', possibly giving the meaning of 'the Homage-Takers'.

A clan owing homage to the Brigantian kings and queens was the Carvetii. Occupying the Eden Valley, the area around Carlisle, the hill country to the east and probably the Lake District, they carried a name with a much simpler derivation. It means 'the Deer People'. Some other British kingdoms also had descriptive names. The Catuvellauni were 'Good in Battle', the Atrebates were simply 'the Inhabitants' and the Ordovices of Wales were 'the Hammer-Fighters'. Like the Carvetii many of the northern kingdoms of early Britain adopted animals as their talismans. The Lugi, the People of the Ravens, lived in Sutherland and Easter Ross, the Epidii, the Horse People, in Argyll and the Venicones, the Kindred Hounds, in Fife and Stirlingshire. If the habit of tattooing first identified by Pytheas had survived in the north (as the later name 'the Picts' suggests), then perhaps the warriors of the Carvetii wore stylised representations of antlers on their manly chests. A Celtic legacy lingered around the high fells of the Lake District and the Pennines for a long time. As late as the nineteenth century, Cumbrian shepherds still counted their flocks in a version of Old Welsh, and the name of Cumbria is itself is cognate to Cymru, the Welsh name for Wales.

Further east, towards the Hexham Gap and the Tyne Valley, lay the lands of the Tectoverdi and the Lopocares. Their names appear to be impenetrable, but beyond them, nearer the mouth of the Tyne were the Corionototae. The first part of the name lives on in Corbridge, known as Coria in the Roman period. It means 'a hosting-place', a muster-point where armies gathered. Corionototae may be an elaborated version – the warband, even the Great Army. There are several Corias in the north, and hosting-places were always chosen by geography: accessible from several directions, near a good water supply and often at a fording place on a routeway. They remained traditional meeting places for centuries, often into the Middle Ages.

North of the Corionototae, perhaps beyond the valley of the Aln, stretched the fertile territories of the Votadini. Probably taking in all of the Tweed basin and north Northumberland, the Lothians and part of Stirlingshire, it was a country of farms and corn production, much as it is today. Across the Firth of Forth, the Kindred Hounds, the

Venicones, were almost certainly allied, and on the well-drained soils of Fife also reaped good harvests. When the Romans marched north, it appeared that the kings of the Votadini had struck a bargain. Across their lands there are few signs of intrusive military activity. Now called the Devil's Causeway, a road ran from the fort at Corbridge northwards to Tweedmouth, and between there and Kelso are the faint outlines of five temporary marching camps. And that is all. Compared with the density of Roman military remains over Brigantian lands, it seems no more than the legacy of a reconnaissance.

Votadinian kings controlled something that Roman quartermasters needed. If the north of Britannia was to be conquered, the army had to have a secure supply of corn available. Retreating enemies would scorch the earth in front of an advance. Probably in return for client status and the right prices, the Votadini seem to have come to an accommodation.

Their kings ruled from at least four centres of power, perhaps the places where they received Roman envoys. The Votadini held the Castle Rock at Edinburgh, Traprain Law (where a huge hoard of Roman silver was found) in East Lothian, Eildon Hill North on the banks of the middle Tweed and Yeavering Bell near Wooler in north Northumberland. On the summits of these impressive hills stood forts. Constructed by work-gangs using mattocks, shovels and baskets to shift the huge volumes of earth and stones, the outlines of their ditches and ramparts can still be seen – except at Edinburgh where a mighty castle has obliterated almost all ancient archaeology. On Eildon Hill North and Yeavering Bell the circuit of the ramparts is long, too long to be effectively defended. Inside, the footprints of hut platforms have been found – and yet there are no sources of water. On Eildon Hill North 300 platforms imply a population of around 2,500. If these really were strongpoints, forts, then their military rationale looks ill thought out. Other, smaller forts – and there are hundreds in Votadinian territory – look even less defensible. Despite elaborate rings of ditches and ramparts, some are overlooked from higher ground, places where determined attackers could rain down missiles. And at other sites the total area of the defences is significantly larger than the area defended.

It is much more likely that hillforts were indeed power centres but were not built with a military purpose in mind, at least not in the sense that we would understand it. They were intended to impress, to make a show of power. Kings and their warbands may have lived in these high places all year round. Logistics did not matter if you had slaves and warriors. But the mass of farmers from the valleys probably climbed up to the summits only at the time of festivals.

An agricultural, stock-rearing society, the Celtic kingdoms of northern Britain and Ireland arranged their year around four turning-points. At Imbolc in late February ewes began to lactate in anticipation of lambing, providing much-needed sustenance at the end of a long winter. Up on the hillforts, great bonfires were lit, kings spoke to their people, and rituals and prayers were offered up to the gods. Beltane in May was the signal to drive flocks and herds up to the high summer pastures, while Lughnasa in August celebrated the first fruits of the year's harvest. At Samhuinn in October the animals were led from what were called the summertowns back down to the wintertowns in the valleys.

These festivals still flicker on, sometimes in heavy disguise. For example, Halloween is the modern name for Samhuinn, and some of its ancient paganism still peeps out of hollowed turnips and pumpkins. With a candle inside to give the appearance of life, they represent the skulls of the dead who used to walk the Earth on Samhuinn Eve.

The festivals no doubt served a practical purpose for the native kings. On and around their hillforts they received their rents, mostly food renders, from their people or their local lords. Some of this would have been sold to Roman quartermasters, but much of the remainder was consumed. Julius Caesar and other writers remarked on how the Celts loved to feast, to eat and drink huge quantities at certain times of the year. The *Tain Bo* sings of such occasions, and there is a description of a Gaulish king setting up a vast feasting-place, more than a mile square, so that his people could come to enjoy his bounty. They were expected to drink and feast for several days. In a Gaelic phrase, the king wished to be seen as *a river to his people*.

Not until the fourth century AD do the shadowy names of Votadinian kings appear on any sort of historical record, but there is no doubt that they had power long before. Some time around 250 BC large numbers of people from the Tweed basin and north Northumberland were moved into the foothills of the Cheviots. Probably as a result of overpopulation, and no doubt unwillingly, farmers were resettled in the upland valleys of the eastern ranges. And it seems that they all trekked into the hills at the same time. The remains of terracing and the results of soil erosion can still be seen.

The location of the frontiers of British kingdoms are often little more than informed guesswork by historians, but in the case of the western neighbours of the Votadini, Roman generals supplied some welcome help. The Selgovae occupied the hill country between the lines of the modern north–south roads, the A68 in the east and the A74 in the west. These ancient routes were taken in AD 79 when the Governor of Britannia, Gnaeus Julius Agricola, led the legions north in an invasion of Scotland. A pincer movement around the Selgovae was consolidated by a legionary fort at Trimontium, at the foot of the Eildon Hills near Melrose, and by a string of forts at the mouths of the valleys on the western side.

TROUSERS AND TOGAS

When he began to consolidate his invasion of Gaul, Julius Caesar realised that he would have to bring the provincial aristocracy into the centre of Roman political life. The Senate still exercised real power, but when Caesar promoted Gauls to its ranks, they were derided as 'trousered senators', wearing their distinctive Celtic leggings under their senatorial togas. It was more than a cliché. Celts lived in an equestrian culture and adapted their clothes to the needs of horse-riding. Togas are useless in the saddle. The movement of a pony will chafe the tender insides of even the most manly thigh if it is not protected by leggings or trousers. Neatly fitted clothing, not a flapping toga, is what is needed when a pony canters or gallops. The heat of a Roman summer is, however, another matter and perhaps the Gaulish senators sweltered – if the whole jibe was not a metaphor. Behind it lies the divide between Roman and provincial, town and country. The great general who led the legions into the north of Britannia in AD 79 came from Frejus (Forum Julii) in southern Gaul, the region called Provence, from 'Provincia', and he was called Agricola, 'the Farmer'.

The name Votadini is difficult, likely to mean something like 'the People of Fothad', perhaps a divine ancestor. Selgovae is much less opaque. It is derived from the Celtic-language root *seilg* and it means 'the Hunters'. Perhaps that is how the Romans felt at Crawford, now on the line of the A74. Hemmed in by unfamiliar hills, they were the hunted. The name may point to a long tradition. Much of the territory of the Selgovae was later known as the Ettrick Forest, a huge royal hunting reserve in the Middle Ages. Little trace of the kings and their kingdom can be found on the ground, but at Lyne, near Peebles, there was a large Roman fort. Its characteristic playing-card shape is particularly well defined. Lyne was probably a *coria*, a hosting-place for the Selgovae, and the fort was positioned like a huge police station, keeping an eye out for trouble.

In the same area, hut platforms from the first century BC have been found. Their shape too is characteristic and very different from the rectilinear Roman camp. Roundhouses could be large: with a diameter of more than 30 feet in some cases, they were sometimes home to large, extended families. The circular walls were built from stone or turf and the heavy timbers to support the conical roof were keyed together to form a rigid tipi shape. Thatch or turf could certainly keep out the worst of the weather, but the fact that there were no windows, only a door, meant that, although they were snug enough, roundhouses were also very dark. A central hearth supplied some light, heat and a means of cooking. But if there was no wind to create an updraught, the interior could be very smoky. In a medium-sized roundhouse, modern experiment has shown that the smoke hovers at about 1.5 metres, making sitting pleasant enough – although standing up could be eye-watering until the door was reached. Modern anxieties about sparks from the fire catching in the thatch have proved unfounded. The smoke creates a cone of carbon monoxide at the apex of the roof, and all rising sparks are immediately extinguished before they can reach the thatch. The reality was that, like nineteenth-century Highland crofters still living in their ancient blackhouses, the Celtic peoples of northern Britain lived and worked in the open air whenever they could and went indoors only to sleep or when it grew dark or very cold.

The Selgovan kings were dangerous. With an intimate knowledge of a difficult landscape, and the ability to melt away into its wastes and bogland, they were a hard enemy to pin down. Roman commanders much preferred to fight in the open where the disciplined ranks of the professional legionaries were unmatched in Europe. But the Selgovan warbands are unlikely to have obliged. In any case they were almost certainly horse-warriors.

Direct confirmation of this comes from the Roman fort at Vindo-landa, 15 miles west of Corbridge and just south of the line of Hadrian's Wall. The site is an archaeological treasure-house – but not because quantities of conventionally precious objects have been found. In the early 1970s Vindolanda's director, Robin Birley, began to discover letters written by Romans, most of them dating towards the end of the first century AD. Wafer-thin leaves of wood, about the size of postcards, were preserved in the peaty soil around the fort and, after close examination, faint traces of writing were found on them. These letters are unique and invaluable, absolutely authentic voices from 2,000 years ago. Informal, everyday, sometimes mundane, sometimes exotic, they also offer some insight into the lives of the native peoples who lived around Hadrian's Wall. The Vindolanda letters and lists will be much more fully dealt with in later chapters.

EAGLE POWER

As the king of birds, the eagle is a powerful, almost majestic symbol. But there is another reason why eagels are revered. Eagles live a very long time: some hen-birds in European aviaries are recorded to have reached age AD 100 or more. As the standards of Roman legions, eagles were adopted by the Republican General, Gaius Marius, when he campaigned in the east. The Persians venerated the great birds, and the Romans imitated them. The heirs of imperial pretensions carried on the tradition. Napoleon's regiments were led by eagle standards, and the Kaisers and Tsars borrowed the bird for their coats of arms – along with Caesar's name.

On one of the letters, Haterius Nepos, a cavalry officer, stationed in the north some time around 100, left a record of a census he undertook. It mentions a previously little-known people, the Anavionenses. They lived to the west of the Selgovae, in the valley of the River Annan – clearly the names are cognate. Another officer made a report on the military capabilities of native warriors:

> . . . the Britons are unprotected by armour. There are very many cavalry. The cavalry do not use swords nor do the wretched Britons mount in order to throw javelins.

The word *Brittunculi* is used; it means 'the wretched Britons' or, more colloquially, 'the nasty little Brits'. And another document found in the peaty soil of the fort turns out to be a petition intended for presentation to the Emperor Hadrian. He was expected to visit Vindolanda in 122. It sheds more light on how the Roman colonists treated the nasty little Brits. The petitioner complained that he had been beaten even though he was a *transmarinus*, someone from overseas. The clear implication is that it was acceptable to beat a Brit, and that some mistake had been made in his case.

None of this should be surprising. Barbarians/natives in virtually every empire have been similarly dealt with. More informative is the emphasis on cavalry. Archaeology has discovered the remains (usually the metal parts of bridles) of a good deal of native horse-gear, some of it high quality.

Since the outset of the first millennium BC, and probably much earlier, horses had been domesticated in Britain. But perhaps they should really be thought of as ponies. Skeletal remains show riding horses as very small by modern standards, sometimes standing no more than thirteen hands high. Even though first millennium BC people were also small and light (and, according to the Vindolanda reports, not in the habit of wearing heavy kit on horseback), they would still have looked big on their mounts, legs dangling well below the horses' bellies. This mattered less than it might now, because of different riding styles and tack. Stirrups had not yet been introduced in the west, and horsemen were consequently in the habit of using their legs to grip the flanks of their little ponies.

Sophisticated bitted bridles were developed in Gaul in the fourth century BC and these allowed warriors precise and rapid control over their ponies. Nimble, very fast over short distances and hardy, these shaggy little beasts belied their appearance. They could turn on a sixpence and halt in a moment. This sort of athleticism, and the bond of heightened sensitivity which often developed between rider and horse (sometimes a wish can be anticipated and, before any signal is actually given, a pony will move as its rider wants), could be a matter of life or death in close-quarter cavalry warfare. By fiddling their feet, ponies could get a warrior out of trouble and, by turning quickly, allow him to deliver a telling back-handed blow. These were fighting techniques honed over centuries and 1,500 years later could still be seen when the descendants of the Selgovae, the Brigantes and their neighbours – the Border Reivers – saddled up their ponies and sallied out to raid and fight.

The Vindolanda record of *very many cavalry* is puzzling. It claims that the nasty little Brits had no swords and did not throw javelins while mounted. Like the Huns who invaded Europe in the fourth and fifth centuries, perhaps they were expert mounted archers. But it is unlikely. The Huns rode with stirrups and, able to manoeuvre their ponies using only their legs, they could use both hands to fire deadly volleys at packed ranks of infantry and then ride off quickly. It may be that the Celtic cavalry of Britain used their ponies as transport, to ride to the battlefield like modern dragoons and then dismount and fight. Or it may be that the Vindolanda reports are wrong. Not every written Roman source is to be implicitly trusted.

The discovery of native horse-gear, with its expensive emphasis on precise control, argues against the notion of dragoons. They would not need it. More archaeology supports the view that the warbands of the north fought on horseback. Their shields appear to have been small. Not the large, slightly curved, rectangular infantry shields carried by Roman legionaries, but small ones used for parrying blows, able to be handled on horseback while gathering reins in the same fist. There is even some Roman corroboration for this alternative view. When describing Agricola's great campaign in the north and the battle at Mons Graupius in AD 83, Tacitus remarked:

> . . . whereas it was awkward for the enemy with their small shields and enormous swords – for the swords of the Britons, having no points, were unsuited for a cut-and-thrust struggle and close quarters battle.

This is because they were cavalry sabres. Known as *spathas*, these slashing swords had fearsomely sharp edges, at least at the beginning of a battle, but sometimes no point. They were designed for use by a mounted warrior and were best against infantry where a height advantage, even on a small pony, could be decisive. Archaeologists have found examples specially weighted towards the tip of the blade, and they could be devastating in a downward cut. It is at least interesting to note that the most famous Celtic sword in history was known as *Hard Dunter* or, more brutally, *Basher*. These are good, if free, translations of the Old Welsh 'Excalibur'.

The puzzlement over weaponry from the observer at Vindolanda may be less significant than the simple observation that *there are very many cavalry*. The native warbands were almost certainly feared by Roman commanders, and did not deserve the sneer behind the report.

Like their reiving descendants, the natives both reared and raided cattle. Herds were a key indicator of wealth in Celtic society. The *Tain Bo* and other Irish sources talk of raiding as though it were almost an institution. The warrior-cult of the *Fianna* was widespread. Literally meaning 'the Soldiers', these were bands of young aristocrats who spent a period, a rite of passage, roaming the countryside on horseback, living in the open. Sustaining themselves by plunder and rustling, they were easily recognised by terrified farmers because they wore their hair in a traditional style – the *ceudgelt* – which was the Druidic tonsure. Cut across the crown of the head, from ear to ear, it showed a high, shaved forehead with flowing locks allowed to grow long behind. Celtic priests cut their hair in the same way.

Once again, it is Roman writers who supply most of the sources for even a sketchy understanding of the Druids and Celtic religion. In fact writing was expressly forbidden. All Druidic lore was painstakingly committed to memory. Prodigious passages were learned and had to be available for immediate recall. When the Druids perished, so did much of native history.

THE GORSEDD

Edward Williams was a dreamer. In 1792 he took a group of his Welsh friends to Primrose Hill in London and created a stone circle. In fact he laid some pebbles on the grass. It was the setting for a revival. The first Gorsedd was inaugurated, and the ancient order of Bards existed once more. In 1819, in the back garden of the Ivy Bush Hotel in Carmarthen, the Druids reappeared – at the National Eisteddfod. Wearing strange costumes, they performed ceremonies invented by Williams and presided over by the Archdruid. At the Gorsedd of 2000 at Llanelli, the Recorder, James Nicholas, was stranded after the ceremonies had ended, his car having been removed. Wearing long white robes, white leather boots, a head-dress of oak leaves and carrying a staff, he was forced to catch a bus. His fellow passengers laughed and then heartily applauded the old man. Daft though the kit and the ponderous Victorian ceremonial might be, the Gorsedd had been central to the rescue of the Welsh language and a real sense of Welshness. And the bus passengers in Llanelli knew that.

There were many gods; one count has 400 in the Celtic pantheon. But most are mentioned only once and the inference must be that there were many local cults, many gods of a particular place, the *genii loci*. Along the line of Hadrian's Wall, shrines and dedications to the native deities, Belatucadros and Cocidius, have been found. Their nature is uncertain but both appear to have been war-gods. Cocidius may have been widely revered, and the site of the Roman outpost fort at Bewcastle was also known as *Fanum Cocidii*, Cocidius' shrine or sanctuary.

The Celts' contract with their gods differed from the Romans'. The altars raised at Newcastle in 120 were in thanks for a safe sea voyage. Generally for the Romans the gift of the gods came first and the thanks second. With the Celts this sequence worked in reverse. Often seen as malign, difficult trouble-makers, their gods needed gifts or a sacrifice *before* any important enterprise was undertaken. What was called propitiation can be seen at a shrine on Hadrian's Wall. At Coventina's Well, near Chesters Fort, thousands of coins and other metal objects were thrown in over a very long period. Even in the first century AD it was already a very old practice. Many caches of prehistoric metal have been retrieved from lakes, wells, bogs and other watery places. Often these were weapons, and the most famous deposit was Sir Bedivere's hurling of Excalibur into the lake – where it was of course caught by an arm *clothed in white samite*. The habit of propitiation remains longstanding, and in Western Europe coins are still thrown into fountains and wells – *for luck*.

The role of the Druids in Celtic society appears to have been central, so important that the Romans determined to destroy them. They seem not merely to have been priests. Citing all sorts of flimsy pretexts (a revulsion at the human sacrifice supposedly common in Britain sits ill from a culture which routinely slaughtered thousands for public amusement in the Colosseum and other arenas), Roman historians described a sustained campaign against the Druids. In AD 60 Suetonius Paullinus led an assault on the island of Anglesey, known to the Celts and the Welsh as Mona. Probably a shrine and almost certainly a redoubt of Druidic power, it lay within the territory of the Ordovices. When the XX Legion formed up on the mainland side of the Menai Strait, even seasoned veterans paused at the sight which greeted them. On the opposite shore, the warriors of the Ordovices waited, but not quietly. Their warhorns blasted, men jeered, but more terrifying, wild, black-haired women, their bodies streaked with ash, carrying torches, leapt into the water and capered around the beach, screaming curses at the Romans. Behind the ranks of warriors, a circle of Druids stood, their arms aloft, imploring the sky-gods to descend and destroy their hated enemies.

At Suetonius Paullinus' command, the legionaries and auxiliaries splashed into the Strait, attacked the Ordovices and defeated them utterly. In the days after the battle, the killing went on; Paullinus ordered his men to cut down the sacred groves of oak trees on Mona, and as far as possible extirpate the cult of the Druids. This was done not because of revulsion at the blood-soaked religion of a bunch of barbarians, but because the Druids were powerful, able to stiffen native resistance to the Roman invasion.

3

The North Road

It was like a monster from a nightmare as it snaked through the countryside. Wearing uniforms, marching in columns, moving as one, almost certainly singing soldiers' songs, the II Augusta Legion made its way westwards from the south-east coast, penetrating deep into the kingdom of the Durotriges. Those who saw the monster pass had never known its like. Cavalry had scouted the countryside ahead of the line of march, ever watchful for ambush, and the 5,000 crack troops of the Augusta were supported by many regiments of auxiliaries. Their commander, Titus Flavius Vespasianus, rode at the head of the column and, with his senior officers, he had considered all the available intelligence. Immediately following the invasion of AD 43, they had decided to strike at the heart of the territory of the Durotriges. It lay before them on the horizon, the huge hillfort of Mai Dun, now known as Maiden Castle.

From the ramparts, the warriors watched their enemies approach. Four rings of deep ditches and a high timber palisade defended the capital place of their kings. Ammunition had been stockpiled. Thousands of slingshot pebbles the size of plums had been picked up on nearby Chesil Beach, arrows lay in sheaves, and in their hands warriors held spears at the ready. But when the legion approached the huge hillfort, Vespasian kept his men well out of range. No attack appeared to threaten. Instead oxen pulled forward a series of machines. Next to mangonels with throwing-arms the length of trees, ominous piles of large stones were set down. A battery of smaller engines was strung out in a line, and men took much trouble in adjusting their height. The Durotriges could do nothing but watch and wait. A handle on one machine was slowly cranked, and ropes made from sinew groaned and stretched as a bolt was placed on what looked like a large crossbow. More like a javelin than an arrow, it was suddenly released with a tremendous snap and, to the astonishment of the warbands sheltering behind the palisade, it flew more than 300 metres, clearing all the ditches and tearing into the grass paddocks inside the enclosure. Once the range had been found, Vespasian ordered a murderous volley fired into Maiden Castle. It struck home hard. Archaeologists have found the skeleton of a Durotrigan warrior with the iron point of a ballista bolt embedded in his spine.

Once the defenders had been both thinned out and terrified by the Roman artillery barrage, an assault on the east gate was launched. Almost certainly using the testudo formation, which had served so well at Bigbury on the Medway, the legionaries got close enough to fire the gates and break into Maiden Castle. There followed the screams of a massacre. Near the gateway the bodies of men, women and children were found buried in shallow graves. Perhaps they were the Durotrigan royal family or aristocrats. Clinical, disciplined and ruthless, the attack of the II Augusta must have seemed like the wrath of the gods.

Maiden Castle was in reality not a castle at all. With a perimeter far too long to be effectively manned, an outward military appearance more symbolic than practical, Maiden Castle occupied a huge 50-acre site. Also misnamed as hillforts, these elaborate rings of ditches and ramparts were very difficult to defend. More likely a combination of sacred enclosure and royal or aristocratic compound, the hillforts were probably believed to have power of a different sort. The occupants prayed that their gods could somehow descend and repel the Roman defilers. Their warbands could never hope to.

Between the invasion of AD 43 and the summer of 47, Suetonius later wrote that Vespasian *fought thirty battles, subjugated two warlike tribes, and captured more than twenty towns [meaning hillforts], besides the entire Isle of Wight.* The armies of the southern British kings no doubt fought as hard as they knew how, but their strategists faced an irreducible problem. The legions were trained for combat in pitched battles across open ground and were near-invincible in close order. British armies depended on the impact of a tearaway charge and, when it became clear that the Romans could counter this very effectively with volleys of javelins and an iron discipline, native kings were forced to turn to guerrilla tactics. The rolling countryside of southern England, with many open fields, high ridgeways with little cover and few forests, did not make ambush or surprise attack easy.

TWENTY-FIVE SKINS

When a Roman army was on the march, its men carried all of their personal kit. But as the army penetrated further and further north, the men began to need tents to keep out the wetter and windier weather. Each leather tent slept a *contubernium*, a platoon of eight men, and had to be tall enough in the ridge to allow standing. Approximately twenty-five animal skins, usually goatskin or calfskin, were required to make each tent. It was very heavy and impossible for one man to carry, so a legion's tents were rolled up into fat cylinders and loaded onto the pack-saddles of mules. The arithmetic and logistics are remarkable. Each legion had to have at least 30,000 animal skins to make its tents. The auxiliaries and the cavalry will have added greatly to that total. With a garrison of four legions, the Roman army in Britain needed around 120,000 skins to keep the rain off and the wind out. Statistics like these show the amazing scale of what Rome achieved.

The British were compelled to retreat to their hillforts and the desperate hope that their gods would drive back the many-headed monster which trampled through their sacred lands.

After the capture of Camulodunum in 43, the invading legions fanned out across the south. The IX Hispana pushed north towards Lincoln and the Humber estuary beyond. In the Midlands lay the kingdom of the Catuvellauni, the people of Cunobelin and the dominant force before the invasion, and the XIV Gemina marched to subdue them. The XX Valeria was left in reserve at Colchester while the II Augusta drove into the West Country.

As they won victory after victory (at other hillforts the legionaries only had to set up a single ballista to persuade the defenders to surrender), Vespasian's cavalry troopers searched for Caratacus, the son of the great British king Cunobelin. As the focus of resistance, and no doubt the leader of a substantial refugee warband, he could prove a source of continuing trouble, tying up much valuable manpower.

By 47 Caratacus was doing exactly that. Having allied himself with the vigorous Silures of South Wales, he led raids into the Roman-controlled areas of the Midlands, possibly the kingdom of the Cornovii, around modern Birmingham. Showing immediate strategic flair, the new Governor of Britannia, Publius Ostorius Scapula, drove a wedge north-westwards, pushing the legions into the Cheshire Gap and to the shores of the Irish Sea. By the end of the campaigning season of 48, he had put his men between the Welsh kingdoms and those in the north.

No frontier was created. Lines on a map mattered little to Roman army commanders. Control was what counted and, to make that effective, the legions began to build. Metalled, free-draining roads soon patterned the landscape of Britain and they connected mighty fortresses planted at strategic places – river-crossings, valley-mouths, trading centres. *Speed in war*, wrote the military theorist Vegetius, *is more important than courage*. And a highly mobile, well-trained and well-led army could hold down vast swathes of territory.

When the Romans extended their reach further westwards and built legionary fortresses at Gloucester and Wroxeter, near Shrewsbury, Caratacus and his warriors retreated deeper into the Welsh mountains. The British king made an alliance with the Ordovices – but foolishly found himself forced to fight a set-piece battle at Caersws, at the headwaters of the Severn. After the inevitable defeat, a desperate Caratacus fled north. His support had probably begun to melt away.

As the invaders' grip tightened, the fleeing king made his last – and fateful – move. The most populous kingdom in all Britain, the kingdom of the Brigantes, remained free of Roman occupation, and was as yet unconquered. While its queen, Cartimandua, had concluded an alliance, it was surely becoming clear to her that the Roman advance might continue north. Client realms might fall in its path. If Caratacus had hoped to persuade Cartimandua, or, more likely, detach some of her aristocracy, he was to be quickly disappointed. In 51 she had him arrested and handed over to the Romans.

Caratacus had become famous. Throughout the Empire his exploits had been marvelled at. Few resistance leaders had been as successful and lasted so long against the might of the legions. Much in the way underdogs are still supported, it appears that the Roman public had taken to its heart this king from the edge of the world.

The Emperor Claudius was delighted at Caratacus' capture. It set the seal on his glorious conquest of Britannia, but a second triumph through the streets of Rome was out of the question. Instead the parade ground of the Praetorian Guard was chosen for a march past of all the British prisoners. Huge crowds gathered and the Guard turned out in all their menacing finery. Warriors from the royal warband, Catuvellaunian aristocrats, Caratacus' brothers, his queen and his daughter were all laden with chains and forced to walk past a dais. There Claudius and his court sat, basking in all their power, making the unmissable point that Rome ruled the world, even to its farthest margins.

The chained captives were awed and terrified by all the panoply and show. And they will have known the fate of those led in chains through Rome and its baying crowds. Many pleaded for their lives. But even great kings like Jugurtha of Numidia in North Africa and Vercingetorix, the resistance leader of the Gaulish rebellion against Caesar, had been humiliated in this way and then taken to the dungeons of the Mamertine prison. Under the Capitoline Hill, this dark and hellish place had witnessed many miserable ends. Originally a water cistern with two levels, it was entered from above. Bound in their chains, Jugurtha and Vercingetorix were lowered through a hole in the floor into the black darkness of the bottom level, where an executioner waited in the shadows to garotte them. It was said that their bodies were then despatched into the sewer system which led to the Tiber.

Walking at the very end of the procession into the Praetorian parade ground, Caratacus knew that a sinister death in the Mamertine waited. When he reached the imperial dais, it was said that he turned and looked up at Claudius. In his *Annals of Imperial Rome*, Tacitus put these fine words into Caratacus' mouth:

> . . . humiliation is my destiny, glory is yours. I had horses, men, arms, wealth. Can you be surprised that I am sorry to lose them? If you wish to rule the world, does it follow that everyone else should welcome enslavement? If I had surrendered without a blow before being brought before you, neither my downfall nor your triumph would have become famous. If you execute me, they will be forgotten. Spare me, and I shall be an everlasting token of your mercy.

It is more likely that Caratacus spoke Latin than Claudius had a command of Old Welsh. And even more likely that Caratacus made no speech at all. But Tacitus' invention does echo the politics of the time. Caesar had had Vercingetorix strangled after his triumph, but Claudius would not only exceed the deified Julius in actually conquering Britain, he would also show himself more merciful in sparing its most famous warrior-king. Politics had already decided Caratacus' fate.

However all that may be, the story of this failed rebel does have one illuminating effect. For at least a moment, it lifts the grey portrayal of native British kings out of the background shadows and puts words, albeit invented, into their mouths.

While all this was being played out on the parade grounds of Rome, war in Britain blazed into life once more. Without their captured leader the Silures had nevertheless defeated a legion and struck back hard against the tide of invasion. Their own kings believed that they faced extinction – the Governor, Ostorius Scapula, had said that they must be annihilated – and they fought like a people with nothing to lose. In the north, Cartimandua's consort, Venutius, took over Caratacus' role and led opposition amongst the Brigantes. If it had been a matter of imperial policy in Britain to gain control of the fertile and wealthy south, and only contain Wales and the north, that policy was no longer tenable. Trouble was flaring on two fronts.

In AD 54 Claudius died in suspicious circumstances, possibly from poison. His stepson, Nero, became emperor, and although it was said that he considered abandoning Britain, his actions spoke of the momentum of more conquest. Highly capable soldiers with experience of fighting in difficult terrain elsewhere in the Empire were sent as governors during his reign. Suetonius Paullinus led the assault on Anglesey in 60, and as his men ravaged the island in an attempt to extirpate the cult of the Druids, urgent messages galloped along the coast road. Far behind his lines, far to the south, in the heart of what the Romans believed was now a peaceful part of the province, a rebellion of extraordinary violence had exploded.

In Colchester in 43 Claudius accepted the submission of the kings of the Iceni. Famously wealthy, they ruled the north of East Anglia and the Fens. Trouble had flickered briefly in 47 when Ostorius Scapula had been forced to campaign amongst the dangerous marshes and creeks in the east of the kingdom, but under King Prasutagus there had been peace. When he died in 60, the blundering ineptitude and sheer greed of Roman officials converted a difficult transition into the fire and slaughter of the great rebellion led by Queen Boudicca.

In order to protect the integrity of his kingdom and preserve part of its wealth for his family, Prasutagus had named the Emperor Nero as one of the beneficiaries of his will. But not the only one. The king's daughters, the royal princesses of the Iceni, also stood to inherit a great deal. The Romans ignored Prasutagus' wishes. In their view the kingdom should revert entirely to the Empire and be absorbed without delay. In Roman eyes women had the same rights as children – and perhaps for that reason Boudicca's vigorous objections to their take-over astonished them. Their reaction was brutal. The queen was stripped and whipped with rods while the young princesses were raped by soldiers. Wealthy Icenian landowners were cast out of their estates, and the rest of the royal family treated like slaves. Cash bounties thought to be gifts from the Emperor turned out to be loans and Roman aristocrats began to demand repayment. These included the surprising figure of the philosopher Seneca, Nero's tutor. The Iceni had not only seen their queen humiliated and her daughters viciously defiled, they also felt they had been grossly deceived.

The effect was incendiary. As the warbands of the Iceni armed and mustered to evict those who had attempted to steal their lands and possessions, they were joined by the Trinovantes of the south. When Colchester had been designated a *colonia*, a settlement where retired Roman veterans were given plots of land, much abuse had taken place. Not content with their allotted plots, the veterans had grabbed more, and were encouraged by serving soldiers with an eye to their own retirement.

Boudicca's growing army swept down to Colchester, a hated imperial symbol. There were no walls and few defenders. Suetonius Paullinus and his legions were far away in North Wales. The Iceni torched the streets of the *colonia* and drove all who could resist to take refuge inside the ultimate focus of their fury, the temple of the Imperial Cult. Built over a sacred native site, it was a desecration to be erased. The gods would smile as it blazed. Boudicca's warriors surrounded the temple, but they had no equipment to besiege it. The garrison inside fought bravely and held out for two days before the Iceni stormed the makeshift defences and slaughtered everyone they could find.

From the vexillation fortress at Longthorpe, near Peterborough, Petilius Cerialis hurried south with detachments of the IX Hispana and a squadron of cavalry. They were overwhelmed. The legionary infantry stood no chance and were surrounded and annihilated. Cerialis scrambled onto his pony and galloped for his life and the safety of the walls of Longthorpe. Rome's hold on Britain was loosening.

When he received news of the rebellion, Suetonius Paullinus immediately abandoned his campaign in North Wales, and with extraordinary speed he and his advance guard reached London before Boudicca could swing her army south. London had grown into the principal town of Roman Britain, but when Paullinus heard of Cerialis' defeat he decided to abandon all hope of a successful defence. This ruthless but sensible decision was to prove a turning-point in the campaign, and without delay the Governor rejoined the main force of his legions somewhere on Watling Street.

Meanwhile the Iceni rampaged into Roman London, the newly paved streets ran red with blood, and smoke blackened the skies over the banks of the Thames. Brimming with confidence, Boudicca led her warriors north and went to find Paullinus, probably to meet him head-on, and kill more Romans. St Albans was destroyed in her wake, and reports of appalling atrocities began to circulate. Dio Cassius wrote that female Roman captives were bound and taken to a grove sacred to the Celtic war goddess Andraste. There they were tied to trees, and had their breasts cut off and stuffed into their mouths. Then they suffered the unimaginable agonies of impaling, when a sharpened stake was inserted into their anus and shoved up through their bodies.

Paullinus knew that a decisive battle was coming and he sent to Exeter for the battle-hardened II Augusta. But its commander, Poenius Postumus, refused to follow orders and leave his fortress. The Silures were not subdued, were near at hand and might join the rebellion. Perhaps Postumus believed the whole province would go up in flames, perhaps he had heard stories of the savagery of Boudicca's warriors.

In any event Paullinus prepared for battle with the troops he had and, fatally, Boudicca allowed him to choose his ground. The legions formed up in a defile somewhere near Towcester, on the line of Watling Street. The tactics were familiar, the outcome predictable. After a volley of javelins had fatally slowed the charge of the warbands, the legionaries fell into the flying wedge formation and tore into the disorganised ranks of the British. They drove them back into their baggage train, no doubt swollen with loot, and the battle turned into a massacre. Boudicca fled and probably committed suicide soon afterwards. Paullinus scoured the countryside for fugitives, allies, even neutrals. Roman vengeance was terrible, and smoke rose on every horizon as the soldiers punished southern Britain for daring to rebel.

It was, to paraphrase a more recent general, a close-run thing. In the calm after the fire and sword, the legions were showered with honour; the XIV Gemina added Martia Victrix to its name, while the XX became Valeria Victrix. In Rome it was decided that further conquest would bring tighter control and a more certain peace. It did not. There would be frequent spasms of warfare in Britain for almost sixty years.

GLADIATORS

Perhaps one of the most common and potent symbols of ancient Rome, gladiators and the public games they appeared in were a bloodthirsty but fascinating phenomenon. Professional fighters were first seen at funeral games, celebrations mounted in honour of dead soldiers. Caesar widened out this tradition, and games were mounted to gain favour with the Roman mob. Augustus had 5,000 pairs of gladiators fight in eight separate series of games. Not just any weapons and armour were used. There were four sorts of combatants. Most alike were the Murmillo and the Samnite who wielded short swords (a *gladius* in Latin, hence 'gladiator'), wore visored helmets and protected themselves with oblong shields. Perhaps the most recognisable was the Retiarius. With little armour, he used a net and a trident. The Thracian had a broad-bladed scimitar and a round shield. Sometimes slaves, sometimes free men, all gladiators were expensive and, contrary to Hollywood convention, the baying crowds often voted to spare their lives. The Colosseum was the largest venue in Rome, and Domitian ruled that gladiatorial games could only be mounted by the Emperor. In 325, Constantine banned them.

The chaos of the summer of AD 60 was followed by a winter of retribution of a different sort. Boudicca's army had been largely made up of farmers. It is very likely that little seedcorn had been sown in that fateful spring, and only a meagre harvest was ripening in the fields. But calm and common sense did eventually arrive in the shape of Julius Classicianus, the new provincial procurator. His was a pivotal role. As chief financial secretary in Britain, responsible for the man-agement of taxation and the imperial estates, Classicianus reported directly to the Emperor and his chancery. The previous incumbent had been Decianus Catus, and it was his greed and incompetence which in part goaded the Iceni into open revolt. When Boudicca threatened London, he wisely fled to Gaul.

In contrast to Paullinus' lust for vengeance, Classicianus preached moderation. He was himself of Gaulish origin and may have been able to understand and talk to British aristocrats in a language which was cousin to Old Welsh. There were also clear political motives. How could the imperial procurator raise tax revenues while Paullinus' legions continued to terrorise the countryside? After the recall of the Governor to Rome, Classicianus was joined by someone who had not seen the savagery of Boudicca's warriors or the baleful remnants of their atrocities. Petronius Turpilianus shared the procurator's view that Britain badly needed a period of calm, a time for recovery. Tacitus did not approve, and in *The Annals* he sniffed:

> Publius Petronius Turpilianus, neither provoking the enemy nor provoked, called this ignoble inactivity peace with honour.

As the wounds healed, the Governor and procurator began to rebuild – both civic buildings and political trust. They knew that the role of the British kingdoms had to be absolutely central in the new province. Basing their administrative structure on their old territories, Turpilius and Classicianus reinvented them as *civitates*. It was continuity of a sort. Towns were founded as centres for commerce and local government, and the native aristocracy was encouraged to become magistrates and councillors at the likes of Durnovaria (Dorchester, capital of the Durotriges) or Venta Icenorum (Caistor by Norwich, capital of the Iceni). Whether through exhaustion and a weary compliance, or a genuine acceptance that Rome was not going to go away, these administrative arrangements began to take. In 67 the XIV Gemina, the legion which had defeated Boudicca, was withdrawn. The British garrison shrank to three legions, enough to hold what had quickly become a peaceful province. There was never to be another rebellion in the south.

It was different in the north. Old enmities simmered. It was almost two decades since the Brigantes had been divided between the pro-Roman Queen Cartimandua and the independent-minded Venutius. Surprisingly he had not ridden to Boudicca's side in AD 60, and perhaps he and his wife had reached some accommodation. But in 69 resentments reignited. Cartimandua renounced her marriage to Venutius and replaced him with a younger man, his own armour-bearer, Vellocatus. Unmistakable echoes of melodrama sounded around the Pennines as this soap-opera subplot played out. Shamed and insulted, Venutius rose in rebellion once more against his head-strong queen. This time he called for help from outside. North of the Brigantes lay the lands of the Selgovae and the Novantes, and it seems that their captains led warbands down the hill trails to Brigantium.

LATIN OR ELSE

In the fifth century BC Latin was a dialect of Italic spoken by a very few people around the small and insignificant town of Rome. Other languages and dialects were much more widely spoken in the Italian peninsula. Greek was common in the south and Sicily; Lepontic, a Celtic language, in the north, the Po Valley and as far down the Adriatic coast as Ancona. Osco-Umbrian was a much larger speech community and it stretched down the centre of Italy from Arezzo to Calabria. Politics changed all that. As Rome gained dominance, so did its language. But Latin did not obliterate local dialects entirely. When Italy reunified in the middle of the nineteenth century abrupt regional differences still existed – so much so that a standard Italian (based on Tuscan) had to be imposed by the government. But even now, even in Tuscany, dialect is still strong. The small town of Pitigliano has its own dictionary and, without it, those who imagine they are fluent in Italian discover that they are most certainly not.

International politics also promised to help the rebels. The increasingly unstable and psychotic Emperor Nero had been forced to suicide. Rome was reeling in a bitter civil war. In 69 there were no less than four emperors. Venutius will have followed the ebb and flow, and he knew that the provincial armies all over the Empire were involved in supporting different candidates. There would be confusion and uncertainty amongst the depleted garrison in Britain. Now was the time to summon his northern allies and strike.

The provincial Governor, Vettius Bolanus, sent troops to support Cartimandua and her young consort, but all they could manage was a desperate rescue. Venutius had made himself undisputed king of Britain's most populous realm. Rome now had a powerful enemy in the north.

Once Vespasian had established himself as Emperor, he turned his mind to Britain. After his campaigns in the 40s with the II Augusta, he understood the strategic situation well. The north could not be left like a wolf prowling outside the fold, able to strike at any time. Another veteran of British warfare was appointed Governor; Petilius Cerialis had suffered defeat by Boudicca's warriors and been forced to make an ignominious retreat. He was not likely to underestimate the Brigantes.

What greeted Cerialis on his arrival in Britain in 71 was not encouraging. After a few years of relative peace, discipline had slackened amongst the legions and there appears to have been a mutiny. Having brought the newly formed II Adiutrix and stationed them at Lincoln, Cerialis led the IX Hispana up the north road. At York they built a legionary fortress in a bend of the River Ouse. In the first century AD the tide washed up from the Humber as far as York, and the small *liburnae* (sixty-man patrol ships) could supply the army base from the sea. If a long campaign was anticipated, this sort of ready access was more than usually important.

As important as geography and logistics, politics also placed the IX Legion at the bend in the Ouse. It looks as though York lay between the kingdom of the Brigantes and the territory of the Parisii. Occupying much of the old East Riding, the Parisii were recent immigrants from Gaul (and their cousins gave the French capital its name). It is not known whether or not these neighbours were hostile to each other, but the site of the new headquarters at York seems to have been a version of the old Roman dictum of *divide et impera*, divide and rule.

York grew into an impressive citadel. Much of the Multangular Tower at the west corner of the fortress is still upstanding and other massive foundations recall an imposing symbol of imperial power. At least three emperors came to York and none will have felt out of place. It was a good place to locate a garrison, and the city has a long and distinguished military history.

Cerialis appears to have struck north-west into the Pennines. Near what is now called Scotch Corner, Venutius' warbands and his allies mustered at a huge hillfort at Stanwick. The outer perimeter measured almost 8 miles in length, and even an inner ring of defences was more than a mile in circumference. The Brigantes were overrun.

SIN! DEX!

Roman soldiers still drill on British parade grounds. Centurions and optios still roar the Latin equivalents of Left! Right! That is, *sin* for *sinister* (left) and *dex* for *dexter* (right). No records of legionaries marching to these commands exist, and the Roman re-enactors who bark them admit that they are improvising. But little else is done without regard for the finest degrees of historical accuracy. Their gleaming uniforms are faithfully reproduced and the result of astonishing cost and commitment. For example, a chain-mail shirt takes 800 hours to make, and the more common sort of armour to protect the abdomen, the *lorica segmentata*, is also very expensive. At summer events along Hadrian's Wall and elsewhere in Roman Britain, several groups of re-enactors can be seen. They drill, form a testudo, charge, fire arrows at targets, and their cavalry soldiers show feats of genuine horsemanship. There are six or seven groups in Britain but each has only twenty or so members at most. What would be most impressive is a combined force – close to a legionary double century. But this is apparently impossible. The different groups do not get on well, each one sniffing at the others' lack of attention to detail, commitment and, well, general Roman-ness.

In the ditches of the old hillfort, archaeologists have found the remains of broken beliefs and failed gods. Below the ramparts guarding the gates several skulls were uncovered. Unrelated to any skeleton and probably older than AD 71, the date of the battle for Stanwick, they formed part of a ghost-fence. To turn back the ranks of hard-bitten legionaries, Venutius' Druids had set up rows of skulls on the stockade. Their magic would surely be strong. No man would dare to cross the fence they made. As the legionaries stormed the gates safe under the testudo, the IX Hispana will not even have noticed what was staring hollow-eyed down at them.

By tracking Cerialis' marching camps across the Stainmore Gap and down into the Eden Valley, archaeologists have traced his advance north. At Carlisle, on a low rise between the Caldew and the Eden, another navigable river, the IX and the XX built a legionary fortress. From its ramparts they could see the distant shores of Galloway, the territory of the Novantae and the Selgovae. Allies of the Brigantes,

The Wall

their *help from outside*, some of their warbands probably fought in the hopeless rout at Stanwick.

The XX Valeria Victrix were under the command of a young man soon to become famous, Gnaeus Julius Agricola. He already knew Britain well and had fought with Suetonius Paullinus in the Boudicca rebellion. This was also Cerialis' second tour of duty, but neither had ever come as far north as Carlisle and the Cumbrian Mountains. Their intentions were governed by imperial policy. In the reign of Claudius, a successful and glamorous general, Domitius Corbulo, had led his soldiers across the Rhine and beyond the limits of the Empire. Whatever the compelling strategic motives, Claudius would have none of it. There would be no freelancing, and Corbulo was quickly recalled. Conquest was an exclusively imperial prerogative, and from that time on no general could extend the frontiers of Rome without an express commission to do so. Cerialis and Agricola knew that very well, and if they were tempted to seek retribution across the Solway and in the Southern Uplands, they resisted it.

Recent historians of Roman Britain have argued that Vespasian had encouraged Cerialis to push northwards as far as seemed logistically sensible. Perhaps the Emperor's own knowledge had persuaded him that a conquest of the whole island would settle all strategic issues. As ever at the beginning of a new reign, the prestige of military success at the edge of the world would do no harm. It is difficult to be sure what happened when the legions reached the Tyne–Solway isthmus in AD 73.

Often archaeology is all that remains of the historical record, and rickles of stones and the humps and bumps of earthworks rarely have much to say about individuals, their motives and actions. But the movement of Roman armies across the landscape can be accurately tracked by following the line and type of marching camps dug by the legionaries. Aerial photography can pick up the location and outline in great detail, often when nothing much can be seen on the ground. It has been suggested that Cerialis did indeed march up the north road from Carlisle, probably on the line of what is now the A74. Some believe that he penetrated as far as the Firth of Tay. This assertion is not merely a facet of one of those entertaining and occasionally vicious academic squabbles, it touches on a very important issue. Either Cerialis or Agricola (when he became Governor of Britannia) was responsible for the Gask Ridge frontier system, a line of forts and watchtowers linked by a road which ran north-westwards from Doune, near Stirling, up the Allan Water valley, along the ridge and ultimately to Perth. It was almost certainly designed to divide the territory of the Venicones in Fife and Kinross from the Caledonians of the Eastern Highlands. Its greater significance was that it was a first. If Cerialis ordered its construction, it predates similar arrangements in Roman Germany. The Gask Ridge may have been the first frontier.

Whatever the reality, Cerialis' initiative cannot be proved, at least not until a definitive archaeological find changes the picture. All the watchtowers and forts are the right sort of shape and style to suit the period but no certainly datable objects such as coins or inscriptions have been discovered. By contrast it is absolutely confirmed that Agricola was on the Gask Ridge in 79 and the story of the construction of its frontier system will wait until he and his legions arrive.

Meanwhile, Cerialis was recalled to Rome in 73 and another battle-hardened general replaced him as Governor of Britannia. Julius Frontinus turned his energies to the west. Having seen that Cerialis had contained the problem of the Brigantes, the new commander-in-chief wanted to secure all of Britain to the south of them. Wales had never ceased to resist. The Silures had defeated a legion and were clearly highly capable warriors. For the first time the legions marched into their territory to build a mighty fortress. At Caerleon on the Usk (now the northern suburbs of modern Newport), a site was chosen which could be serviced and supplied from the Bristol Channel. Interestingly the present place-name is derived from Latin. Caerleon is a flattened-out rendition of *Castra Legionis*, while the Roman name was Celtic in origin. Usk is from *Isca*, which means 'water' as in the sense of river and is cognate to Esk, of which there are several in the north; it is also related very distantly to *uisge*, the root of 'whisky'.

Frontinus attacked the Silures. Their fierce independence had glowed undimmed since the first invasions. The new Governor led the II Augusta, the men who stormed Maiden Castle and subdued the West Country, out of their new base and into the fertile cornlands of the Vale of Glamorgan. The campaign appears to have been successful and there are reports of forts being built in mid Wales. Cavalry squadrons patrolled the north, the territory of the Ordovices and the Deceangli. At last, it seemed, the West had been won.

TOURING THE PROVINCES

At Caerleon the amphitheatre is well preserved. Built conveniently near the legionary fortress, its customers, at least in the early days, will have been mostly soldiers. Touring companies of actors, acrobats and wrestlers will no doubt have tailored their material to suit. Mime appears to have been popular, a universal language without words, with actors wearing masks to signify stock characters. Multilingual audiences will have understood everything. For the rough-and-ready sense of humour of the soldiers sitting on the tiered seating, this will have been ribald, knockabout stuff: adult pantomime. Troupes of travelling acrobats, like those who sent the Emperor Claudius a golden crown, and musicians may also have been on the bill, but one of the most puzzling entertainments was boxing. Sculpture and illustrations of boxers show not gloves on their fists but a pair of brutal, thick knuckle-dusters. Around their forearms and wrists were wound iron-studded thongs; blows landed with this equipment will have been devastating – teeth, skin and bone flying. The face of a defeated boxer would have been a pummelled mess of shattered cheekbones and severe cuts. The mystery is – why did they do it? Equally matched professional boxers (unequal matches would have been short and less entertaining) would have had very brief careers, having literally knocked lumps out of each other.

Agricola had departed with Cerialis in AD 73 and become Governor of Aquitania, a province in south-western Gaul. His tenure pleased the Emperor and, in 76, Agricola was given the great honour of a consulship. It was no less than he might have expected. In the chaos of the Year of the Four Emperors, Agricola had been quick to pledge his support to Vespasian – even before he had emerged as a claimant to the imperial throne. There were family reasons behind this gamble. One of the four emperors, Otho, had sent his fleet to harry the Ligurian coast of north-western Italy. In the confusion and the fighting, Agricola's mother had been killed. And Vespasian trusted him for another reason: he was a man largely untouched by the poisonous politics of Rome. Agricola's family came from Frejus (Forum Julii) in Provence and his cognomen (Agricola, 'the Farmer') spoke of the bucolic virtues of the provinces.

In what was to turn out to be as significant a move as his consulship, Agricola allowed his daughter to marry Publius Cornelius Tacitus. The historian would guarantee that both their names would become famous. A year after the marriage, Agricola was appointed Governor of Britannia, by now a prestigious posting, and it is very likely that he took his new son-in-law with him as a military tribune.

As soon as he arrived in the province, Agricola hurried north to the legionary fortress at Wroxeter, the headquarters of his old comrades-in-arms, the XX Valeria Victrix. It was late in the campaigning season but the new Governor wanted to make an immediate impression, set the tone for his time in the province he knew so well. The cavalry patrolling the lands of the Ordovices in North Wales had been attacked and destroyed. Vengeance moved swiftly as the XX marched along the coast road. Retreating in front of Agricola, the Ordovices sought the sanctuary of the Welsh mountains, refusing pitched battle, hoping that the onset of autumn, and the winter behind it, would persuade the Romans to return to their barracks and their granaries.

Knowing that time was short, Agricola pursued the warbands into the high valleys with *himself at the head of the column so as to impart his own courage to the rest by sharing the danger.* It was a bold, even foolhardy, decision to take on the Ordovices in the landscape they knew intimately. Snowdonia is known in Welsh as Eryri, the Eagles' Lair, impregnable, almost sacrosanct. Snowdon itself is Yr Wyddfa, the Throne of Kings, the place of heroes. But the strategy worked. In a brutally brief sentence, Tacitus reported: *Almost the entire people was cut to pieces.*

Agricola quickly followed his success in the mountains by returning to a place he will never have forgotten. In AD 60 with Suetonius Paullinus, as a twenty-year-old tribune, he had faced the Ordovices and the curses of their Druids at the Menai Strait, and almost immediately afterwards raced southwards at the news of the Boudicca rebellion. This time Agricola did not hesitate. The Batavians and their ponies swam the Strait once more, and the sacred island of Anglesey was forced into submission and into the Empire.

To cement his gains, Agricola moved the II Adiutrix up to a fortress at Chester. Close to the Dee estuary and the Irish Sea, a naval base was established. Having been recruited only eight years earlier from the sailors of the Italian fleet at Ravenna, the II Adiutrix was in essence a naval legion, staffed with shipwrights who could build the ships needed in western waters. Piles for a huge jetty were driven into the mudflats below the fortress, and the jetty stretched out into the midstream of the Dee to allow ships to dock and sail in all tidal conditions. Out of Chester, the army could be supplied up the Irish Sea coast and beyond. Agricola was clearly planning a move up the north roads.

The following summer he made it. Brigading the legions and auxiliaries into two battle groups, he advanced from the new fortress at Carlisle and from the Tyne, from a base built at Corbridge. Diplomacy paved the way and dictated the line of march. The Votadini of the Tweed basin and the Lothians were productive farmers, able to grow a corn surplus and, as had been established before a legionary set foot out of his camp, willing to sell it at reasonable prices – which was of great importance to Roman quarter-masters.

The eastern battle group pushed north up the line of the modern A68, reaching the watershed ridges of the Cheviots a few miles east of where the road now crosses into Scotland, at the Carter Bar. Agricola was probably riding at the head of the western army. Following the line of the modern A74, they proceeded with great caution. The planned pincer movement hoped to encircle the Selgovae, the one-time allies of Venutius and the Brigantes. But like their Border Reiver descendants fourteen centuries later, these warriors knew their wind-swept hills and hidden valleys very well. They could disappear into nowhere and appear out of nowhere. Roman caution is recalled by the decisions of the engineers who built the road north of the fort at Crawford. Instead of following the flat ground by the headwaters of the River Clyde, the road zigzags up a hillside and onto a boggy plateau. It seems a perverse decision – until the alternative route is looked at closely. If the Roman road-builders had taken the easier option, they and their comrades would have had to march through a narrow defile between steep slopes on one side and the river on the other. A perfect place for a Selgovan ambush.

Seventeen hundred miles to the south, the political weather was changing. On 23rd June AD 79, the Emperor Vespasian died (enga-gingly, his last words were those of a tough and sceptical old soldier: *Dear me, I think I am turning into a god*). Having made his eldest son, Titus, commander of the Praetorian Guard, the soon to be deified Vespasian will have had few anxieties about the succession. And, as usual, there was an immediate imperial need for prestige. Titus had served in Britain with Suetonius Paullinus. He knew and trusted Agricola, and as the Governor halted his advance to await orders from the new emperor, there will have been little doubt that the word from Rome would be *Onward!*

Success was suitably spectacular. By the late summer of AD 79 the legions stood on the shores of the Firth of Tay. Titus celebrated. And it seems that Agricola decided that his men would build Rome's first identifiable frontier in Britain, perhaps in the Empire: the Gask Ridge.

Tacitus is disappointingly vague at this point. The legions had encountered *new peoples* but he does not say who they were. Later sources suggest that the kingdom of the Venicones lay to the east of the new frontier along the Allan Water and the Gask Ridge. With territory comprising Fife and Kinross, the Venicones seem to have been allies of the Votadini and, interestingly, their name translates as 'the Kindred Hounds'. Like their cousins across the Forth, the Venicones were corn producers, and in the second century AD map of Britain drawn by Ptolemy, he marks a place in Fife called Horrea. It means granaries. Perhaps there was more than one collection point for corn in the kingdom of Fife. The fort of Birrens, just north of the Ridge, was known by the nickname of Blatobulgium, 'the corn sack place'. Between Cupar and St Andrews lies the hamlet of Blebo and its name derives from the same source.

On the western side of the Gask Ridge were the hill peoples collectively known as the Caledonii. Later place-names whisper at their presence. Dunkeld means 'Fort of the Caledonians' and Schiehallion is 'the Magic Mountain of the Caledonians'. The name Caledonii itself may mean something unhelpful like 'the Warrior People'. Other names flit around the historical record. More than a century later the Romans encountered a warlike people known as the Maeatae, and again place-names remember them. On the southern rampart of the Ochil Hills stands Dumyat, 'the Fort of the Maeatae', while a few miles further south is Myot Hill. It seems that the new frontier lay along a pre-existing boundary, one which divided the Caledonii from the Venicones, hillmen from plainsmen, shepherds from ploughmen, those friendly towards Rome from those hostile.

Traces of eighteen watchtowers have been found in the valley of the Allan Water and on the Gask Ridge. Two-storey buildings of timber and turf, they were manned by a platoon or *contubernium* of eight soldiers, and placed approximately a mile apart so that each could be easily seen by its neighbour. They were connected by a road which also linked four forts at Doune, Ardoch, Strageath and Perth. Smaller fortlets lay between each tower. It appears to have been a considered design, which ought to have worked well.

If it does date to the time of the Agricolan invasion (or even earlier), then the Gask Ridge is the first example of an artificial frontier in the Empire. A similar arrangement was laid out in Germany east of the natural barrier of the Rhine – but probably in the reign of Trajan (AD 98 to 117).

UP POMPEII

Sandals supply a telling clue to the presence of women in the Roman forts. Because of their size and the particular points of wear found on their soles, leather sandals preserved in anaerobic, peaty ground have been identified by archaeologists as definitely belonging to women. They appear only occasionally in the written record, but there is no doubt that at Roman forts there lived more than just a few women. A tiny minority were the wives of senior officers, some were the common-law wives of soldiers (who were not officially allowed to marry until retirement or discharge) and some were prostitutes. As forts settled into permanent garrisons in Britain, many of the civilian villages which grew up around them will have had a brothel somewhere. When the Italian town of Pompeii was submerged under 5 metres of volcanic ash in AD 79, several brothels were preserved. And they show how differently the Roman saw this unsavoury aspect of life. Menus and prices were clearly advertised. Some women were very cheap, others expensive, others offered specialities. Their working names showed versatility – Panta (Every-thing), Culibona (Lovely Bum) and other much more graphic attributes. Entertainingly their patrons' nicknames are occasionally recorded: Enoclione (Brave Toper) and Skordopordonikos (Garlic Farter) appear both to have been regulars. Britain, and particularly the large garrison in the north, will have supported a thriving sex industry. But it was not driven underground. The Romans blushed at other things.

Forward of the frontier three forts were built in the mouths of glens which reached into the Highland massif. Bochastle, Dalginross and Fendoch were positioned to detect and observe movement: if the numbers made sense and it was hostile, challenge it. Behind these forts, the watchtowers could do only that, watch for trouble and report to the commander of the nearest fort along the line.

In times of peace, movement across the frontier was controlled. In Germany the native peoples were only allowed into the Empire during daylight, if they were unarmed and at particular crossing-points. No doubt a toll was collected, especially if travellers were carrying goods to trade. The Gask Ridge is very likely to have operated in the same way.

Agricola commanded a large army, perhaps 20,000 legionaries, auxiliaries and cavalry. Wherever they halted to consolidate, they had the numbers and the skills to achieve a massive building programme. Such speed and skill was an integral part of military strategy. After terrorising an area and then offering surprisingly reasonable – and therefore attractive – terms to whomever had suffered the short, sharp Roman shock, they then tightened their grip by building roads and forts. This not only gave an immediate impression of tremendous power, it also allowed Agricola's soldiers to stay on through the winter. There was no respite for native kings to regroup. The Romans had come and conquered.

In 81 it seems that forts were built across the Forth–Clyde isthmus before Agricola returned to the XX Legion's base at Carlisle. While it was not a precursor for the Antonine Wall of the next century, the building programme was certainly a recognition that the narrow waist of Scotland was a good place for a frontier. Here is Tacitus' appraisal:

> . . . a frontier had been found within Britain itself. For the Firths of
> Clota (Clyde) and Bodotria (Forth), carried far inland by the tides of
> the opposite seas, are separated by a narrow neck of land. This was
> now being securely held by garrisons and the whole sweep of the
> country on the nearer side was secured: the enemy had been pushed
> back, as if into a different island.

As the arms of his pincer had struck through southern Scotland in 78, Agricola cut off the kingdoms of the south-west – Dumfries and Galloway, and Ayrshire – from their former allies in the Cheviots and the Pennines. The Novantae appear to have been a naval power. The Solway coast is indented with dozens of natural harbours, sailors are rarely out of the sight of land in the Irish Sea and it was much more of a highway than a barrier. One of the most sheltered harbours faces north. From Loch Ryan modern ferries sail for Ireland but their journey is an ancient one. The name is a remnant of Rerigonium, a place marked by Ptolemy at the foot of the loch, near where Stranraer stands now. It means 'Most Royal Place' and may have been the seat of Novantan kings.

Agricola's push north needed consolidation behind it, and he knew that he could not safely leave a hostile people on the northern shores of the Solway. *He crossed in the leading ship,* reported Tacitus, *and defeated peoples up to that time unknown in a series of successful actions. He lined up his forces in that part of Britain that faces Ireland, an expression of hope rather than of fear.* Since Agricola believed that Ireland could be taken and held by a single legion and some auxiliaries, it is well he did not attempt to confront the warriors of the Ulster kings – even if Cuchulainn had long before fought his way into legend.

HOW MANY?

As those who read the New Testament will know, the Romans were keen on making a regular census of populations in even the farthest reaches of the Empire. It was done mainly to make tax-raising more efficient. Sadly, no census of the province of Britain has survived, but historians have estimated that Roman England, essentially, was inhabited by about a million people. Rome itself was at least as populous (probably two million if slaves are counted) and other cities around the Empire were also very large. Alexandria, Carthage, Antioch, Pergamum, Ephesus and Lyons in Gaul had between 100,000 and 300,000 people living in each of them and the territory immediately adjacent. At the death of Augustus in AD 14, there were around 54 million in his empire.

Like that of all victorious armies, Roman military intelligence was good. As a matter of routine, Agricola's staff officers interrogated prisoners, traders, disaffected native aristocrats, anyone who could supply information about enemy positions, strength, even morale.

When the first rumbles of rebellion in the north reached Agricola, he began to plan a general advance into Scotland. But he could not move without imperial approval. Titus had died suddenly, perhaps suspiciously, and his younger brother, Domitian, followed him onto the throne. Tacitus thought him loathsome, a despicable tyrant. And since Tacitus was a senator for most of Domitian's reign, he was close enough to the imperial court to form a firm view. Much of the tone of the *Agricola* is set by the notion that good men can still behave honourably and achieve good things even when a bad emperor rules in Rome. Suetonius shared a poor opinion of Domitian, listing his many vicious cruelties and the names of the good men he had had unjustly executed.

Nevertheless, the order from Rome was positive and Agricola began the long march north. Scotland's geography dictated his strategy. Forced to advance up the eastern lowlands of Perthshire and Angus and the Mearns, Agricola decided not to brigade his legions and auxiliaries into one huge army group. Intelligence reports had warned that the Caledonians (probably a federation like the Brigantes) had massed a vast host and fearing *encirclement by superior forces familiar with the country, he himself divided his army into three divisions and advanced.*

Perhaps with the expert advice of the officers of the II Adiutrix, Agricola had organised for a fleet to shadow his land invasion. The east coast of Scotland is blessed with several beaches suitable for landings by supply boats and their protective warships. Lunan Bay, the Montrose basin and Bervie Bay all lie close to the line of march and forts dug by the legionaries. The natural harbour at Stonehaven is less than two miles from the marching camp at Raedykes.

Agricola's caution was not rewarded. Having committed the fundamental error of dividing his forces (something not pointed out by the loyal Tacitus), disaster almost struck. The IX Legion was the smallest of the three divisions and, as it moved north, Caledonian scouts counted its numbers and watched and waited. Once a halt had been called in a likely location, a ditch dug and a rampart piled up, the scouts sent gallopers to alert native generals to the opportunity. And the warbands massed for a night attack.

Roman marching camps were all very similar in layout. Tent lines were pegged out in the same places each time and units always pitched in the same part. This was not simply a matter of habit or bureaucracy.

In moments of emergency, soldiers knew exactly where to run to and muster when trumpets sounded or commands were shouted. Even in the darkest, moonless night, they could fall properly into their ranks. Between the lines of tents and the rampart a wide space known as the *intervallum* was left. This ensured that missiles, slingshots, arrows or javelins launched from outside the perimeter could not reach where the soldiers slept and kept their kit. It also served as an area where units could form up into battle order. The Roman military instinct was always to get out into open field to fight. In restricted spaces their great advantages in equipment, tactics and discipline were less determinant. Visitors to the ruins of Roman fortresses are often surprised at the number and width of the gates. Used to looking at medieval castles with only one heavily defended entrance, they wonder at such obvious points of weakness. But in fact the gates were designed to allow Roman soldiers to get out of their forts in as large a number and as quickly as possible.

ROMAN NEWSREEL

Trajan's Column is an extraordinary historical object. Standing in the centre of Rome, having miraculously survived for nineteen centuries, its sculpture tells a highly detailed story of the Emperor's wars in Dacia, modern Romania. Like a film with no soundtrack, the narrative winds up the column, recording several triumphs and hard fights on its way. The reliefs supply an invaluable insight into Roman military methods: battlefield tactics, uniforms, weapons, how marching camps were dug, and a wealth of other information illustrated nowhere else. It is now 95 feet in height (originally 125 feet) and stood on top of Trajan's mausoleum. Despite a vigorous use of colour (now all gone) to pick out the busy, action-packed scenes, those near the top must have been almost invisible. Hadrian was Trajan's immediate successor, and the style of almost everything depicted on the column will have looked exactly the same as on the Wall and in the province of Britannia.

Marching camps had no wooden gates, only defended openings in each of the four sides. As darkness fell in the summer of AD 82, the Caledonian generals who watched the IX Legion light their campfires and settle down for the night will have noted that the gateways were heavily guarded but not blocked by anything solid. The ramparts were also not formidable, able only to slow down an assault but not to stop it.

To launch a night attack, it is likely that warhorns sounded the charge, and out of the shadows the Caledonian warriors raced towards the gates, roaring their war-cries. *They cut down the sentries and burst into the sleeping camp, creating panic*, wrote Tacitus. With little or no time to buckle on armour, the legionaries grabbed their helmets, shields and weapons and fought back as best they could, blundering amongst the tents and guy ropes. Earlier in the campaign the warbands had attacked forts and knew what to expect. It looked as though there would be a great slaughter and, just as three legions had been annihilated in the forests of Germany seventy years earlier, the IX would be wiped out in the fateful shadow of the Scottish Highlands.

But help came. Perhaps the commander of the IX had somehow got horsemen away out of the mêlée and they had found Agricola's division. Perhaps Tacitus was telling the unspun truth, rather than promoting his father-in-law's acumen, when he wrote that it was his scouts who had reported the enemy attack. But he seems to suggest that Agricola's men were still on the march – at night? Whatever the reality, reinforcements arrived in the nick of time, and by dawn the warbands had been driven off. Memorably, Tacitus wrote: *At first light the standards gleamed.*

The ability of the fleet to supply his land army allowed Agricola to penetrate far to the north. But it also had another advantage. When Caledonian commanders saw Roman ships appear on the horizon again and again, keeping in step with the army pushing up from the south, they must have felt that there was no escape. So they began to turn their minds from guerilla warfare and night attacks to preparation for a battle, a mighty battle which would bring *either revenge or enslavement*.

In consecutive passages Tacitus talks of alliances, exchanges of embassies and a united front amongst the kings of northern Scotland. It was clearly a federation which fought the advance of the Romans. Ptolemy noted the names of its probable members. The kings of the Vacomagi ruled in Angus and the Mearns, and north of the Mounth, the Taexali were in Aberdeenshire and the north-east, and the Decantae, the Smertae and the Lugi in Ross and Sutherland. These peoples remain mysterious. Little sense of their personality has survived, only the occasional glint of meaning flickers. The name of the *Lugi* translates as 'the People of the Raven' and, as it hints, *Smertae* means 'Smeared', the warriors who smeared themselves in blood before battle.

Tacitus does identify one man, the first named Scotsman (forgetting the anachronism for a moment) in history. The Caledonian federation was commanded by a war-leader supreme over all the kings of the north. Calgacus may well have been his nickname for it means, simply, 'the Swordsman' or 'good with a sword'.

In 83 the confederate army of the north chose its ground. Calgacus arrayed his men in battle order at a place called the Graupian Mountain. In time-honoured style Tacitus put a long speech in his mouth. It contains several ringing phrases: *We are the last people on earth, and the last to be free*, and *They make a desert and call it 'peace'*, and there is much talk of the virtues of freedom and the evils of slavery. It ends with a telling exhortation:

> On then into battle and as you go, think both of your ancestors and of your descendants.

The atmosphere in the ranks of the warbands will have been unmistakable. On the slopes of the Graupian Mountain there stood an army of families, of fathers and sons, brothers and cousins, and they had come to that place to fight for more than their lives. The land, those who had gone before and would come after them, their whole sense of themselves – for all of these they stood with all their courage and stared hard at the legions massing below them, at the most feared army the world had ever seen.

Almost seventeen hundred summers later another army of brothers, fathers and sons mustered to fight for the same things. There are of course many differences between what happened at Culloden in 1746 and at Mons Graupius in 83. But both were battles between a professional army and a host, people who fought with passion rather than for pay. They were contests between the power of a furious Celtic charge and a front of disciplined, trained ranks whose officers implored them to stand fast. But, most of all, these two battles were fought between groups of men who shared ties of blood and soil and an army of individuals who had been welded together by hard-won experience and comradeship. Before Culloden the *sloinneadh* began, the naming of the ancient names. Many of the clansmen recited their genealogy, remembered who they were and where they came from before raising their broadswords and tearing across the heather into the murderous hail of musket fire.

Once Agricola had made his speech (oddly, not as rousing or poignant as Calgacus'), he put his battleplan into action. Facing the warbands directly were the auxiliary regiments, 8,000 soldiers in all, and protecting their flanks were 3,000 cavalry. The legions were *stationed in front of the rampart*, clearly near a camp, but behind the auxiliaries to act as a reserve. Tacitus was quick to point out that a victory was esteemed all the greater if no *Roman* blood was shed.

The preliminaries were dominated by charioteers racing back and forth on the ground between the two front lines. Volleys of javelins were exchanged. And then Agricola ordered the Batavian and Tungrian auxiliary cohorts to advance in close order. There appears to have been no Caledonian charge at this point. The long Roman shields and short stabbing swords were far more effective than the cavalry sabres and small parrying shields of the native warriors, and the auxiliaries began to gain ground, moving up the slopes of the mountain. Then Calgacus engaged the bulk of the confederate army in a flanking movement, an attempt to roll up the Roman line and encircle them. But Agricola sent in his reserve cavalry and they themselves not only prevented this but managed to work themselves in behind the warbands.

At that moment everything changed. Panic seems to have seized the Caledonian army. From Tacitus' description, the battle broke into a series of separate rearguard actions. The warbands retreated, regrouped and fought back. But momentum was with Agricola's men and by nightfall they had won the field. They could not follow victory with annihilation, the sort of mass slaughter which often disfigured Roman strategy. The bulk of Calgacus' army vanished into their mountain heartlands. Agricola continued his march but, since the campaigning season was almost over and winter was threatening, the army returned to camp.

Domitian professed himself delighted at the victory at Mons Graupius (Tacitus was doubtful: *what he dreaded most of all was for the name of a subject to be exalted above that of the Emperor*) and awarded Agricola triumphal insignia, a public statue and an honorary triumph. At Richborough something even more spectacular was created. On the site where Claudius' troops invaded Britain in 43, Domitian had a huge triumphal arch erected to mark the moment when he completed the conquest of the province with the battle at Mons Graupius. The arch was clad with Carrara marble and had gilded bronze statuary to decorate it. The imperial family, Domitian's father, brother and uncle, had all served in Britain and it seems that he saw its final subjugation as a personal Flavian triumph. Perhaps a state visit was planned. It never happened and all that remains are some impressive foundations at Richborough.

Tacitus was bitter about Domitian's shoddy treatment of Agricola on his recall to Rome:

> So that his entry would not attract attention by crowds flocking to welcome him, he avoided the friends who wanted to pay their respects and came into the city by night, and by night also, just as he had been instructed, to the Palace. He was greeted with a perfunctory kiss and then dismissed without a word, into the crowd of courtiers.

TACITUS

Historians are never objective, and while Tacitus did not waver from his adulation of Agricola, his father-in-law, he does sometimes make surprising comments – for a Roman aristocrat. For example, he affords some dignity to barbarians and is occasionally cynical about the motives and methods of the Empire. His own life story may offer some clues to the origin of these unexpected sensitivities. Publius Cornelius Tacitus was born around AD 58, and his father had been an imperial official of some sort in the Rhineland. The family may have come from southern Gaul, like Agricola, and may have spoken Latin with a slight Celtic accent. The name is unusual and was probably coined as a nickname – the Quiet Man. Tacitus did not live up to it. After being made a senator by Vespasian, promoted by Titus and even by the hated Domitian, he became famous as a public speaker as well as a historian. The ultimate accolade came in 97 when Tacitus served as a consul.

With the conclusion of the *Agricola*, the written historical record for Britain is plunged suddenly into darkness. After so much detail for the years from AD 77 to 84, there is very little surviving material between then and the mid 90s. Even the name of Agricola's successor as Governor of Britannia is unknown.

It is clear, however, that Mons Graupius was the stimulus for a huge building project in Scotland. At Inchtuthil, on the River Tay near Perth, a legionary fortress was begun in 84. The XX Valeria Victrix, Agricola's own legion, was to be stationed there and, much in the way that Caerleon glowered at the Silures of South Wales, Inchtuthil was to keep the defeated Caledonii in check. But the fortress was never completed. Trouble threatened elsewhere in the Empire and a legion was withdrawn from Britain. Deliberately and carefully dismantled (a million iron nails were found buried in a pit), Inchtuthil was abandoned in 86 and the edges of the Roman Empire retreated south from Caledonia – and stayed there. Tacitus could not restrain his disgust: *Britain was completely conquered – and straight away let go.*

Much further south Agricola's consolidation and good government began to have its effect. The Romans were not only in Britain to stay, but they and their empire also presented opportunities. Those who wanted to do business with the garrisons had to learn Latin, and there is evidence that many merchants and manufacturers did. This process of acculturation is partly reflected in the nature of the 600 or so loan-words from Latin which are still detectable in modern Welsh. These were adapted for things new to Britain after 43 and they say something about cultural difference. For example, *llyfr* is from *liber* for a book, *ffos* is from *fossa* for a ditch, and *ffenestr* from *fenestra* for a window. Even Welsh christian-names remember the Empire. Iestyn is from Justinus and even Tacitus survives as Tegid.

In the *Agricola*, Tacitus relates how the Governor had fostered Romanisation as a matter of policy:

> . . . those who had once shunned the Latin language now sought fluency and eloquence in it. Roman dress too became popular and the toga was frequently seen. Little by little there was a slide towards the allurements of degeneracy: assembly rooms, bathing establishments, and smart dinner parties. In their naivety the Britons called it civilisation when it was really part of their servitude.

4

Dinner on the Stone Road

Claudia Severa to her Lepidina greetings. On the third day before the Ides of September, sister, for the day of the celebration of my birthday, I give you a warm invitation to make sure that you come to us, to make the day more enjoyable for me by your arrival . . . Give my greetings to your Cerialis. My Aelius and my little son send him their greetings.

I shall expect you, sister. Farewell, sister, my dearest soul, as I hope to prosper, and hail. To Sulpicia Lepidina, (wife) of Cerialis, from Severa.

Only the names and the word *hail* give away the dates of this birthday invitation. It could have been written at almost any period in the last two thousand years of our history. The formalities, the gushing sign-off, the evident warmth and the slightly superior tone might as easily have come from the memsahibs of the British Raj as from a woman living on Rome's northern frontier some time around the year 100.

Sulpicia Lepidina was the wife of Flavius Cerialis, the commander of the IX Cohort of Batavians stationed at the fort of Vindolanda. It lay on the Stanegate Road, the Stone Road, midway between Newcastle and Carlisle, a mile or so south of the line of what was to become Hadrian's Wall. The invitation from Claudia Severa was miraculously preserved in the anaerobic mud of Vindolanda and, along with many hundreds of other wooden writing tablets, it was discovered in a series of brilliant excavations directed by Robin Birley, which began in the 1970s and are ongoing. The tablets form what is considered the greatest archaeological treasure ever discovered in Britain. Not gold, not silver, nor precious gemstones, the Vindolanda letters and lists are priceless because they allow us directly into the thoughts of people from the long past. In the cloying, black mud of soaking trenches, Robin Birley found Roman voices.

They whispered stories of remarkable immediacy. From the small change of everyday life – shopping lists, parcels of socks and underpants, schoolroom exercises – to the great affairs of state – a visit from the Governor of Britannia, a petition to the Emperor Hadrian, an assessment of regimental strength – the Vindolanda letters and lists take us into the Roman world of northern England, 2,000 years ago.

WOODEN POSTCARDS

The Vindolanda Tablets were slightly larger than a modern postcard and they were made from very thinly cut pieces of the sapwood of young trees. Using a very sharp and broad knife, the wood was almost peeled off and then pressed to stop it curling and warping. The technique is very similar to the production of veneer. An ancient craft, it was used by the Egyptians, who applied very thin panels of exotic or beautiful woods to furniture and sarcophagi. Veneer was very widely used in the Roman Empire and its specialised tools will have been readily available at Vindolanda. When the sheet of wood was cut into tablet-size sections, the surface was smoothed down before a scribe or the author of a letter, list or report began to write with a steel-nibbed pen and ink made from iron gall or soot. Once the tablet was complete, it was scored down the middle, folded and dispatched. When Robin Birley found the first of these in 1973 at the bottom of a muddy trench, it was folded. Only when the thin sheets were carefully prized apart could he see that the tablet was covered with writing. The first was apparently about supplies of beer and barley. Birley at first thought the script might be in Greek characters, but in fact it turned out to be Roman cursive (joined up) script. Extremely difficult to read, partly because there were no breaks between the words, the tablets formed an immensely detailed picture of life on the northern frontier of the Empire. They also supplied a means of tracing the development of the Latin language in the 1st and 2nd centuries AD. But perhaps one of the most surprising discoveries was the high degree of literacy amongst the soldiers, most of whom at Vindolanda and the other Stanegate forts were Batavians and Tungrians and not Italians.

Their discovery was the result of a problem. When the Vindolanda Trust began life in 1970, its sole source of income was from entrance fees to the site. Excavation and its unpredictable excitements drew visitors and it was first undertaken outside the western gate of the fort, in the civilian settlement. To get at the Roman layers, Robin Birley and his team had to remove modern field drains. Water then collected in the hollow between the settlement and the long mound covering the western wall of the fort. Sometimes it was so deep that the precious visitors could not get into the fort. Something had to be done, and instead of Roman remains, a drainage ditch was dug.

As the excavators moved south towards the slope and the stream running below, they were forced to dig deeper to achieve sufficient fall for the drainage pipe. And they ran straight into what was first believed to be a Roman rubbish dump. Then the stumps of two timber posts were uncovered and Robin Birley realised that they had come upon the buildings of the early timber fort. It being too late in the year to begin a comprehensive excavation, the trench was quickly backfilled for the winter.

In March 1973, Birley moved his team back into the drainage ditch. He quickly saw that, before each phase of rebuilding, soldiers had flattened the site, covering over demolition with clay or thick turf. This process had effectively sealed each layer, trapping material in an anaerobic, or oxygen-free, environment. All sorts of organic remains came up. The carpets of bracken which had lain on the floors of rooms were at first brightly coloured, brown, green and yellow, just as they had been 2,000 years before. But as they came into contact with the oxygen in the atmosphere, they quickly turned black and also began to smell and rot.

Wood was well preserved, as was leather and other normally rare sorts of finds. In a room of what appeared to be a timber building, some thin and oily shavings were noticed amongst much larger objects, like barrel staves. But because there was such a volume of material, much of which needed to be conserved urgently, they were ignored. Then one of the excavators picked up two of these shavings which seemed to be stuck together. Separating them, he noticed that the inside surfaces were covered with illegible markings. *I had another look,* wrote Birley, *and thought I must have been dreaming, for the marks appeared to be ink writing.* He later commented:

If I have to spend the rest of my life working in dirty, wet trenches, I doubt whether I shall ever again experience the shock and excitement I felt at my first glimpse of ink hieroglyphics on tiny scraps of wood.

Hastily collecting as many of these scraps as they could find, Birley and his assistant raced down to Durham to find a leading expert on ancient handwriting, Richard Wright. When they unpacked the shavings from their moss-filled box, they had turned black. Birley wrote:

We were shattered. But Richard Wright had faith in us, and suggested we contact Miss Alison Rutherford, at the Newcastle University Medical School, to see whether ultra-violet or infra-red photography could reveal the texts again. It took time, but the infra-red photography produced the images, and when we saw them, we realised we were no further forward, because it was impossible to read the scripts. Even Richard Wright had to admit defeat, but one of our Trustees, Professor Barri Jones, put us in touch with Dr Alan Bowman at Manchester University, who was an expert in dealing with papyrus records from Egypt, and with the assistance of Dr David Thomas at Durham University, the long process of reading the texts began. At the time, no-one realised the magnitude of the task.

But it turned out to be immensely rewarding. As scores of finds grew into hundreds and then thousands, a unique record of Roman life began to form. Life on the northern frontier only decades before the Wall was built.

The writers of all this extraordinary material, it should be made clear, were not in fact Romans, or at least not Italians. Flavius Cerialis was a Batavian, an aristocrat from the peoples who lived on what Tacitus described as *the Rhine Island*. This was the land lying between the old course of the Rhine and the River Waal, the area around the modern city of Nijmegen in the Netherlands. *Batavi* means 'the Better Ones' and the legacy of the name, a certain superior attitude, often leaps off the page at Vindolanda.

Considered exceptional cavalry warriors, Batavians formed the Imperial Horseguards and, from the reign of Augustus to Nero, a detachment was stationed at Rome. Very unusually, the eight cohorts and one purely cavalry regiment drawn from these people were commanded by their own aristocracy, and Flavius Cerialis may even have been a member of the royal family. Like most commanding officers in the Roman army, the Batavian officers were permitted to bring their wives and families to live with them wherever they were posted. It was not approved of by everyone. The stern Republican virtues of discipline and gritty sacrifice come through in this speech by the historian Tacitus to an old-fashioned senator, Caecina Severus:

> An entourage of women involves delays through luxury in peacetime and through panic in war. It turns the Roman army into the likeness of a procession of barbarians. Not only is the female sex weak and unable to bear hardship but, when it has the freedom, it is spiteful, ambitious and greedy for power. They disport themselves amongst the soldiers and have the centurions eating out of their hands.

Out of a total population of only 35,000 or so on the Rhine Island, almost 5,000 Batavians had enlisted in the Roman army. Few able-bodied young men can have been left at home. The reason for this was another unusual arrangement. Along with their southern neighbours, the Tungrians, the Batavians were exempt from taxation in cash or in kind. Instead their ruling families supplied recruits to swell the ranks of Roman auxiliary regiments. Their military prowess must have been impressive for the normally grasping imperial procurators to prefer soldiers to cash or goods.

And they were undoubtedly crack troops. Batavians served with distinction in Britain. As part of the Claudian invasion force, it was almost certainly they who swam the Medway in full armour with their ponies, the decisive tactic in winning the first, and critical, battle. They were also at Mons Graupius with Agricola in 83, fighting alongside the Tungrians in the first rank. Having become embroiled in the ebb and flow of the Year of the Four Emperors, they showed great loyalty – in several directions. Under their commander, an ex-gladiator called Tiberius Claudius Spiculus, the Imperial Horseguards fought for the doomed Nero to the last. Revolt erupted on the Rhine Island in AD 70 and Petilius Cerialis hurried north to suppress it. He negotiated with the alarming Batavian leader, Julius Civilis, who had lost an eye in battle, grown his hair very long and dyed it red. Proclaiming his loyalty to Vespasian, claiming to be a friend of the new emperor – and he probably was, having fought at his side on the Medway and at

Maiden Castle – Civilis appears to have extracted a pardon for his people from Cerialis. Some Batavians had not joined the revolt, and it was because of this that the family of Flavius Cerialis were probably granted citizenship in 70. Taking the name of Flavius for the family of Vespasian and Cerialis from Petilius, who had agreed to the rehabilitation of the Batavians, it was almost certainly Flavius Cerialis' father who first became a Roman citizen.

Family wealth appeared to be untouched by the rebellion. Commands in the Roman army demanded property qualifications, and the rank of prefect of an auxiliary regiment was second only to the senatorial class who led the legions. These equestrians, or knights, had to be worth 400,000 sestertii to qualify as commanders, or prefects. There was real wealth washing around the northern frontier in AD 100. More than twenty men of equestrian rank are mentioned in the Vindolanda letters and lists and, in Britain as a whole, sixty prefects were appointed to lead auxiliary regiments. By contrast, the average legionary earned 1,200 sestertii a year – before deductions.

Flavius Cerialis appears not to have been a career soldier, and Vindolanda and the IX Batavians may have been only his second command, possibly his last. Unlike his friend mentioned in the invitation, Aelius Brocchus, his name disappears from the historical record after his tour of duty on the frontier in Britain. Brocchus' name is found in Pannonia, modern Hungary, some time after 105.

The surviving letters and lists suggest that Cerialis left the daily grind of military life to his senior officers. Centurions seem to have organised training, duty rosters and manoeuvres. These men were the backbone of the Roman army, many dedicating their entire adult lives to its service. They not only stiffened discipline, usually able to back their commands with an implicit threat of violence, they also added a deep reservoir of experience. Most centurions did not retire after twenty-five years of soldiering. Several appear on inscriptions on both Hadrian's Wall and the Antonine Wall, and there were cases of men still in active service at the age of 80. Like many young officers who relied heavily on their sergeants in the modern British army, Cerialis would have been wise to listen to the advice of these gnarled old veterans.

If most military matters were of little interest to him, some administration did engage the fort commander, and twelve applications made to him for leave were found in the black mud: *I ask you, Lord Cerialis, that you hold me worthy for you to grant me leave.* Another soldier supplies more information. For his period of leave, he wants to make for the bright lights of downtown Corbridge, only a few miles to the east. Corbridge was growing into a substantial Roman town, and the stumps of the massive columns on its main street suggest an urban substance not yet seen elsewhere along the Stanegate. Yet another man requests time off *so that I can buy something*. Perhaps it was a gift for family or friends, perhaps a night on the tiles and a prostitute. Before these applications were found, it was assumed by historians that the Roman army granted leave, but at Vindolanda (and almost certainly elsewhere), it seems to have been normal practice.

COSTS AND MEASURES

The Romans were very interested in money. Although coinage was invented by the Mesopotamians and developed by the Egyptians and Greeks, the Romans were the first to create an economy based purely on money. Around 300 BC their first coins were closely related to livestock; the Latin word for money is *pecunia* and it is derived from *pecus* for cattle, while *denarius* meant sixteen asses' worth. But once coins acquired an intrinsic value and began to be mass-produced in many centres, money drove imperial expansion as hard as political ambition. In 61 BC, before his conquest of Gaul, Julius Caesar owed his bankers 25 million denarii, but after he had subdued and taxed what is now modern France, he made a fortune many times larger than his debts. Caesar's nephew, the first Emperor Augustus, used the expansion of the Empire to make himself by far the richest man the world had yet known, or at least the first whose immense wealth was quantifiable. Equivalent values for currency are very difficult to measure but relative values are useful to know. A silver coin known as the denarius was worth four sestertii and there were four asses to each sertertius. Measures were also standard and the most common in the Vindolanda lists is the modius. It was 8.62 litres.

Like almost all aristocrats in almost all periods, Flavius Cerialis loved hunting. In a letter to Aelius Brocchus, he pleaded: *if you love me, brother, send me hunting nets*. They were used to catch everything from a charging wild boar to the sort of small songbirds whose consumption (especially in modern Italy where *uccellini* are a delicacy) appalls the tender-hearted British. Like several local ducal families until very recently, Cerialis also kept hounds to hunt in north Northumberland. Perhaps like the men and women in pink and black jackets, he rode to them. Batavian culture was certainly equestrian and there can be no doubt that Cerialis would have been schooled into an accomplished horseman.

WITLESS, CLUELESS AND WORTHLESS

Insults rarely stand the test of time. Most of the best were spoken, spontaneous and probably shouted, and others contain contemporary references which have lost their force. But Cicero, the great Roman politician, lawyer and orator, was a past master. Because some of his best insults were launched in the law courts, they were written down – and he did not hold back when attacking his opponents: *You were such a moron that throughout your speech you were at war with yourself, firing out statements which were not just inconsistent, but which were utterly devoid of any coherence or logic, to the point where your adversary in battle stopped being me and became yourself.*

Aristocrats playing at being soldiers were not spared: *These weakling softy-boys . . . how in the hell do they expect to survive the frosts and snows of the Apennines? . . . Unless they imagine that they are better armed against winter on account of their expertise in dancing naked at banquets.*

Nor was a political opponent: *No-one can say whether he spent more time drinking, vomiting or relieving himself.*

Ancient hunting methods lasted a long time, well into the nineteenth century. Hounds were of two sorts. Sight hounds (*vertragi* in Latin) were bred and trained for speed, able to run down a quarry such as deer over long distances. Greyhounds and wolfhounds are modern versions – although mastiffs went after wolves, their spiked and studded collars not a matter of show but designed to protect their necks from vulpine fangs. Scent hounds (*segosi*) picked up a trail, like bloodhounds, and led huntsmen to their prey. Sometimes an animal might have been wounded by spears or arrows, but not brought down, and scent hounds would follow the trail of gore until the weakening creature slowed and was at last found. Hunting dogs were a famous British export to the rest of the Roman Empire.

These young aristocrats were also intensely competitive in the hunting field and, after a few cups of wine before dinner, they may have become boisterous in their boastfulness. In one amusing record, it is possible to hear more than a whisper of triumph. Gaius Tetius Veturius Micianus, who commanded a cavalry regiment at Binchester, near Bishop Auckland, was so mightily chuffed with a kill that he set up an altar to give thanks. It was dedicated to the god of the woods and the fields, *Silvanus the unconquered, for the capture of a boar of exceptionally fine appearance, which many of my predecessors have been unable to bag*. It sounds like the boar had evaded capture for some time and, like many big salmon or pike, was known to those who hunted it.

The Romans may well have also hunted in the sett. Beaters would drive through cover, as they do now to put up grouse and pheasants in front of guns, and, in a semi-circular sweep, push wild boar, deer and smaller game towards a defile, or a geographical feature otherwise suitable, where hunstmen waited with spears or arrows, or even nets. The hunting horn is ancient, used as a means of communication when a hunting field became extended or confused, or lost, and it may be that Flavius Cerialis' *venatores*, or hunters, used a version of the *cornu*. This was a parade-ground and battlefield horn which could blow at least seventeen notes and was as useful as a modern bugle to give commands. The yelping of excited dogs, the pluming breath of panting horses in the frosty air, the piping notes of the horn will have echoed across many a winter morning.

The land around Vindolanda is prime hunting country. High moorland along the line of the Wall descends gradually to the South Tyne Valley with virtually every variety of cover in between. Cerialis and his men celebrated it. Near Crow Hall Farm, almost 3 kilometres south of Vindolanda, a relief of Diana, the goddess of hunting, was found. Like Micianus' altar, it may have been set up at the scene of a particulary exhilarating kill. There was another shrine to the goddess at the fort and, when he was stationed in Pannonia, Aelius Brocchus set up yet another.

Without doubt these young men hunted for the thrill of the chase, but also to enrich their supper tables. There were few better introductions to a dish at a smart dinner party than *I caught this myself*. And few better follow-ups than the story of how and when. The rivers and lochs around the fort were fished, swans and geese were snared, ducks, thrushes and other birds netted.

All of this food was prepared at the commander's house at Vindolanda by slaves in the kitchen. Astonishingly, buried in the bracken and rushes on the kitchen floor, an incomplete inventory of the dinner service it was served on was found. Here is the list:

Shallow dishes – 2
Side plates – 5
Vinegar bowls – 3
Egg plates – 3
A platter, or shallow dish
A container
A bronze lamp
Bread baskets – 4
Cups – 2
Bowls or ladles – 2

The Romans dined very differently from us and, to make sense of what seems to be an odd collection of plates and vessels (no cutlery), some explanation is needed. For the people who lived at Vindolanda, and all over the Empire, breakfast and lunch (if available) were no more than snatched snacks: pieces of fruit or cheese, a hunk of bread, leftovers, a cup of water. *Cena*, or dinner, was the main meal of the day, as it still is in Mediterranean cultures, and in the commanding officer's house at Vindolanda, it will have been an elaborate affair, especially if guests were staying.

Diners reclined on couches around a central, low table. Before food arrived, there was always a drink. *Mulsum* is on at least one shopping list found at the fort. It was a mixture of wine and honey, a precursor of the upper-class habit of a glass of sherry before dinner. At banquets, food was often carried in by slaves on a pre-set table and laid down where the reclining diners could reach it.

Otherwise food was plated in the kitchen on large ashets or in round bowls, and put in front of the diners. They took small cuts and quantities and, from their side plates, ate the food with their fingers. In her dinner service, Sulpicia Lepidina lists five such small side plates. Eggs were a favourite for the *gustatio*, the first course, as were oysters and fish. The *ovaria*, or egg plates, in the inventory would have been used often. Salad, olives and bread also appeared, and *isicia*, meatballs, were also often on the menu at dinner parties. Throughout the meal, slaves will have brought in bowls of dipping sauces; two recipes are mentioned in the Vindolanda lists: a garlic paste and a spicy dip simply called *conditum*.

The *mensae primae*, literally the first tables, were more substantial. Roast haunch of venison, joints of all sorts, baked fish and game pie (probably Hadrian's favourite) were all carved and sliced by slaves. Diners took small pieces for their side plates and dipped them in the sauce bowls. The pace of a Roman dinner was slow and steady, different from the modern habit of piling up a single plate with a meal and devouring it. Evidently dinners could go on for many hours.

DAYS OF WINE, OLIVE OIL AND TOMATOES

Neither wine, olive oil nor tomatoes were first made or grown by the Romans, or the Greeks, or in the Mediterranean. Olive oil production began in Mesopotamia, roughly modern Iraq. It was introduced into Italy by the Greeks in the eighth century BC. Homer called it 'liquid gold', and winning athletes at the original Olympic Games were presented with it instead of medals. It is a very healthy food and one of the reasons why the peoples of the Mediterranean suffer much less from heart disease. Wine was first made in the area between the Black Sea and the Caspian before its manufacture spread westwards. Some of that eastern heritage is preserved in the occasional word. 'Shiraz', for example, is a Persian name for a popular style of red wine. The best vines in ancient Italy were not grown in free-standing rows, as now, or on trellises, but trained to climb up the trunks of trees. Tomatoes are seen as the quintessence of Italian cooking, but the Romans did not eat them. The Spanish first saw tomatoes when they conquered the Aztecs of Mexico, and they brought them to Europe. The early varieties were yellow and that is why they are called *pomodoro* in Italian: golden apples.

Wine featured in the Vindolanda shopping lists, but it must have been expensive, having been brought so far north. River traffic could reach as far up the Tyne as Corbridge, but amphorae will have been loaded onto carts and shoogled the last few miles to Vindolanda – at some cost, both financial and to its taste and condition on arrival. Most wine came from Gaul and southern Spain, but the lists do mention *Massic,* an expensive brand from Campania in Italy. Unlike modern purists, the Romans did not hesitate to add things to their wine, and in winter they used an even further-travelled additive. Pepper is recorded at Vindolanda, and along with other exotic additives such as dates and saffron, the Romans used these to made a spiced wine to warm themselves when the bitter west wind blew through the Hexham Gap.

In late summer Sulpicia Lepidina's kitchen slaves probably gathered wild berries and apples to make a sort of fruit cocktail. Wine was poured over the bilberries, raspberries and brambles and the resulting mixture left to infuse and ferment. The process produced either a sweet drink with bits in it or a runny pudding but, however it was described, it was very alcoholic.

An amphora found at Newstead, near Melrose, has the word *vinum* scratched on the handle. This meant vintage wine and, from records elsewhere in the Empire, fort commanders appear to have ordered it from vineyards in southern Italy and Sicily. Ordinary soldiers, by contrast, had to be content with *posca*, a drink made from *acetum*, sour wine mixed with water. At Vindolanda and no doubt elsewhere, wine lees, the bits left at the bottom, had water added to them to make what seems to have been an acceptable beverage.

Beer appears regularly in the lists and it must have been a staple for the soldiers, a drink they knew well from home in Batavia. Known as *cervesa*, or Celtic beer, it was brewed from local barley, or *bracis*. No hops were used and, as a result, Celtic beer did not keep for long. It probably did not need to. One of Vindolanda's many claims to fame is the name of the first brewer recorded in the north-east. Atrectus began a long and honourable tradition still carried on with distinction along the banks of the Tyne.

When the beer ran out, it could be a problem. Cerialis received a plaintive request from one of his cavalry officers: *the comrades have no beer, which I ask that you order to be sent.* It should be pointed out that beer was drunk as much for its calorific content as its alcoholic.

ROMAN EMAILS

Between St Paul's Cathedral and the Tower of London lay the heart of the Roman city of Londinium. Through the centre of it a ghost river ran into the Thames and, preserved in the anaerobic, muddy banks of the Walbrook, the earliest letters and messages written in the province of Britannia have been found. Similar to the Vindolanda Tablets, scratched on thin wooden postcard shapes through a film of wax, these documents have been described as the emails of the Roman world. Written in the decade immediately following the Claudian invasion of 43 AD, they comprise requests for loans to be repaid, lists of goods and the first surviving record of the name of London itself. One tablet refers to Tertius the Brewer, almost certainly a man called Domitius Tertius Bracearius. He appears to have built up a successful brewing business that had outlets along the length of the new province because a tablet found in Carlisle dated to 85 AD also mentions him. Tertius may have supplied the Wall garrison with beer. Just as at Vindolanda, the tablets were discovered embedded in rubbish as new house platforms were built over ground where they had been dropped. Some were found inside the foundations of a small, square timber building, what has been described as 'the oldest office in Britain'. The site will be built over by 2017 and the treasures of the ghost river of the City of London will be lost once more.

Flavius Cerialis, Sulpicia Lepidina and their guests dressed for dinner. Another list details the sorts of clothes they wore and, appropriately for the family of a wealthy equestrian, they seem to have been fashionable, of high quality and made by a specialist. What is surprising is the gender of the sender and the receiver of this list of garments. Aelius Brocchus sent clothes for formal wear, some *synthesi* (matching items, probably in different combinations), scarves, capes or cloaks, a plain tunic, half-belted tunics more appropriate for dining and one or two more utilitarian items. No doubt Flavius Cerialis was glad to have a new wardrobe. Were these two wealthy young aristocrats dandies as well as keen huntsmen? It seems so.

Lepidina was not to be outdone, and a remarkable correlation between the Vindolanda lists and archaeology at the fort demonstrates her awareness of fashion in an eerily vivid way. In the anaerobic mud one of her sandals has been found. The Jimmy Choo or Gucci of its day, the acme of contemporary Roman footwear for the wealthy, and something which would not look out of place in the streets of Milan or Paris today, it is something almost certainly worn at a very smart dinner party. Preserved by the black mud, it is almost complete, showing only a break in a small strap – probably while Lepidina was wearing it. Perhaps she threw it out of the window in fury? Stamped on the sole is the maker's name, L Aebutius Thales, a shoemaker with a factory in Gaul – serving the luxury market. On the other side, there is enough wear to show that Lepidina wore the sandal for some time before the strap broke. In the Vindolanda lists, her expensive shoes are of course itemised.

Footwear probably belonging to Cerialis has also been found. One pair of shoes in particular seems to reinforce the image of him as a dandy. The design for the uppers is a latticework pattern, and it would only have shown up if Cerialis had worn brightly coloured socks. Can there be any doubt that he did – and Brocchus too?

TOGA

The principal garment of a free-born Roman, the toga, was huge; it must have been very warm in a hot Mediterranean summer. Usually made from undyed wool, it was shaped like a semi-circle and measured up to 5.5 metres along the straight edge and 2.75 metres at its widest point. Unlike the kilt, which in some ways it otherwise resembled, it was worn without a clasp or fastening – anywhere. As many Roman statues suggest, toga wearers had to keep their left arm crooked to cope with the volume of cloth. To put it on, one corner was laid at the feet while the straight edge was pulled up the back and over the left shoulder, then across the back, under the right arm, or over it, across the chest and then over the left shoulder again, leaving the other corner to hang down behind the knees. How it caught on is a mystery.

If the talk at these smart dinner parties was of the chase, of fashions in Rome and of the politics of the wider world, there was sometimes someone whose decorum slipped, lowering the high tone. In a letter which may have been sent to Cerialis, a correspondent warns him about a difficult guest: *you know that he is* [often?] *drunk . . . and kindnesses are ruined by envy.* That last reference smacks of long-lost gossip. Other guests were more considerate. In a letter sent to Flavius Genialis, Cerialis' predecessor at Vindolanda, an invitation is politely declined: *. . . that I could not come, for a headache is affecting me very painfully.*

Sulpicia Lepidina was almost certainly a Batavian aristocrat, possibly a princess. Her cognomen suggest that her family were granted Roman citizenship during the brief reign of the Emperor Sulpicius Galba (AD 68–9). Like most Roman brides, she would have been much younger than her husband. Analysts of the letters have calculated that Cerialis was about thirty years old in AD 100, but Lepidina is likely to have been little more than a teenager. In the ancient world, girls as young as 12 were encouraged to marry and begin bearing children. Inasmuch as the literary conventions of the letters allow an interpretation, the relationship between Lepidina and her friend Claudia Severa has the atmosphere of breathless intimacy and intensity associated with teenage girls. Here is another letter sent to Vindolanda:

I, sister, just as I had spoken with you, and promised that I would ask Brocchus, and that I would come to you – I did ask him, and he replied that it is always, wholeheartedly, permitted to me, together with . . . to come to you in whatsoever way I can. There are truly, certain intimate matters which [I long to discuss with you (?). As soon as I know for sure(?)] you will receive my letter, from which you will know what I am going to do . . . I was . . . and I will remain at Briga. Farewell my dearest sister and my most longed-for soul. To Sulpicia Lepidina from Severa, wife of Brocchus.

What *is* going on? What is this matter needing such urgent and private discussion? Such is the power of the Vindolanda material that the reader, at a distance of 2,000 years, wants to know. Perhaps these young women were very lonely, marooned in a sea of soldiers with little or no female company of the same age. Another letter, only a fragment, from an unnamed woman to the wife of the later Tungrian prefect Priscinus, whispers at a sense of isolation:

[as?] my Lady has done, whereby you console me eloquently, just as a mother would do. For my soul . . . this state of mind . . . [during these(?)] days . . . and I was able to convalesce comfortably. As for you . . . what will you do with your Priscinus?

There yawned an unbridgable social gulf between regimental commanders, their wives and families, and the men they commanded. It would have been unthinkable for Lepidina or Severa to have any social commerce with the men in the camp or any of the women associated with them. That made these letters and the meetings they facilitated all the more important.

Letters were important to ordinary soldiers too. News was hungrily devoured in the forts and contacts kept up as good wishes were passed on the acquaintances in other units. Here is Sollemnis beginning a letter to his errant friend Paris:

So that you may know that I am in good health, which I hope you are in turn, you most irreligious fellow, who haven't even sent me a single letter – but I think I am behaving in a more civilised way by writing to you!

The substantive part of the letter has been lost, but the sign-off survived:

. . . you are to greet my messmates Diligens from me and Cogitatus and Corinthus, and I ask you to send me the names . . . Farewell dearest brother.

Paris was another Batavian, stationed with the III Cohort at the unidentified fort of Ulucium. It is mentioned several times in the lists and letters and was likely to have been near Vindolanda. Perhaps it was at Newbrough, a few miles to the east.

When Robin Birley unearthed the first letters in 1973, Alan Bowman and David Thomas deciphered the text. Because of what the first letter to be published said, public reaction immediately warmed to these discoveries and a flush of recognition lifted its contents and context out of the academic or abstruse.

. . . I have sent you . . . pairs of socks from Sattua, two pairs of sandals and two pairs of underpants, two pairs of sandals . . .

Greet . . . ndes, Elpis, Iu . . . enus, Tetricius and all of your
messmates, with whom I pray that you live in the greatest good
fortune.

Like the mothers and sweethearts of modern soldiers, someone had
sent a welcome parcel to a loved one on a remote and chilly
northern posting far from home. The letter conjured up images of
knitting socks and scarves by the fireside for our brave boys. In
fact it is much more likely that the letter accompanied goods
ordered and was sent to Vindolanda by a fellow former soldier.
But it was fortunate that the very first letter carried such a homely
message and it allowed an interested public to relate immediately to
the garrison of the Roman frontier two thousand years ago. It
conveyed how different, and how important these amazing finds
were.

The socks and underpants in themselves also contributed new
information – as often with the contents of the letters. Hitherto there
had been no evidence that the Romans wore either, although bare feet
in leather sandals in a Northumberland January would have demonstrated unimaginable hardihood. And underpants no doubt supplied
much needed manly support.

The reference to messmates, *contubernales*, suggested a male
sender who understood something of army organisation. Perhaps
he was a Batavian veteran who had returned home. In any case he
knew that each century in an auxiliary regiment, and a legion, was
divided into ten platoons of eight men. On the march they shared a
tent, and at Vindolanda a barrack room. Bunk beds probably made
these more spacious and congenial than the archaeological remains
imply.

Each platoon cooked its own meals, the men probably taking
turns. There was no communal dining (although a club, the *scola*,
existed for non-commissioned officers) and the army did not supply
rations. The fort appears to have sold barley to its soldiers as well
as chickens and eggs, perhaps through some accounting mechanism
which reverted the cash to the commander or the army. Not
surprisingly, large volumes of beer were sold; one individual order
was for the equivalent of 50 pints and it seems to have been very
cheap.

COOKING APICIUS

Slaves usually ran the kitchens of the well-off in ancient times, and they also invented many recipes. The best-known collection is thought to have been compiled by Marcus Gavius Apicius, a gourmet who sailed the Mediterranean in search of giant prawns. In fact it is much more likely to have been written by a series of scribes who were given recipes by slave-cooks. Sally Grainger and her husband have translated many of these and, in an excellent new edition of *Cooking Apicius*, have made them very accessible to modern methods; blenders are unblushingly used. The recipes are superb and unusual: favourites might include a starter of soft-boiled eggs in pine kernel sauce, a side dish of spicy mushy peas. The Romans made good vinaigrettes for salads and called them *oeno-garum*. In addition to several dipping sauces for meats, two of the best *mensae primae* are the roast lamb and the belly pork known as *ofellae*. Almond and semolina pudding is surprisingly light. As with modern Mediterranean cooking, the emphasis is always on the excellence of the ingredients.

Far to the north of Vindolanda and built forty years later, Bearsden Fort in Glasgow revealed much about the diet of ordinary soldiers. Through painstaking analysis of the contents of a blocked latrine drain, strong-minded experts have been able to show that porridge was a staple. In season, wild fruits, berries and nuts could be gathered by soldiers and mixed in to add some variety and flavour. Hazelnuts, brambles, bilberries, crab apples and raspberries would have been almost farmed and protected by each platoon. This wild harvest also had the attraction of costing nothing, no deductions from pay. The men were probably allowed to fish, and to trap and snare small animals, but just as medieval kings guarded their hunting reserves, it is likely that commanders like Cerialis and Brocchus forbad the pursuit of bigger game by anyone else.

The arrival of so many men in northern England at the end of the first century AD transformed the local economy. Although their numbers were small compared with the 30,000 or so who came to build Hadrian's Wall in AD 122 and its subsequent garrison of 12,000 auxiliaries, the soldiers stationed at Vindolanda and the other early forts strung out along the Stanegate Road provided a substantial new market for goods and services. There were perhaps 5,000 of them – and they all needed something.

Once the countryside had recovered from the initial shock of conquest – and this is not to be underestimated – trade began. But it must be remembered that the forts were built on good land which was worked by the native peoples. The Romans did not enter an empty landscape. Summarily driven off wide swathes of pasture and arable ground, the farmers will have nursed their fury for at least a generation. It is estimated that a cohort of 500 men needed the yield of 700 acres of cornfields each year. Add to this at least an equivalent amount of pasture for 200 oxen (used to pull the regiment's carts), 200 or so ponies, and woodland for the fort's pigs and chickens to root around in and the result is a very large appropriation of land, a dispossession and hardship on a huge scale. Vindolanda's *territorium* may have run to 1,500 acres. This sort of deprivation took place all along the Stanegate, and on a renewed and greater scale when the Wall builders came. It will have taken some time before local producers began to trade significantly with the invaders who had evicted so many.

But trade they did. Markets developed as goods and food were brought for sale to the gates of the forts. And while the occasional complaint about prices and supply surface in the Vindolanda letters and lists, it was in everyone's interests for these markets to benefit both buyer and seller. Local goods were almost always cheaper than anything shipped from the south.

Perhaps the most radical economic shift is nowhere explicitly recorded, or at least no record has survived. The Romans operated a money economy, and the natives seem to have used barter. In order for trade to function at all, cash must have been universally adopted. How else could transactions have been completed? The soldiers had little to offer in the way of goods to barter, and cash was what they were paid. The only hint of rapid adoption is in the Vindolanda lists where people with native-sounding names do write of the cash costs of items. But it must at first have been bewildering.

In order for trade to transact smoothly – there was after all money and livelihoods involved – it is inevitable that the native peoples will have had to learn to speak Latin. Many loan-words made their way into Old Welsh but the linguistic traffic did travel in the opposite direction in one significant way.

The names used by the Romans for their forts were almost all Celtic in derivation. And this process of adoption took place early. Within less than twenty years of the building of the first timber fort, letter writers marked their address clearly as Vindolanda. The meaning of the name is a rare insight into native reaction to the Roman invasion. From *uindo* (*gwyn* in modern Welsh), the first element means white or bright. This is almost certainly a native reference to the Roman habit of plastering their buildings with render to help keep out the weather. A deposit of wall plaster was found outside the northern rampart, and it more than suggests that the fort's gatehouses were rendered as the IX Batavians rebuilt Vindolanda around AD 100. There are several other *Vindo* names in the Celtic regions of the Empire and at least four in Britain. They probably echo a similar reaction to the rapid appearance of bright, white buildings in the landscape; Vindobala is nearby at Rudchester in Northumberland, Vindomora is in County Durham, Vindogara in Ayrshire and Vindocladia in Dorset. These foreign, new and threatening structures stood in startling contrast with the earth colours of the native roundhouses built out of natural materials which blended into the soft greens and browns of the Northumberland landscape.

The second element of the place-name is simpler. It comes from *llan*, a modern Welsh term for a church or, more correctly, a churchyard. Originally it described a fenced or walled enclosure. The White Fort is probably the native name for what its soldiers knew as Vindolanda.

The Tungrians were first on the scene, perhaps around AD 85, and the earliest letters and lists say a good deal about their tenure of the White Fort. But some of the most detailed archaeological and documentary information is confusing. Excavation indicated a standard layout for the early fort, probably built for a cohort of 480 men. Significantly the ditching defending the western wall was deep and elaborate (the other three walls overlooked downslopes), a reminder that the Tungrians were digging in hostile country. So far, so predictable. But a fascinating list came to light early in the excavations. It is a strength report of the I Tungrian Cohort, and it describes the state of a regiment of 752 men, far more than could be accommodated in the new fort:

18th May, net number of the I Cohort of Tungrians, of which the commander is Julius Verecundus the prefect, 752, including 6 centurions.

Of whom there are absent:	
Guards of the governor	
at the office of Ferox	46
at Coria	337
including [?] 2 centurions	
at London [?] a centurion	6
including 1 centurion	9
including 1 centurion	11
at [?]	1
	45
total absentees	456
including 5 centurions,	
remainder, present	296
including 1 centurion	
from these:	
sick	15
wounded	6
suffering from inflammation of the eyes	10
total of these	31
remainder, fit for active service	265
including 1 centurion.	

Most striking is how few soldiers there were at Vindolanda fit and able to deal with any emergencies. Only a little more than half a standard cohort held down a wide swathe of, at best, unsettled countryside. The neighbouring forts of Carvoran in the west and Newbrough in the east lay only 8 or so miles away, but too far to be helpful in the event of surprise or night attack. Morale amongst the native kings must have been low, to say nothing of their military intelligence.

The dangerously sparse garrison at Vindolanda was probably in the process of being upgraded. The large detachment at Corbridge, 337 soldiers, may have been new recruits undergoing some sort of induction. Their origins are uncertain. They cannot have been local – too much bad blood had been too recently shed – but they might have been drafted from southern Britannia. More likely they were tax-equivalent Tungrians fresh off the boat.

The Vindolanda letters and lists often provide a disconcertingly everyday background to the grim grind of the Roman military apparatus. While his soldiers were sweating at the bottom of deeper ditches dug below the western wall to protect their fort from a threatening hinterland, their commander, Julius Verecundus, was being very particular about the sort of apples he liked. Another aristocrat from the Netherlands, he owned at least one slave; here is the shopping list he gave him for what sounds like a trip to the more sophisticated market at Corbridge:

Two modii of bruised beans, 20 chickens, 100 apples – if you can find nice-looking ones – 100 or 200 eggs, if they are on sale there at a fair price . . . mulsum [honey-flavoured wine] . . . eight sextarii [about four litres] of fish sauce [muria] . . . a modius of olives . . .

Vindolanda was enlarged to accommodate a double-strength cohort, but Army Command North, in the legionary fortress at York, sent orders for the infantry of the I Tungrians to move out and be replaced by the part-mounted Batavians. From this time onwards the volume of letters and lists increases markedly, and they paint a vivid picture of what garrison life was like in the White Fort.

The day began with a morning muster when a roll call was taken and duty rosters read out. At Vindolanda both a list of these duties and the names of the men who worked at specialist tasks has been found. One morning, two thousand years ago, a centurion or his second-in-command, the *optio*, barked out that detachments were to be assigned to building work at the new bath house (recently discovered outside the south wall), making shoes, collecting lead and rubble, working in the lime and clay pits, and carrying out general plastering and building work. If it was raining and cold, the *immunes*, the men with inside clerking jobs, might have smiled a sly smile.

Another list detailed the regiment's specialists. Because it was a part-mounted outfit, the IX Batavians had two *veterinarii*, who looked after their ponies, the large herd of oxen and all the other livestock. Horses were particularly valuable and, with mounts for 240 cavalry troopers and a reserve of remounts to cope with, the vets will have been busy.

Horsemanship was clearly premiated amongst the Batavians, and some Vindolanda correspondence leads to insight on this. Letter-writing appears also to have been an important business, and much valued. Here is Chrauttius complaining that Veldeius has not been keeping up:

And I ask you, brother Veldeius – I am surprised that you have not written anything back to me for such a long time – whether you have heard anything from our kinsmen, or about Quotus – in which unit he is – and you are to greet him in my own words – and Virilis the vet. You are to ask him whether you may send through one of our people the shears which he promised me for a price. And I ask you, brother Virilis, that you greet me from sister Thuttena and write back to us about Velbuteius, how he is. I wish you may be very happy. Farewell.

The address on the back of the letter is London, and Veldeius appears to have been a groom on the Governor of Britannia's general staff. The Tungrian strength report showed 46 men on secondment in London; the practice of drawing men from the northern frontier to serve in the Governor's bodyguard was not uncommon.

ROMAN WOAD

Julius Caesar and other Roman commentators noted the British habit of wearing tattoos and decorating their bodies with paint. But the Romans did it too, albeit more discreetly. It seems that soldiers were allowed to wear a legionary tattoo once they had completed some sort of test, perhaps an initiation. Some auxiliary regiments did the same thing. In his fourth-century treatise 'The Epitome of Military Science', Vegetius wrote that the tattoo was earned by a physical test, perhaps one concerned with endurance. The tattoo may have been an eagle and, after discharge, it was a handy proof of military service.

When the Governor visited Vindolanda in 105, it seems that Veldeius was in his retinue, and that he brought Chrauttius' complaining letter with him. Once again written sources link with archaeology to produce a rich picture of life in the fort. Preserved in the black mud, a piece of leather was found with Veldeius' name stamped on it. Perhaps it was an offcut from a tanned hide he had bought and brought to a saddler to have some piece of tack made. A chamfron, a beautifully worked mask worn to protect the heads of cavalry ponies (but in reality used mainly in parade-ground displays) was also discovered. It belonged to Veldeius, and if it was made for his own horse, then he owned a beauty. The chamfron best fits a pure-bred Arab mare, a big horse for its type, standing more than fifteen hands high.

The vets at Vindolanda will have seen many fancy horses, but their main concern was with the shaggy little ponies grazing in the regimental paddocks, the cavalry mounts. Most would have been smaller than Veldeius' Arab, and much more strong-boned and chunky. Their brood mares must have interbred with local native stallions to refresh their bloodlines. Native hill-ponies were hardy and well used to the uncertain ground and the wet and windy conditions which often obtained. The Vindolanda lists and letters have maddeningly little to say about the people who rode them, the native British, and when one Roman observer sniffs at their poor military prowess, he focuses as much on their ponies:

> the Brittones, rather many of them cavalrymen, are naked [perhaps meaning 'without body-armour']. The cavalrymen do not use swords, nor do the Brittunculi mount to throw javelins.

The most revealing aspect of this fascinating passage is perhaps the least suprising. As has been noted, *Brittunculi* is a dismissive diminutive meaning something like 'pathetic little Brits'. Invaders and colonists always look down on the natives they have conquered, and *Brittunculi* could not have been worse than many names conferred by the British Empire – wogs, niggers, kaffirs, fuzzie-wuzzies are even more offensive.

The *rather many cavalry* of native hosts is observed elsewhere on the frontier and the society appears also to have been a horse-based one. But it sounds as though the pathetic Brits not only fought on horseback but, as seems to have been the case in the north and at Mons Graupius, also sometimes used their ponies for speed and mobility, dismounting to throw javelins, fire arrows or use sabres and shields. The memorandum mentioning the *Brittunculi* may have been a disparaging comment on raw British recruits who needed licking into shape. But the date is early, and training local warriors in advanced military methods seems a little risky, even if they were to be posted elsewhere. British regiments turned up on the Rhine frontier in the late first century AD and into the second century.

The morning roll call and duty roster will have held no surprises for some of the men. In peace-time they did the same things every day. Candidus looked after the piggery, making sure farrowing sows did not squash their litters (or indeed eat them). And then once they had been weaned, he found them safe access to the delights of the wood-land surrounding the fort. The swineherd was an important man. Archaeologists have found enough bones to know that the garrison was very fond of pork. Bacon and ham was cured and kept well through the hungry winter months.

Oxherds are also noted on the rosters. These men, who looked after the feeding and safety of 200 oxen, probably lived in shielings outside the fort so that they could be near the 100 or so acres needed to keep the beasts fit and strong. At one point, a supply of food is sent *to the wood* to feed the men and keep them in good condition.

Condition, or well-being, could also be found at the bath house, which had been built by a work-party. Archaeology has discovered something which may have caused the workmen to shout and shoo. The *caldarium* and *laconicum*, the hot rooms, were heated by a hypocaust, a system which worked on the principle of warm air circulating under the floor. This needed a series of supports made from tiles. They could stand the heat and also allowed more precision in holding up a flat floor. When the workmen made the tiles from puddled clay, they laid them out on the grass to dry off before being fired in a kiln. It was at that stage the shouting and shooing took place. Several tiles have been found with clear animal paw and hoofprints on them. While they dried on the grass, dogs, cats, cows, pigs and either sheep or goats, or both, stepped on them. Perhaps no one was around to do any shooing.

Other skilled workers went about their tasks on what must have been a daily basis when they were not soldiering. Only one cartwright, Tullio, is mentioned, but he probably had charge of a workshop of several men. Oxcarts were vital to the running of the fort, and soldiers were careful with them:

> The hides which you write are at Cataractonium [Catterick] – write that they be given to me – and the wagon you write about – and write to me what is with that wagon. I would have collected them already – except that I did not care to wear out the baggage animals while the roads are bad.

Bad Roman roads! Another revelation. Despite the above writer's consideration, carts often broke down, and Vindolanda's cartwrights will have been busy. Evidence of trade with a man who sounds like a local supplier suggests a large number of wagons were used by the fort. Metto wrote the following to Advectus:

> I have sent you goatskins . . . sent through Saco . . . 34 wheel-hubs; 38 cart axles, one of them turned on a lathe; 300 spokes.

Other traders also supplied Vindolanda with hides. The regimental cobblers, the *sutores*, made hob-nailed boots, not sandals, for the soldiers, and there are several mentions of small numbers of nails being bought to make do-it-yourself repairs. Holes were deliberately punched through the uppers to allow water to squelch out. Boots were designed to protect the feet from sharp stones and worse, but not to keep them dry. Waterproof footwear for soldiers is a recent invention. The Highland army which crossed Hadrian's Wall in 1746 wore very similar shoes. The Gaels called them *brogan*. Changed only a little into brogues, the principal design feature of these modern shoes is the tooling on the uppers which resembles half-cut holes.

The duty roster included other roles such as the *scutarius*, or shield-maker, the *venetus*, the butcher, and of course, most important, the *cervesarius*, the brewer. The roster itself had probably been compiled by the men with the cushiest number of all, and their boss was known as the *cornicularius*, the chief pen-pusher. Records were kept in the *principia*, the headquarters building in the centre of the fort, and files were copied in duplicate and sometimes triplicate before being stored in *capsae*, document boxes. It is astonishing how few files have survived. From the beginning of the reign of Augustus in 31 BC to the beginning of Diocletian's in AD 284, one historian has calculated that the pen-pushers generated about 225 million records of Roman army pay, but only three have been found in reasonable condition. Clerking may have been dull, but it was also dry and warm, a lot better than road-building and ditch-digging, and a lot better paid.

Training was considered essential to maintain the physical fitness of all soldiers, and at Vindolanda the centurions organised it. It must have been difficult to dodge. Every ten days a route march in full kit was undertaken and the required rate was at least three miles an hour. More elaborate manoeuvres were planned and executed, temporary marching camps dug in remote locations and mock attacks mounted. Hadrian approved heartily of these as means of maintaining discipline and avoiding the ever-present danger of mutiny. But Army Command North at York had to approve manoeuvres in advance in case native kings misread them as genuine acts of warfare.

CARRYING COALS TO HOUSESTEADS

Carbo marinus, or sea-coal, was first picked up on Northumberland and Durham beaches a very long time ago. Prehistoric peoples probably burned it. The Romans certainly did. Coal holes have been found at both Housesteads and Vindolanda, but not for sea-coal; this sort came straight out of the ground. Along the banks of the Tyne and in isolated pockets inland, there were outcrops known as coal-heughs and, until the late Middle Ages, miners could get at them easily. Water transport for such a bulk item was handy, and barges may have brought it up the Tyne as far as Corbridge. Coal was probably used for heating up the bath houses. Until the nineteenth century there was a resistance to using coal for cooking. The fumes and gases which sometimes hissed out of big lumps persuaded people to use wood to cook on.

Vindolanda was kept busy – perhaps precisely because, in all the lists and letters, there is not one solitary reference to war or fighting. All along the frontier, the Roman garrison spent 99 per cent of its time doing something else. Idle soldiers can become undisciplined and dangerous, and their commanders kept them almost neurotically at work.

Building seems to have been a near-constant activity. Until 122 and the construction of Hadrian's Wall, Vindolanda and the other Stanegate forts were made from timber. Posts rammed and chocked directly into the ground rotted quickly and that meant that the life of such buildings was no more than eight to ten years. Even the stockaded rampart could weaken, and soldiers packed a bank of earth and rubble against the inside to add strength and also allow rapid access to the rampart top in the event of a surprise attack. Later, ovens and kilns were dug into the back of this internal mound. Needing fiercely hot fires to be efficient, both could also be dangerous if let out of control, and their location at the rampart was safer than in the body of the fort. Ovens and kilns are also found in gatehouses. There is a particularly well-preserved example at Birdoswald Fort. It will have had the welcome effect of keeping sentries warm on long watches through winter nights. At Housesteads their famous latrines were also dug into the rampart bank, well away from the barracks block, but not for reasons of safety.

THE LAST ROMAN BUILDING

Under the floor of Hexham Abbey, surely one of the most beautiful and atmospheric churches in Britain, lies a remarkable structure. The crypt is all that remains of St Wilfrid's seventh-century foundation. Before work began, a huge hole was dug and a small chapel built in it. Every stone came from the ruined Roman town at Corbridge. Still legible is an inscription dating from the visit of the Emperor Septimius Severus in 208. Unfortunately this stone has been removed now and put in the nave. *In situ* is a fragment of a pagan altar to Maponus Apollo holding up a passageway. Much of the Roman masonry has been broached so that render would stick to it. A leaf and berry design from the frieze around the walls of a fine house at Corbridge is visible in several places. It probably still had its roof on when Wilfrid's masons robbed out the stone. The tiny chapel housed a shrine to St Andrew. Wilfrid had been to Rome, bought a relic of one of the disciples and brought it back to Northumberland. A direct link with Christ, it would have been visited by many pilgrims, and its planting under the church sanctified the ground it was built on. The seventh-century mason work is crude, some of the robbed stones are upside down, but it is, after a fashion, a complete Roman building.

In some ways the timber forts were like more solid versions of marching camps, not designed to be defended like medieval castles, but to slow down an attack. The Romans' instinct to get out into the open to fight is well illustrated at the cavalry fort at Chesters, near Chollerford. It abuts Hadrian's Wall but has three of its four gateways to the north of it – so that squadrons of troopers could gallop out and get at an attacking force quickly. At Ambleside in the Lake District, an exception was recorded. The tombstone of Flavius Romanus, a regimental clerk, notes that he had been killed by the enemy *inside* the fort.

THE ROMAN CENTURION'S SONG

British admiration for the Roman Empire springs partly from a recent memory of our own imperial centuries. One of the great bards of the British Empire may have been recalling stories of old India hands who had sailed home to an uncomfortable retirement in the Home Counties, far from the country they had come to love. In this moving poem, Rudyard Kipling cleverly reverses the compass:

Legate, I had the news last night – my cohort ordered home,
By ship to Portus Itius and thence by road to Rome.
I've marched the companies aboard, the arms are stowed below:
Now let another take my sword. Command me not to go!

I've served in Britain forty years, from Vectis to the Wall,
I have none other home than this, not any life at all.
Last night I did not understand, but, now the hour draws near,
That calls me to my native land, I feel that land is here.

Here where men say my name was made, here where my work
    was done,
Here where my dearest dead are laid – my wife – my wife and son;
Here where time, custom, grief and toil, age, memory, service, love,
Have rooted me in British soil. Ah, how can I remove?

. . .

Legate, I come to you in tears – My cohort ordered home!
I've served in Britain forty years. What should I do in Rome?
Here is my heart, my soul, my mind – the only life I know.
I cannot leave it all behind. Command me not to go!

As the frontier settled on the line of what was to become the Wall, and the province of Britannia quietened, the Romans began to rebuild their fortresses in stone. The garrison consolidated into a permanent army of occupation. By AD 122 many auxiliary regiments had been in Britain for eighty years. As soldiers completed twenty-five years of service and were discharged as Roman citizens, some will have returned to Batavia and Tungria with their savings, their bronze diplomas and their stories. Others undoubtedly stayed. As Kipling judged in 'The Roman Centurion's Song', many had known no other place as home. Some will have formed lasting relationships with local women, and although army regulations forbad marriage while in service, they will have settled into a common law arrangement. A blind eye was usually turned. What happened to these men? Where did they go after all those years in the army?

Not far, is the likely answer. When Tacitus wrote of smart dinner parties and the subtle process of Romanisation, he was describing the subversion of the native aristocracy. With ordinary soldiers who decided to stay in Britannia, the process took a different route. Having spent most of their adult lives in the army, they were the living agents of Romanisation, at least in the north. Those who married local women and had children by them created a slim but significant stratum of society with a direct stake in developing a more Roman culture. Enfranchised by marriage to a veteran, citizen-families settled in Britannia, and it is likely that those who left their posts in the frontier forts moved only a short distance, going to live outside the gates rather than inside them.

Vici, or civilian settlements, appeared early around forts and most, like the one outside the west gate of Vindolanda, were built very close to the walls. This is surprising because the presence of these houses removed a vital defensive advantage. Fort builders usually cleared wide areas on all sides, so that an attacking enemy was forced to approach over open ground, and thereby be seen and be vulnerable to fire from the ramparts, or at least be quickly seen. The houses of the *vici* huddle so close that they must have been the homes of absolutely trustworthy people. And who could be more so than regimental veterans? They would also understand if their homes had to be fired or levelled if there was war and the fort was threatened. In any case the *vici* were built on the territorium belonging to the army – portions of which could be granted to veterans on their discharge.

These small villages set up an important link between the native and military communities. In addition to holding regular markets, they supplied services. The Emperor Hadrian disapproved of *vici* and, in listing his reasons, he outlined exactly what was attractive to soldiers: *drinking booths, gambling halls and prostitutes*. In most there were at least two buildings which appear to have been standard; a bath house and an inn, called a *mansio*. The latter is usually primly interpreted as a place where travellers or visitors to the fort might lodge. It was also almost certainly a whorehouse. With either 500 or 1,000 young and unmarried soldiers living mostly bachelor lives inside Roman forts, the notion that they were *not* serviced by a large number of whores is entirely absurd. Of course no trace of them remains, no archaeological or literary evidence has yet been found at Vindolanda, but its absence does not mean that the White Fort was populated by whiter-than-white, clean-living young men with a wide variety of hobbies to occupy them in the evenings. They were soldiers and they behaved in the way soldiers have always behaved.

Gambling, by constrast, has left a mark, and it certainly went on in the bath houses. Many games revolved around dice and a throw-board. A favourite was *ludus latrunculorum*, or robber-soldiers. It was a battlegame like chess. At the fort of Segedunum at Wallsend a board and a set of counters were found, and it seems that pieces were moved according to throws of the dice. All of them moved in straight lines like the rook in chess, and could be captured and removed if both their advance and retreat were cut off. According to contemporaries, the wedge formation was most effective – just as on the battlefield. No doubt substantial sums changed hands as players bet against each other and others bet on them.

The Romans seemed fascinated by gambling. A good deal of literary evidence survives – the Emperor Claudius even wrote a history of dice-games and was apparently devoted to them. Another game, called *duodecim scripta*, or twelve points, and resembling backgammon, inspired the poet Ovid to describe it: *A sort of game confined by subtle method into as many lines as the slippery year has months.*

Played without a board, *tesserae*, or dice, were often marked with different values, and players would bet on how they landed. At Birdoswald four dice were found as a complete set and each face had I, III, IV or VI inscribed on it. The principle was the same as for modern poker dice. Venus was the best throw since it showed all of the different values at once, and Dogs was the worst with four Is. Poor throws were penalised by adding more stakes to the pot, which was scooped by the first player to throw a Venus. Sums could spiral. Gambling chips came into use: there were three denominations, I, V and X. As the stakes rose, a crowd must have pressed hard to watch the high rollers in the warmth of the caldarium. Perhaps it was not just the hypocaust that made men sweat.

Snacks were served in the bath houses. Oysters, mussels and other titbits were on sale, and Hadrian's third vice, drinking, must have washed down many a plateful. There is no doubt that overindulgence, sexually transmitted diseases and indebtedness through gambling were all a danger, but camp commanders were more than likely glad of the diversions of the *vici*. They allowed soldiers to let off steam, kept up morale and broke up the dull, quotidian routines of guard duty, route marches and cleaning out the latrines.

Over time the fort-villages grew. Outside Chesters, which had a garrison of a thousand cavalry troopers, there were four streets arranged around a crossroads. And at Old Carlisle in North Cumbria surveys have hinted at a sizable settlement of several hundred souls. To the army one of the most attractive aspects of these villages was probably as a reservoir of recruits. Many sons of veterans will have followed their father's footsteps onto the parade grounds. Batavian and Tungrian military traditions might even have been sustained by a second generation, perhaps a third as the army renewed itself. An inscription found in Egypt and dated to AD 194 records the retirement of forty-six veterans from the Legio II Traiana Fortis. Unusually it lists the origins of the soldiers, and more than half (twenty-four) said that they had been born at a fort. In order to enlist in a legion, they will all have had to be citizens, and they were probably enfranchised on the discharge of their fathers and their formal marriage to their mothers. As in modern times the names of the regiments never changed to reflect different recruiting grounds, and it would be a mistake to assume that the men of the Batavians or the Thracians later came from either of these places.

Later altar dedications at four forts show that the villages were assuming a measure of self-government. At Vindolanda, Old Carlisle and Housesteads cash seems to have been contributed, perhaps through taxation, perhaps donation, to pay for altars. Two are dedicated to Vulcan, the god of blacksmithing, and the army may have been happy to see fire-hazardous smiddies set up outwith the walls of its forts. At Old Carlisle the inscription was specific: *dedicated by the village elders with money contributed by the villagers.*

SMELLS

To our sensitive noses the ancient world would have stunk to high heaven. Worst, by far, were the leather-tanning pits. These used a disgusting soup of urine and dog turds to produce the tough, treated leather that the Roman army badly needed. Next on the scale was probably animal dung. Oxen splatted the streets of Vindolanda regularly, ponies piled out their muck, chickens shat their eye-watering guano, and no one bothered – unless it landed on them. Almost all the soldiers had been raised on farms and they were used to it. In fact, up until the early twentieth century, most people were – from the farm workers who shared their cottages with their cow in the winter (imagine steaming piles of dung dropped only a few feet from where people slept) to the dainty ladies of the cities dodging street manure of all kinds. There were good smells at Vindolanda too: cooking, baking, woodsmoke and someone who had just visited the bath house.

A macabre discovery by Eric Birley in his 1930 excavation of the *vicus* at Housesteads suggests that civilian life on the Roman frontier was occasionally as wild as the equivalent in nineteenth-century America. Under a false floor he found two skeletons. One had a knife blade embedded in its ribs. The site became known as the Murder House, for no one doubted that was what had taken place. All Roman burials had to be located outside settlements and forts, and the obvious concealment of two bodies amounted, at the very least, to what the police are fond of calling *suspicious circumstances*. More resembling an incident from Tombstone or Dodge City, it vindicated Hadrian's stern disapproval. The *vici* could be lawless, dangerous places. When Eric Birley reported his find to the coroner at Hexham, as he was bound to do, a verdict came back of *murder by person or persons unknown shortly before* AD 367.

A hundred years before the dark deeds at Housesteads, the *vicus* at Vindolanda seems to have been abandoned. Around 270, it may be that the substantial reduction in the garrison allowed villagers to move inside the fort's sheltering walls. There was plumbing, the buildings were better constructed, and there was running water. By 400, all of these settlements had gone. They existed only to service the forts and clearly made no economic sense without them. Only Carlisle sustained itself. When St Cuthbert visited in 685, the water supply was still working, and medieval chroniclers reported that Roman streets were still paved and buildings still standing as late as the 1200s. But Tacitus' cynical predictions did not come to pass in the north. Despite the four centuries of a large garrison along the line of the Wall, Romanisation simply did not take. Celtic culture was too powerful.

All of this lay far in the future. Around AD 100 the IX Batavians were as busy as ever. Part of the reason why they had replaced the I Tungrians was their part-mounted capability. Their 240 cavalry troopers were also excellent intelligence gatherers and watchers, patrolling the countryside, asking questions, looking out for suspicious movement. Tagged onto their title, the regiment had the additional description of *exploratorum*, the scouts.

The immediate vicinity of Vindolanda appears to have formed part of the territory of the Textoverdi. Only 3 kilometres from the fort an altar dedicated to the goddess Saitada has been found. It is unique. Like hundreds of other Celtic deities whose names appear only once in the historical record, Saitada sounds like the focus of a local cult. Perhaps she was the genius, the patron goddess of the Textoverdi, since the inscription informs that the altar was set up by *curia Textoverdorum*. This may be a mis-spelling of *coria*, the Old Welsh word found in the place-name of Corbridge and meaning the host or the hosting-place. Or it may mean something like council, perhaps in the sense of elders.

The Textoverdi of the South Tyne Valley may have allied themselves with the Brigantes, been part of their federation. Some of the personal names of the people who appear in the Vindolanda letters and lists were almost certainly Textoverdi and will have spoken their dialect of Old Welsh. The name itself is obscure, but it may be related to the Celtic root-word *teach*, which meant something like fleet or fast. Maybe they and their ponies were famously adept at the gallop across the rough country they knew so well.

Like all Celtic peoples the Textoverdi left no written record, no means of confirming such supposition. By contrast the ability of the Vindolanda garrison to use written communication was a distinct military advantage because of the way in which it spread precise information, and made the Roman army more efficient, better able to punch above the weight of its often depleted numbers. Messages could be written quickly and carried at speed along the Stanegate to neighbouring forts where they might be read and acted upon. A sense of this urgency and immediacy was captured in a remarkable record of a mistake. When Flavius Cerialis was dictating to a scribe, he did not make himself clear. Perhaps he stumbled over the words of what was after all his second language. The scribe first wrote *tempestates et hiem*, then scrubbed out the last two words (not well enough – probably because he was being hurried) and replaced them with *etiam*, what Cerialis had really meant to say.

When the Governor of Britannia came to Vindolanda in 105, he may have brought orders from the Emperor, Trajan, who was fighting a ferocious war on a vast scale in Dacia (modern Romania) and against a formidable enemy, King Decebalus. Troop deployments would have to be reorganised to allow reinforcements to be sent to the Danube frontier. Flavius Cerialis and Sulpicia Lepidina packed their many belongings onto oxcarts and, after a long posting and very distinguished service, the IX Batavians left Britain in the summer of 105.

The astonishing detail which careful archaeology can produce shows that much of Vindolanda lay empty for some months before a new garrison rumbled in through the gates in the late autumn. Blown off the trees fringing the fort, dead leaves had rustled into many of the rooms, piling up in drifts in some of the corners. Birds had flown in through the gaping windows and left some feathers and droppings on the floor. Squirrels had hopped into Cerialis and Lepidina's apartments and buried their hazelnuts beneath the carpet of leaves and bracken. Seven caches were found.

The contrast must have been baffling to the native peoples. At one moment the White Fort buzzed with the racket and clangour of soldiers, blacksmiths, wagon trains and parade-ground commands. The next, it was silent as the wind sighed through the buildings and the leaves swept into its rooms and blew down the *via principalis*.

It was the I Tungrians who came back in late 105. Their commander was Priscinus and it is likely that his men occupied the fort until 122. Having no cavalry, the Tungrians were reinforced by troopers from the I Cohort of Vardulli, originally from northern Spain. There seems to have been serious trouble in Britain. The forts to the north, at

Newstead near Melrose, Dalswinton and Glenlochar in the south-west, and Cappuck and Oakwood in hills above the Tweed basin, were all destroyed by fire, most of them deliberately. The army was retreating from the lands of the Selgovae and the Novantae. But it seems that the departure of the Romans was encouraged. Archaeologists believe that Newstead shows signs of having been attacked. Human bones were found charred amongst the wreckage as well as a great deal of valuable kit and some damaged armour. Perhaps the Selgovan kings led their warbands down the Tweed, roared their war-cries and launched themselves at the great army depot at the foot of the sacred Eildon Hills.

High Rochester, impressively sited on the line of Dere Street and commanding much of Upper Redesdale, was also burned, but the flames did not stop there. Corbridge also went up in smoke. It seems certain that these two forts were attacked, possibly also by the Selgovae. Lying too far south to be part of any deliberate withdrawal from Scotland, Corbridge and its growing town presented too tempting a target. It looks very much as though a large and powerful warband rode down Dere Street, from Newstead to Corbridge, leaving fire and destruction in its deadly wake. As the Tungrian strength report showed, forts could on occasion be desperately short of manpower.

After the Selgovan kings and their warriors had ridden back home over the hill trails through the Cheviots, no doubt lugging their plunder after them, the northern frontier grew quiet again. And its line seemed to settle along the Stanegate Road.

Security at Vindolanda probably tightened in the wake of 105, its huge iron-studded wooden gates closed and barred at nightfall, the guards on the platform above scanning the darkening horizon. As a matter of routine each morning a daily password was agreed, written on a wooden tablet and given by the duty officer, usually a centurion, to an orderly. He then toured the gates, ramparts and the principia making sure all the soldiers on guard read and remembered it. This laborious business was designed to preserve the password's secrecy, but it also suggests that ordinary soldiers had some ability to read. Simple words like *courage* or *victory* were commonly used.

The most routine problem encountered by sentries was probably theft. The fort was normally full of supplies and valuable items. Hungry natives and greedy or needy soldiers may have raided granaries and other stores. The Vindolanda letters and lists occa-sionally complain of things going missing. After nightfall it is likely that four-man pickets patrolled outside the walls of the fort to keep an eye on stock and other movables, like carts. They could also have made out the shapes of anyone attempting to climb the rampart. Perhaps they had dogs on a leash. Watches rotated frequently throughout a 24-hour period with around a fifth of the garrison involved on any given day.

Arguably Rome's most dynamic and successful emperor, Trajan had succeeded Nerva in AD 98. His interests lay in the east, both on the Danube and in what is now modern Iraq. Unlike his predecessors, he showed little interest in Britain, certainly none in advancing up into Scotland. Glory lay elsewhere. During his reign the frontier stayed on the Stanegate Road and the forts along its length. It was a well-made, two-way paved road able to carry heavy military traffic. A clear outline of its camber and the drainage ditches on either side can be seen from the western approach road to Vindolanda. The number of Stanegate forts was increased, and the frontier seems to have been extended beyond Carlisle to Kirkbride and Bowness-on-Solway. Seaborne raids across the firth may have been troublesome. Lookout towers were built on the high ridges to the north of the forts in the central section, and one, at Walltown Crags, was certainly incorporated into Hadrian's Wall. But sources for the period between 105 and 117, the death of Trajan and accession of Hadrian, are sparse. The name of the Governor who took over Britannia after L. Neratius Marcellus is not even known.

In the south of the province the legionary fortresses at York, Chester and Caerleon were all rebuilt in stone, and new colonies of veterans had been founded at Lincoln and Gloucester. More troops arrived in Britain around 105, perhaps as reinforcements after the attacks of the Selgovae. The prefect of the II Cohort of Asturians was buried in Alexandria, in Egypt. The inscription recalled his service in Britain with the Asturians when it noted that C. Julius Karus had been decorated for bravery, probably in the war of 105.

At Vindolanda another tombstone commemorated Titus Annius, a centurion of the I Tungrian Cohort, possibly their acting commander, who was killed in the war, fought in 117 in Britain.

THE BIRLEY DYNASTY

Three generations of Birleys have found themselves at the bottom of Vindolanda's wet and muddy trenches and, without their decades of hard work, the state of our knowledge of Roman Britain would be immeasurably poorer. It all began in 1929. The estates of John Clayton were put up for sale. The owner of Chesters, Housesteads, Carvoran, Vindolanda and Carrawburgh, he had done a great deal to rescue Hadrian's Wall from nineteenth-century stone robbers and destroyers. A young Eric Birley had become fascinated by the Wall, and on being told that Vindolanda was a site of huge archaeological potential, he persuaded his father to help him buy the farm it stood on. The first excavations began. Then war intervened, and then Eric Birley's academic career at Durham University took up more and more of his time. By 1950 he had sold Vindolanda. But family interest continued. Robin Birley started to do research in 1956 and became increasingly certain that the site would ultimately reveal a great deal, if only he could get at it. The farm came up for sale in 1970. Mrs Daphne Archibald, the mother of one of Robin Birley's volunteer excavators, bought it and gave what was known as 'the Camp Field' to a newly formed Vindolanda Trust. Work began in earnest. Sustaining itself solely by receipts from visitors and the revenue from excavation courses, the site slowly fulfilled all that potential, and more. Robin Birley's colleague, Patricia Burnham, became Mrs Birley and by 1974 the Trust began to expand. The nearby cottage at Chesterholm was bought and converted into a museum. The discovery of the first letters and lists built momentum, and the publicity they generated helped to bring in more than 100,000 visitors each year. A third generation now runs Vindolanda's excavations. Andrew Birley has taken over from his father and, each summer, the distinguished Roman scholar Professor Anthony Birley finds his wellies and overalls and helps with excavation. Vindolanda is a remarkable place, dynamic and constantly adding to the store of knowledge about the Wall and Roman Britain. Without the Birleys, it might, as with several other important sites, have remained a green field with a few strange humps and bumps.

All around the Empire native peoples were well aware of the shifts of imperial politics and knew that the death of an emperor and the shaky accession of another could herald a period of instability – and opportunity. In a list of the problems facing Hadrian in 117, a third-century historian noted that *the Britons could not be kept under control.* The kings in the north appear to have made a sustained attempt to take advantage of a moment of Roman weakness.

Annius' death suggests that there might have been conflict on the Stanegate. If the Roman army had indeed been attempting to conscript young native men, resentment may have flared into open revolt. When the attacks came, they seem to have been savage – and effective. Both the II Augusta and the XX Valeria Victrix took heavy casualties and, in the initial period of his reign, Hadrian was forced to send 3,000 reinforcements to Britain. The historian Cornelius Fronto, writing not long afterwards, in 157, lamented the killing of many soldiers *at the hands of the Britons.* Even after thirty years of occupation, the hill peoples of the north still hated the Roman conquest and pitched themselves against a mighty empire to be rid of it.

By 119 it was reported that *the barbarians had been scattered and the province of Britannia recovered*, and coins were issued which showed the figure of Britannia (looking not unlike those which used to appear on old pennies) on the obverse in a submissive pose. The war, it seems, had been won – for the moment.

Hadrian knew that Britannia required sustained attention and he determined to give it personally. When news of his impending arrival spread in 122, the commander at Vindolanda put his soldiers to work. The fort would be an excellent base for any survey of the frontier and it is likely that the imperial household had sent word ahead. Well-appointed quarters were quickly built. Spacious, with plastered and painted walls, the house appears to have been a large courtyard building. The Emperor's interest in architecture was well known and the work done will have been finished with great attention to detail.

Once the imperial visit was confirmed, another man went to work. It was well known that Hadrian liked to make himself accessible and was happy to receive petitions from his subjects in person. At Vindolanda the writer of the following probably believed that he had a good chance of getting his complaint into the Emperor's hands. Over twenty centuries the anger is still palpable:

. . . he beat [?] me all the more . . . goods . . . or pour them down the drain[?] . . . As befits an honest man [?] I implore your majesty not to allow me, an innocent man, to have been beaten with rods and, my lord, inasmuch as [?] I was unable to complain to the prefect because he was detained by ill-health I have complained in vain [?] to the beneficiarius and the rest [?] of the centurions of [?] his unit. I accordingly implore your mercifulness not to allow me, a man from overseas and an innocent one, about whose good faith you may enquire, to have been bloodied by rods as if I had committed some crime.

The complainant appears to have been a civilian merchant from overseas. Whatever he had supplied had been thrown away, presumably because it had spoiled or been of poor quality. But the merchant insists that, whatever the merits of the dispute, he should not have been beaten – because he was from overseas. The clear corollary is that it was appropriate to beat Britons.

It is highly unlikely that the petition was ever put into the hands of His Majesty. The scribe asked by the merchant to write out a fair copy had probably gone to see the centurions. They then sought out the poor man, took the draft from him (it was found in the centurions' quarters) and probably gave him another thrashing for his impudence.

The petition and the incidents around it are a fascinating, very human perspective on an event of immense significance. Hadrian had arrived on the northern frontier and, as he rode through the gates of Vindolanda, history was rumbling into place. Within ten years his plans and wishes would transform the north forever, and the greatest monument to Roman power would ribbon through the Northumbrian and Cumbrian countryside.

5

The Day the Empire Came

Carefully coasting up past Flamborough Head, on beyond the reed marshes at the mouth of the River Tees and other familiar sea-marks, the *Classis Britannica*, the British fleet, brought the Empire north. Based at Boulogne, and with depots at Dover, Chester and other ports, the British fleet was impressive. About 7,000 men were under the command of its *trierarchs*, the sea-captains, and by the AD 120s more than fifty ships were in active service. Most of these were biremes, what the Romans knew as *liburnae* after the Adriatic pirates who first built and developed them. Fast, sleek and manoeuvrable, these ships sliced through the water and, when the wind billowed their single square sail and their banks of oarsmen bent their backs, they could make good headway. Each beak had a large and menacing eye painted on either side; the effect was shark-like.

When watchers on the headland at Tynemouth looked south and scanned the horizon some time in the summer of 122, they will have made out many coloured sails and brightly painted hulls glinting in the sunshine. But one ship dwarfed all the others. Pushed forward by a purple sail with the imperial inscription picked out in gold lettering at its top, a trireme surged through the waves. Evidence for the existence of only one trireme in the British fleet has come to light. On a relief discovered at Boulogne, the *Radians* is recorded. Perhaps it was this ship, *The Gleamer*, which made its stately way up the North Sea coast.

In its belly three banks of oarsmen on each side pulled hard to the commands of the *Pausarius*, the cox who called all the different speeds. To keep all in time, the *Pitulus* pounded a wooden block with a mallet, and his stroke-oarsmen on the benches beside him set the rhythm. On deck the *Trierarch* looked anxiously at the approaching river-mouth. Like most estuaries, the Tyne's could be treacherous, sandbars shifting with the tides, silt washed down with seasonal spates. As the great trireme glided nearer, the *Proreta* made his way forward to a station in the prow. Leaning over and searching the surface of the water for telltale ripples and eddies around hidden obstructions or shallows, he called instructions back to the *Gubernator* and his men on the steering oar.

Immense care was taken, no pains spared to make the entrance into the Tyne uneventful, comfortable and impressive. *The Gleamer* carried the world's most precious cargo – the world's most important man. Publius Aelius Hadrianus had become Emperor of Rome in AD 117, the adopted successor of Trajan. He inherited a vast domain stretching from the Tigris to the Tyne. His professional standing army numbered thirty legions, almost 200,000 highly trained men in a state of constant readiness. The Roman Empire seemed to contemporaries invincible – even eternal. In fact it lasted from 753 BC when Rome was founded to 1453 when New Rome, or Constantinople, fell to the Turks and the last Emperor was killed as he plunged into the street-fighting. Unparalleled in history, the mighty Empire endured for 2,206 years. And Hadrian was one of its most powerful emperors, his reign falling in the middle of what historians have labelled Rome's Golden Age, the period between AD 96 and the death of Marcus Aurelius in 180. The Proreta craning his neck over the prow of *The Gleamer* will never have dared take his eyes off the water.

Although its remains have disappeared under the modern town, it is likely that there was a depot of the Classis Britannica at South Shields. So, when the imperial trireme trimmed its purple sail and the Pausarius called for his oarsmen to hold steady, it may be that a local pilot sailed out to advise the Trierarch on the state of the tides. Passage upriver would be much easier and much faster with an indrawn tide running against the current.

The Tyne looked different 2,000 years ago. The banks of the river were not built up and lined with wharves and walls as they are now, and the flow was not canalised except at Gateshead where the gorge forced it into a natural channel. Reedbeds, mudflats such as Jarrow Slake, oxbows and river-islands made navigation more difficult, and the last thing the fleet commanders wanted was the inconvenience and humiliation of running aground as the Emperor looked on.

DYNASTY

Julius Caesar's pivotal role in establishing the Empire and its emperors has been remembered by imitation. The imperial titles of Kaiser and Tsar are corruptions of his name. Irony was at work. In Latin 'Caesar' means 'hairy', but Julius was famously bald. His name was also attached to the first of many imperial dynasties.

The Julio-Claudians were:
Augustus 31 BC–AD 14
Tiberius AD 14–37
Caligula 37–41
Claudius 41–54
Nero 54–68

In the chaos after Nero's suicide came the Year of the Four Emperors:
Galba 68–69
Otho 69
Vitellius 69

And then the brief interlude of the Flavians:
Vespasian 69–79
Titus 79–81
Domitian 81–96

After Domitian's assassination there followed a continuous succession of successful emperors. It must be highly significant that this was not a dynasty of sons following fathers but a series of adoptions of competent soldiers and senators with proven abilities. And Nerva was also the last Italian emperor in this sequence:
Nerva 96–98
Trajan 98–117
Hadrian 117–138
Antoninus Pius 138–161
Marcus Aurelius 161–180

And then the sequence was broken when Commodus, 180–192, inherited the throne from his father and was ultimately removed.

Others were watching too. From the fort at Newcastle a screen of cavalry units will have patrolled both banks of the river. Although the Romans had been on the Tyne for more than forty years, no chances would have been taken. And since prestige and the power of show always played a central part in Roman politics, native princes may have been encouraged to watch as the Classis Britannica brought Publius Aelius Hadrianus, the greatest prince of all, to his most northerly frontier.

PROPINQUITY

Publius Aelius Hadrianus' family came from southern Spain and they were amongst the earliest provincials to be admitted to the Senate. Fascinated by Greek culture from boyhood, Hadrian was known as 'Graeculus' and he also became a passionate huntsman. On the death of his father, the boy became the ward of a family cousin, Trajan (also from southern Spain), and in 97 Hadrian was sent directly into the centre of power when he was despatched to congratulate his patron on being adopted as the successor of the Emperor Nerva. As with modern politics, nothing propinks like propinquity. In Dacia, now Romania, he fought a famous campaign with Trajan. When the Emperor led the legions east to confront the Persians, Hadrian was by his side once more. Timely positioning was everything and, as Governor of Syria at the time Trajan died in the neighbouring province of Cilicia, Hadrian was on hand in 117 when his chance finally came.

The quays at Newcastle were almost certainly his destination. Two years before, 3,000 men disembarked there from transports which had brought them from the legions stationed on the Lower Rhine. They arrived as reinforcements for a campaign against the northern British kings and their warbands. During the journey up the Tyne, one legionary, the unfortunate Junius Dubitatus, dropped his shield into the river. His centurion will certainly have beaten him for such carelessness and probably docked his pay for the cost of a replacement. Buried deep in the murky silt of the Tyne, the wooden shield rotted but its metal boss, the *umbo*, survived and was dredged up 2,000 years after Junius lost it. Nearby, another, much smaller, circular piece of metal was pulled out of the river. A Roman coin, a *sestertius*, shows a trireme with the Emperor Hadrian enthroned under a canopy in the stern. He is flanked by two standards, what seem to be an imperial eagle and a legionary standard. Mounted in the prow is a wind-god, an addition which strongly suggests the erection of a symbol of thanks for the successful completion of a sea voyage. This interpretation is supported by the inscription on the *sestertius*. It reads: *For the good fortune of the Emperor, three times Consul, Father of his Country*. Much more comfortable travelling overland, Romans were very superstitious sailors, especially outside the placid Mediterranean, and the good fortune may represent more thanks for a safe deliverance. The coin was almost certainly struck as a commemorative issue.

Hadrian arrived at the Newcastle quays some time before 17th July 122. By that date Platorius Nepos is recorded as the new provincial Governor of Britannia. His immediate previous posting had been to Germania Inferior, the Lower Rhine, and the outpost of the Empire visited by Hadrian before his journey to Britain. As *The Gleamer* hove to in the Gateshead Gorge, it is very likely that Nepos and Hadrian both stood on its deck.

ACROSS THE OCEAN

Without the inflow of cold water through the Strait of Gibraltar, the Mediterranean would evaporate. Its feeder-rivers and water from the Black Sea are insufficient to maintain its levels. The strong current through the Strait created an anti-clockwise series of ancient trade-routes. Carried on the Atlantic inflow, ships were driven along the North African coast, up to the Syrian shores and Cyprus and on into the Aegean. Mediterranean winds were seasonal and generally predictable. But the Bora, the Scirocco and especially the Mistral could be stormy; the Gulf of Lion is so named because the Mistral could roar like a lion. So it was not bad weather which made the Romans anxious about crossing the English Channel or the North Sea, what they called 'the Ocean'. Unfamiliarity, a fear of currents which might drag them, literally, into the middle of nowhere (the open sea – very different from the comforting enclosure of the Mediterranean) and the much more extreme rise and fall of tides – these conditions were what worried the trierarchs. The Classis Britannica almost certainly depended from the outset on local pilots and local knowledge.

Many others accompanied the Emperor to the Tyne. Wherever Hadrian went – and he travelled the length and breadth of the Roman world – the apparatus of state followed. To all practical intents the place that became Newcastle, and not Rome, was the imperial capital in the summer of 122. Detachments of the VI Legion, the Victrix, sailed up the river but they were not the only soldiers in Hadrian's retinue, nor the most important. First formally recruited by the Emperor Augustus, the Praetorians were the personal imperial bodyguards, an elite drawn from all of the regular army's legions. Politically very powerful, they had dragged the cowering Claudius from behind a curtain after Caligula's assassination and made him emperor, much against his will. And in 193 their commanders auctioned the throne to Didius Julianus for a vast sum.

To protect Hadrian and the imperial court, the Prefect of the Praetorian Guard, Septicius Clarus, brought a substantial force, and he himself would have been a weighty figure, widely feared – not least by the Emperor, as matters turned out. A great historian also sailed up the Tyne, although sadly he did not record the journey. Suetonius Tranquillus was Hadrian's chief civil servant, variously described as Secretary or Director of Chancery. All of the important administrative machinery of running a vast empire of thirty-six provinces implies a great government department packed into the liburnae following the imperial trireme: clerks, accountants, messengers and more clerks.

Much of the flummery and panoply of the imperial court had to be left behind in Rome's palaces and forums. The northern frontier was no setting for elaborate ceremony or set-piece ritual. But the courtiers came. If he had any sense, each emperor brought influential senators with him on his travels. Not only did he need witnesses to attest to his prowess in leading the army and dealing with barbarians, he also wanted to neutralise intrigue and opposition back in Rome. Near-contemporary records of arrangements made for their provisioning and accommodation show hundreds, perhaps more than a thousand people, in the imperial entourage. When Claudius had sailed to Britannia to join the invading army in AD 43, he had had a large contingent of important senators in his retinue and, although they are not named, influential aristocrats would certainly have travelled with Hadrian in 122.

Ever watchful, the Emperor realised that intelligence-gathering was a key to survival and success. In the past the Praetorian Guard had acted as spies and enforcers when the court was in Rome, but Hadrian needed something more reliable and with an Empire-wide reach. The *frumentarii* were tax collectors in the provinces, taking much of their revenue in corn, *frumentum* in Latin. As travelling officials they were well placed to compile information and make regular reports. Letters carried by the imperial postal service were often intercepted, and one in which the wife of a provincial official wrote to her husband chiding him for idleness became famous. When the official appeared before the Emperor requesting leave, Hadrian refused, saying that the man was too lazy to deserve it. *What!?* he is said to have blurted out, *Has my wife been complaining to you too?*

The sinister hand of the *frumentarii* almost certainly caused an eruption in the imperial court in 122, probably in Britain. Hadrian:

> replaced Septicius Clarus, Prefect of the Guard, and Suetonius Tranquillus, Director of the Chancery, and many others, because they had at that time, in their relations with his wife, Sabina, behaved with greater familiarity than the etiquette of the court required.

Why? The reason given sounds like a polite euphemism, or a pretext. If the Praetorians and the Chancery had been plotting with the Empress, then surely heads would have rolled. Suetonius and Clarus certainly survived, as did the Empress Sabina. Perhaps they had simply become too powerful. Perhaps the *frumentarii* had heard what modern security services call chatter, and the Emperor acted quickly to forestall it developing into anything more. Dealing with the Praetorians in particular demanded delicacy. But this curious incident is clear in at least one respect: Hadrian could be ruthless, decisive and dangerous to know – just like most Roman emperors.

At the outset of his reign there was trouble. At Vindolanda, an inscription has been found which tells of war in Britain. Rebellion and war crackled in other provinces, and Trajan's conquests appeared to overstretch resources. Perhaps the notion of limiting the Empire was bruited about early. To stop opposition and the threat of insurrection in their tracks, Hadrian took decisively brutal action. Four *consulars*, soldiers of the highest aristocratic standard who had held the consulship under Trajan, were murdered in the early months of the new regime. Avidius Nigrinus, Lusius Quietus, Cornelius Palma and Publilius Celsus may not have been guilty of treason – more likely they disagreed with the new policy of retrenchment – but Hadrian did not hesitate.

This early purge stained the new Emperor's reputation profoundly, He was hated by the senatorial elite throughout his reign, and the resulting atmosphere may have been an important factor in Hadrian's extended tour of all the provinces of the Empire. In eleven years he visited all thirty-six and must have been the most recognised Roman emperor in history.

Beyond the atmosphere of mistrust that swirled around Rome and also around his close political circle, Hadrian sometimes revealed a more relaxed, informal and even playful side. Annaeus Florus was a poet, teacher and historian who lived at the city of Tarraco (Tarragona) in Spain. Also having significant Spanish connections (he was born in the Iberian city of Italica and was said to speak Latin with a strong Spanish accent), the Emperor appears to have known the poet and while Hadrian was in Britain the two men exchanged a remarkable but, sadly, very brief correspondence. Here are Anthony Birley's translations of two short poems, Florus' first, with the missing third line improvised and added here:

> I don't want to be Caesar, please
> Tramping around the British, weak at the knees
> [Or lurking with the Germans amongst all those trees]
> Or in the Scythian forests to freeze

The references seem to follow Hadrian's first journey along the northern frontiers in reverse order. Scythia was his first destination and an ancient name for the area around the outfall of the Danube into the Black Sea. Then he travelled to Germany and the Rhine frontier, and finally to Britain. Fortunately for Florus, Hadrian was amused and sent back a witty reply:

> I don't want to be Florus, please,
> To tramp around pubs, into bars to squeeze,
> To lurk about eating pies and peas,
> To get myself infested with fleas.

CASTEL SANT'ANGELO

Hadrian fancied himself as an architect, but when he attempted to offer an opinion at a meeting between Trajan and his chief architect, Apollodorus, the latter told him to mind his own business. It turned out to be an ill-advised remark, for when Hadrian at last became emperor, Apollodorus was banished and perhaps worse. Concerned that the imperial mausoleum built for Augustus was full, Hadrian commissioned a new one for himself and his successors. He is said to have had more than a hand in the design. As centuries passed and Rome declined, it looked increasingly as though the mausoleum stood on a vulnerable site, on the west bank of the Tiber, near what became the Vatican City. It was renamed Castel Sant'Angelo and became the principal stronghold of the Pope. All of its decorative sculpture was lost (some of it hurled at besieging barbarian armies by the Byzantine expeditionary force which had retaken Rome for the Empire in 537) and its basic drum shape (not unusual for a mausoleum but definitely so for a fortress) is all that remains to hint at its previous use.

In seeking to set examples, refusing to ask his men to do more than he would do himself, Hadrian bivouacked with his legions, eating simple fare, drinking rough wine around the campfire – and marching 20 miles in full armour the morning after. He was forty-one when he succeeded Trajan, and he enjoyed a deserved reputation for toughness. His eleven years of tramping around the provinces made him fit and hard-riding. Practice with the javelin and frequent hunting expeditions taught him weapons skills and kept him active on into his middle age. Like Alexander the Great, Hadrian had a favourite horse and he loved to ride in the chase with his beloved hounds. Game pie, stuffed with wild boar ham and the meat of game birds, was said to be a dish he ate with great relish. Hard physical exercise and discipline were everything, an ideal which all soldiers should cherish and constantly aspire to. In the waters of the North Tyne a walker came across a Roman altar dedicated to *the Discipline of the Emperor*.

A tall man with a trimmed beard and *his hair curled by a comb*, Hadrian was said to be an imposing figure. Unusually, his surviving portrait busts all look alike, a firm jaw and broad across the cheek-bones. No delicate features, but a mature man of action, a soldier in his prime. Hadrian's hero was Pericles, the bearded Athenian states-man of the fifth century BC. And as the first Roman emperor to wear a trimmed beard (the longer, straggly sort was thought more suitable for philosophers) in the same Greek style, there is a sense of admiring imitation.

And yet the Emperor was devoted to a beautiful Greek boy, Antinous, clearly the love of his life. More than a hundred repre-sentations of Antinous have come down to us, and it seems that he was indeed a very striking-looking young man. Hadrian may have met him in AD 123 when the imperial fleet sailed along the Black Sea coast of what is now Turkey. Pontus-Bithynia was the name of the Roman province, and its coastal cities had originated as Greek colonies. It was a very different place from Britain, where Hadrian had been the year before. Like most Roman aristocrats of the time, Hadrian spoke Greek well and indeed had been governor or *Archon* of Athens before becoming emperor. Perhaps Antinous embodied all that Hadrian admired in Hellenic culture. In any event, he was devoted to the boy and they almost certainly became lovers.

But there may have been a problem. An affair with a young boy was almost acceptable, even amongst the more starchy Roman aristocratic families. But an affair with a young man on the edge of puberty, perhaps sprouting a beard – that was something that caused much more uneasiness. To be the object of another man's desire at that age, and to be penetrated by him, was shaming. But what could Antinous do? He had to obey the most powerful man in the known world, and also put up with all the vicious gossip and malice which slithered around the imperial court. It was an im-possible position and several historians believe that Hadrian's insistent devotion probably drove his lover to commit suicide. Matters seem to have come to a head when the imperial entourage reached Egypt.

When Antinous drowned in the Nile in 130, in mysterious circum-stances, the world turned upside down. Hadrian's grief was immense and some commentators reckoned the remainder of his reign was spent in slow and miserable decline. Perhaps some scant consolation was found when Antinous was declared a god.

Homosexuality in Greek and Roman times carried different connotations. Men who made love to other men were not seen as deviant but just as manly as those who did not, perhaps even more so. And the modern concepts of concealment and shame appeared not to apply at all. While many men seem to have been bisexual, Hadrian's relationship with Antinous does contrast sharply with what is known about his marriage.

GAY ROMANS

There are no words in either Latin or Greek for homosexuality, and although sex between men (and between women) was often commented on, in itself it was not seen as a separate phenomenon or category. Society did not divide into gay and non-gay. Much more significant were sexual relations which crossed boundaries between social class, say, aristocrats and slaves. Modern attitudes do not apply to Roman and Greek homosexuality. There certainly was a distinction between active and passive, between 'male' and 'female' roles in homosexual relationships, but these generally followed pre-existing social or age-related hierarchies. The Romans called homosexuality 'Greek love' and that gloss may have attracted Hadrian Graeculus, the Little Greek.

Hadrian's wife, Sabina, was well connected. The great-niece of Trajan and daughter of Matidia, a favourite of the Emperor, she made a good match for Hadrian. Some time around AD 100 they married. He was twenty-five and about to take his seat in the Senate, and she would have been considerably younger, probably fifteen. Like most aristocratic marriages, the function was political not passionate. What mattered was advantage and advancement, with the incidental possibility of producing children. Hadrian and Sabina failed in the latter, but succeeded in all else. Sadly their childless marriage seems to have withered into lovelessness, antipathy and even sustained anger. Hadrian was said to have grumbled that his position as emperor forced him to stay with Sabina. If he had been an ordinary citizen, he would have divorced her long ago on account of her moods and contrariness. Quotes from a now-lost biography of Hadrian by Marius Maximus asserted that Sabina *had taken steps* to

GYRUS

Thousands of horses lived on or close to the Wall, but their presence is not well understood. The Vindolanda tablets reported many native cavalrymen and in at least three forts, and probably more, alae or Roman cavalry units were stationed. At Stanwix, across the River Eden from modern Carlisle, was a force of 800 troopers commanded by the Prefect, the most senior officer on the Wall. Elsewhere other, smaller units of cavalry were to be found at Benwell on the outskirts of eastern Newcastle and also at Chesters, further to the east. Including remounts, brood mares for breeding, horses too young to be ridden, those used by dispatch riders and by officers, there were probably more than 3,000 Roman cavalry horses on the Wall, and many more ridden by natives. Where were the Wall horses stabled, grazed, backed, trained and fed? And where did they come from? Further north, at the outpost fort of Trimontium, near Melrose, the archaeologist and historian Walter Elliot has found traces of Roman cavalry culture in the distinctive shape of a gyrus. This was a circular structure of posts that probably supported a viewing platform and enclosed a sand-covered area 24 metres in diameter. Ponies were backed and schooled in a gyrus and newly recruited troopers were taught to ride by an instructor. Roman cavalry horses were not shod, and sand was kind to their hooves while they did repetitive work. Near the gyrus at Trimontium a Roman altar was found. It was dedicated to the Campestres, the gods who presided over cavalry parades. The donor was Aelius Marcus, a Decurion in a cavalry unit, the Ala Augusta Vocontiorum. There must have been a gyrus at Stanwix, Chesters and Benwell, but two of these are almost certainly buried under modern housing and roads. Horses were vital to the Wall garrison, and more traces of their presence surely await discovery or recognition.

avoid becoming pregnant by him – because his children would only do harm to the human race. It seems that she needed to consider contraception, and it may be that the bisexual emperor had at least attempted to do his dynastic duty.

By contrast, Hadrian's relations with his mother-in-law, Matidia, were much warmer. Perhaps he was first encouraged by the fact that the childless Trajan treated Matidia like an adopted daughter. Or perhaps he felt more comfortable in the company of a mature woman, relaxing in a version of maternal love, a relationship without the embarrassment of sexual expectations or obligations. Trajan's Empress, Plotina, was also close to Hadrian, and ultimately she took a leading role in persuading her dying husband to adopt her protégé formally in 117. At the risk of reading too much into a scatter of sparse snippets of evidence, it may be that Hadrian's homosexuality played in his favour as he cultivated these older aristocratic ladies.

BRITANNIA RULES THE WALL

Under Hadrian, a shrine was erected at York to Britannia, thus installing her as a goddess in the Roman pantheon. On coins she is shown in a pose very familiar to those now middle-aged people who used to jingle the big old pennies in their pockets. Seated on a rock holding a spear and wearing a helmet, she has a shield propped by her knee. In all its essentials, this Roman image of the national goddess was reproduced on British coins until the present day. Britannia used to have one breast exposed, but in the nineteenth century she was covered up. In 2008, the Royal Mint announced that she would no longer feature on coins. There was, of course, outrage and Britannia's image is now found on È2 coins. France imitated the use of a heroic female figure with Marianne and the USA with Columbia. Neither have the same resonance.

In the fort at Newcastle, Sabina and her entourage no doubt made themselves as comfortable as was possible in trying circumstances. When the VI Legion sailed up the Tyne in 120 to reinforce the garrison of Britannia, their commanders caused two altars to be raised in thanksgiving for a safe crossing of the North Sea. Oceanus controlled the tides of the sea, and Neptune was seen at that time as a river-god. Perhaps the Empress Sabina and the ladies of the court made sacrifice on these altars. She may have known then that this chilly, northern outpost was by no means the last destination on her husband's itinerary. A great deal of travel lay in store.

Meanwhile it was decided to try the favour of Neptune a little more by building a bridge across the Gateshead Gorge. Placed close to where the modern Swing Bridge is, the bridge was a tremendous undertaking but logistically well worth the effort. If the Emperor was considering a permanent frontier north of the river then it was vital to be able to cross the Tyne quickly.

Wooden piles were driven into the muddy river-bed as engineers struggled to establish footings for the piers of a stone bridge but, interested though he was in architecture, it is unlikely that Hadrian hung around to watch. Guarded by the Praetorians and protected by a screen of scouts sweeping the countryside in front of them, he and Platorius Nepos probably rode west to look at the line of the proposed frontier. Only then would the scale of the work have become clear, the practicalities of construction, and the deployment of the legions and their camps. As he rode up into the moorland above the Hexham Gap, the idea of a wall, a stone girdle built across the waist of Britain, had formed in Hadrian's mind.

6

Let One Stone Stand Upon Another

In 1933 Patrick Leigh Fermor disembarked at the Hook of Holland to begin an epic journey. At the age of eighteen, expelled from school, with only a pound a week to live on, he had decided to walk across Europe. Many years later, he wrote down what he had seen, an extended glimpse of a now-vanished Europe, in two volumes of a promised trilogy, *A Time of Gifts* and *Between the Woods and the Water*. Following first the Rhine and then the Danube, he kept a diary (later lost) of his travels, and it ends at the Iron Gates, a sequence of spectacular river-gorges. Between the Carpathian Mountains on one side and the Balkans on the other, the Danube races and swirls, its currents deep, treacherous and violent. As Leigh Fermor passed through on board a steamer, he noticed a Latin inscription incised directly into one of the towering cliffs.

> The Emperor and Caesar, son of the divine Nerva, Nerva Trajanus
> Augustus Germanicus, High Priest and for the fourth time Tribune,
> Father of his Country and Consul for the fourth time, cutting into
> the mountains and on wooden beams, raised up this road.

When the skipper expertly steered his boat around the whirlpools and underwater rocks, he sometimes sailed very close to the sheer rock face. Leaning over the rail, Leigh Fermor could see something remarkable. No more than a few metres above the boiling river a continuous slot had been quarried, hacked directly out of the cliffs. Two and a half metres high and three metres deep, it was large enough to allow men to walk two abreast. But it was not, as Leigh Fermor believed, a Roman road. In AD 102 Trajan planned to lead a huge army to invade and subdue Dacia, much of modern Romania, and he wanted his soldiers to be supplied by river. Because the currents of the Danube were so powerful as it sped through the Iron Gates, barges would need to be towed upriver. A wooden platform wedged into the slot (replacing an earlier and more fragile structure first built under the Emperor Domitian) would not carry marching legionaries but probably teams of men hauling on hawsers, dragging the barges through the gorge.

Further downstream, at the Great Kazan, where the current is calmer and the channel widens, Trajan ordered a bridge to be built across the Danube. Designed by the Greek architect Apollodorus, it was to become one of the wonders of the ancient world. It reached more than a kilometre in length, was 15 metres wide and raised on twenty stone piers. Completed in AD 105, it was the longest bridge in the world, and would remain so for another thousand years.

Apollodorus faced tremendous structural problems. Thirty metres deep in places and liable to seasonal spates of great ferocity, the Danube could be unrelenting, washing away months of work in moments. But using coffer dams and huge water pumps, and building in bricks, mortar and pozzolana cement (which hardens when in contact with water), all twenty piers were finally sunk and the current diverted around them by sharply pointed cutwaters. A wooden superstructure was prefabricated on shore and lifted into place. And in the spring of 105 Trajan led the legions across, crushed the Dacian army and brought their lands into the Empire.

When his steamer arrived at the same place, here is what Patrick Leigh Fermor saw:

> It was the remains of Trajan's amazing bridge that we had come to see, the greatest in the Roman Empire. Apollodorus of Damascus, who built it, was a Greek from Syria, and two great stumps of his conglomerate masonry still cumbered the Rumanian side; a third stood across the water in a Serbian meadow. Swifts were skimming over the water and red-legged falcons hovered and dived all around these solitary survivors of twenty massive piers. Once they had risen tapering to a great height and supported over a mile of arched timber superstructure: beams over which cavalry had clattered and ox-carts creaked as the Thirteenth tramped north to besiege Decebalus in Sarmizegethusa. On the spot, only these stumps remained, but the scene of the dedication is carved in great detail on Trajan's Column in Rome, and the Forum pigeons, ascending the shaft in a spiral, can gaze at these very piers in high relief: the balustered

bridge soars intact and the cloaked general himself waits beside the
sacrificial bull and the flaming altar with his legionaries drawn up
helmet-in-hand under their eagle standards.

As Leigh Fermor saw, only the abutments at either end of the great
bridge are still visible, but in a year of exceptional drought and low
water (1856), all twenty piers were revealed. Trajan's bridge and
towpath were extraordinary structures, two of the greatest feats of
engineering undertaken in Europe before the nineteenth century.
Emblematic of the age, the zenith of the Roman Empire, they set
Hadrian's Wall in a clear context. Emperors saw themselves as the
Lords of the Earth, not hesitating to alter or overcome geography in
pursuit of glory, in the drive for empire.

LUPERCALE

The legend of Rome's origin centres around the unlikely story of a she-
wolf coming to the rescue of the twins Romulus and Remus. Abandoned on the banks of the Tiber, they were taken by the wolf to her
cave and she suckled them and saved their lives. No wolf, no Rome.
The rest was history (rather than legend). Known as the Lupercale, the
cave and the rescue were thought to be little more than myth. But, in
November 2007, Italian archaeologists held a press conference.
Excavating on the Palatine Hill on the site of the Emperor Augustus'
palace, they had found a cave, a cave which had been a shrine. It was
decorated with mosaics, sea-shells, pumice stones and had a representation of a white eagle at its centre. Was this the Lupercale, the
sacred place where the wolf had suckled Romulus and Remus? It
appears that Augustus, who understood well the power of symbols,
had attached himself securely, in architectural terms at least, to the
history and destiny of Rome. Professor Giorgio Croci led the excavation, and became very excited: 'You can imagine our amazement, we
almost screamed.' The Minister of Culture, Francesco Rutelli, was
calmer: 'This could reasonably be the place bearing witness to the
myth of Rome, one of the most well known in the world.' In March
2008 tourists were at last admitted to Augustus' private apartments.
Small and modest, they were decorated with standard frescoes for a
man of his status and offer no clues as to his nature.

Hadrian was with Trajan on the Danube and he saw with his own eyes what could be done. With thousands of battle-hardened and highly skilled soldiers at his command, was there anything a determined emperor could not build?

His bridge allowed Trajan to strike fast and deep into the Dacian heartlands. Their king, Decebalus, retreated in front of the legions, hoping, like Calgacus and the Caledonians, to lengthen their supply lines to breaking point at best, and slow and weaken Trajan's advance at worst. By a remarkable quirk of archaeological survival, what happened next is understood, but through no written source. The spiralling panels of Trajan's Column show a Roman cavalry trooper riding hard towards a Dacian who holds a curved dagger to his own throat. The scene is set in dense woodland and the trooper leans urgently forward, half dismounting, arm outstretched, in an attempt to prevent this man from taking his own life.

This is the capture of the fugitive Dacian king, the great Decebalus. And the trooper is Tiberius Claudius Maximus. Buried in a field in northern Greece, his headstone was recently recovered and it lists his exploits in a long career with the VII Legion. Maximus' troop had been tracking Decebalus and his band of loyal die-hards, but when the king realised that he would be caught, that there would be no escape, he took his life. Refusing to be captured, taken in chains to Rome, humiliated, whipped through the streets behind a triumphant Trajan, he slashed his carotid arteries and bled to death. Better to end by his own hand than be strangled in the black depths of the Mamertine Prison. Maximus cut off the king's head, tied it by the hair to his saddle pommel and rode back to headquarters to give it to his conquering emperor.

Dacia was a vast province, much of it mountainous, all of it difficult to hold down. But Trajan had bridged the mighty Danube, brought the lands to the north into the Empire and sent back to Rome many thousands of slaves and much booty. He used these immense prizes to build a new forum and market in the city, dedicated in 112. The Senate commissioned the great column to take a central place. Rome was marching once more down the roads to glory.

In the east, since the age of Augustus and before, the emperors' only substantial rivals were the Persians, known as the Parthians in the early second century. Based on the old dominions of the Babylonians, their empire was rich, powerful and very attractive. In 114 Trajan assembled the legions at Antioch in the province of Syria. Hadrian was at the muster, as a senior staff officer, perhaps second-in-command.

The Emperor was sixty by AD 114 but his plans betrayed the vast ambition of a much younger man. Like Alexander the Great, he would stride with his soldiers across the east, and the lands of the Tigris and Euphrates would fall before his unstoppable advance. And that is how it began. Armenia, the mountain kingdom to the north of Mesopotamia, the Empire between the two rivers, was to be the first to be defeated, humbled and brought into the orbit of Rome. On the long march from Antioch, Trajan held what sounds like an imperial durbar from the days of the British Raj: *the satraps and princes came to meet him with gifts, one of which was a horse that had been taught to do obeisance, kneeling on its forelegs and placing its head beneath the feet of whoever stood near.*

Armenia fell, then Mesopotamia, and by 116 the legions saw the sea once more. Incredibly, Trajan had led them from one stunning victory to another, and when he and Hadrian gazed on the waters of the Persian Gulf, Rome had reached right across the known world. From the seas of Arabia to the chill waters of the River Tyne, the legions had conquered. It was breathtaking – and impossible.

Even Trajan knew it. In 117 a client Parthian king was installed in southern Mesopotamia, and Roman soldiers withdrew from the Gulf. The price of glory could not be paid. The old Emperor had hoped to consolidate and stabilise in Dacia, complete a wide-ranging subjection of the east and hold the line elsewhere. But it was very precarious. Imperial overstretch on this scale needed only two major wars to break out in different parts of the Empire to descend into imperial collapse. As Trajan lay dying in Antioch, and the Empress Plotina moved quickly to manoeuvre Hadrian into the line of succession, it was clear that policy had to change.

Five years later, when Hadrian sailed up the Tyne to the Newcastle quays in 122, he had formally renounced almost all that the great Trajan had achieved. While he still ruled an empire larger than Augustus and all the emperors of the first century, Hadrian was forced to *give up what could not be held*. While the Parthians had been cowed, the east shrank back to its frontiers before 114. Dacia was retained but no more wars of conquest were planned. As he progressed around the boundaries of his empire, Hadrian set about the work of consolidation. The map began to settle.

HADRIAN'S TRAVELS

Having visited virtually every province in the Empire, Hadrain was almost certainly seen in the flesh by more of his subjects than any of those who reigned before or after him. In 121 he began his first tour by riding from Rome to Lyon and then to Germany and Middle Europe to inspect the defences of the Rhine–Danube line. Perhaps his fleet called in at London before sailing on to the Tyne in 122. After the Wall was begun, the sprawling imperial retinue packed its bags to travel right across France to Tarragona in Spain. Then, in perhaps his most spectacular year, 123, Hadrian crossed the Strait of Gibraltar into Africa, the province of Mauretania. From there he sailed the length of the Mediterranean, following the Atlantic current, to Antioch in Syria, where he was first proclaimed Emperor, thence across eastern Turkey to the Black Sea coast and its Greek cities, where he met Antinous. Back in Rome by 125, Hadrian left for Africa in 128, Greece and southern Turkey in 129, Palestine and Egypt in 130, and finally back to Rome in 133–4. His backside was well used to the saddle and his stomach to the roll of the waves.

Before his arrival in Britain, the new Emperor had ridden through the German forests inspecting his garrisons – and making a more emphatic frontier. In the first century a policy of defence in depth had been pursued. There had been frontier zones dotted with forts, depending on good communication, good roads and good intelligence. A *limes* or frontier path (giving the English word 'limit') was more likely to lead directly into enemy territory than lie transverse on a boundary between the Empire and the barbarians beyond. Control, not physical borders, was what mattered.

Nevertheless, in Germany and Middle Europe, handy natural lines of demarcation flowed through the landscape. Until Dacia was taken, the Danube supplied a clear frontier in the east, and in the west the line of the Rhine defended the Empire. To connect what geography had already done for him, Hadrian caused a very long timber palisade to be built in 121–2 between the two great rivers. In some ways the original arrangements resembled the Gask Ridge in Scotland of forty years before. In Germany, Domitian had sanctioned a line of watchtowers half a kilometre apart and linked by a *limes*, a path. Turf and timber forts were raised along a line which stretched for an immense distance through the forests. It ran for more than 500 kilometres between the Upper Danube and the Rhine, through the Taunus, Wetterau and Odenwald regions. When Hadrian arrived, he made radical alterations, converting the open system of defence into a solid barrier.

In 121–2 the legionaries embarked on building a vast fence. Ditches were dug, and on the upcast a timber palisade was driven in. Oak was the wood of choice and, once a huge number of trees had been felled, perhaps a quarter of a million, they were sawn into lengths. Laid on their sides, the trunks were rived lengthways with wedges and sledgehammers. The flatter, rived surface of white heartwood was turned outwards to present a more wall-like obstacle. Then it was stiffened and tied with rails nailed cross-ways. A later biography of Hadrian in the *Historia Augusta* recorded that *at that time and frequently at other times he marked off the barbarians in many places, where they are separated not by rivers but by limites with great posts driven into the ground and joined together like a wall*. Either side of the new barrier the forest was cleared and a military zone created. Clearly the palisade, made from perishable materials available close at hand, was not intended as a solid rampart designed to repel an assault. Rather, it acted like the perimeter of a Roman camp or fort, able to slow down an attack but not stop it in its tracks.

Less dramatically, the new German frontier was also a matter of clear definition, a *marking off*. South of it was Rome, the Empire, the lands of the citizens, cities and civil order. North lay the trackless forests of Germania Barbarica. The fence also controlled movement in and out of the Empire. Those who wished to pass between could do so peacefully at a crossing-point, and also pay the *portaria*, a version of customs dues. As at all places of international exit and entry, intelligence could be gathered from the hinterland and, if required, Roman legionaries and auxiliaries could act on it and travel quickly through the barrier if trouble flared.

This was different. A tangible break with the forward policies of the immediate imperial past, the new frontier set an unambiguous limit on the ambitions of Rome. Virgil's god-given destiny of conquest had been repudiated by Hadrian, and those aristocrats who craved the excitement, the honour and the wealth which came with an expanding empire will have been disquieted as the oak trees crashed to the ground in the German forests.

But a fence? A wooden fence in the depths of the woods? Compared with the blaze of glory trailed by Trajan as he fought his way to the Persian Gulf, and the creation of a mighty bridge to reach into the heart of Dacia, the building of a fence certainly struck a minor key – which did not suit Hadrian's nature.

A year later, in 122, when the Emperor and his new Governor of Britannia, Platorius Nepos, watched their engineers drive iron-tipped wooden piles into the muddy bed of the Tyne at Newcastle, they must have talked and planned. There had been war in Britain in 117, and probably fighting close by, along the line of the Stanegate. But Hadrian would not lead a punitive expedition north; that was short-termism and in any event looked very like more conquest. Nor would he order the construction of a frontier like the Gask Ridge or the German forests. If Rome was to retrench, then let it be a triumphant retrenchment. Timbers rotted in the ground and collapsed, ditches caved in. Britannia would be different, the scene of a different version of glory. Let one stone stand upon another: let there be a mighty stone Wall.

There was, in any case, no convenient forest to hand. When Hadrian, Nepos, the Praetorians and his surveyors and labourers set out westwards from Newcastle, they rode through a cleared landscape. But stone could be quarried from it, and once it had been established that there were in fact quarries accessible and sufficient to the task – surely the first issue to be dealt with by the military planners – then a stone Wall offered the opportunity not only to build but to build on a spectacular scale.

As the imperial retinue progressed, they moved through the valley of the lower Tyne, a flattish stretch of farmland. The line of the Wall hugs the north bank of the river as the land rises gently towards Benwell. The Celtic name of the Roman fort, Condercum, meant something like Viewpoint Fort and from the crest of the rise it is possible to see some considerable distance both downriver and up as well as north across the Northumberland Plain and south to the high ground at Birtley, where the Angel of the North now spreads his wings.

Decisions were probably made on the hoof. Based on research doubtless done by forward parties of surveyors and scouts, Hadrian and Nepos laid down the line of the Wall as they went. Not only did the Emperor fancy himself as an architect, he was, like most famous Roman generals, reputed to have an eye for good sites for forts and roads. And he had an irresistible urge to interfere, to become involved in detail. Following his directions, the *mensores* pegged out the line with stakes or marked it with small cairns. No one cared whether or not the Wall cut across good agricultural land. Native farmers were simply removed, lock, stock and barrel. Perhaps they were compensated.

When the frontier had moved up to a new line in Germany in AD 83, the Emperor Domitian specifically ordered that farmers who lost land as a consequence were to be paid for the loss of that year's harvest. The issue of ownership and any transfer which may have taken place is not clear, but Roman politicians were fussy about property rights (they generally owned a good deal of property themselves) and it is likely that along the line of Hadrian's Wall some sort of transaction was worked out between the army and local farmers.

At Throckley, a little way west of Benwell, archaeologists have found the marks of native ploughing under the Wall and it looks as though it was fresh. Farmers had probably ploughed in the spring of 122 and sown their fields before the Emperor and his army arrived to obliterate them. It must have been baffling as well as savage. Building a wall? Plough marks have also been found under the forts at Wallsend and Carrawburgh as well as at Wallhouses, 8 kilometres west of Throckley. No doubt many other sites were built over farm fields.

After Rudchester the landscape begins to change, climbing from the coastal plain up to 120 metres above sea level. Further west, at Haltonchesters, there is little trace of the fort but the modern road runs arrow-straight, following the line of the Roman road. Hadrian will have noted Dere Street as the old north road disappeared over the horizon and given thought to how it might penetrate the new Wall. Only a short way to the south lies Corbridge, the Roman fort and settlement at Coria, on the banks of the Tyne. Having clattered down the paved road, it is likely that the Emperor, his Governor and their entourage stayed there, perhaps using it as a base for their reconnaissance of the eastern sector.

At Chesters Fort near Chollerford, the line of the Wall dips down into the beautiful valley of the North Tyne. Clearly a second bridge would be needed and the sites of its abutments were duly fixed on.

Once the imperial party had moved on from there, the landscape began to change again. On the long hill up to Walwick, the contour lines crowd together, and upland pasture takes over from arable farmland. At Black Carts a substantial run of surviving wall shows how steep the incline is and, at Limestone Corner, it reaches its most northerly point. This is the beginning of the central section and its geography may have been one of the most persuasive factors in following the line Hadrian chose.

The vantage from Limestone Corner in all directions is breathtaking, especially to the north as the ground falls away to the valley of the North Tyne. And if the view *from* the Wall was good, then the view *of* it must have been equally impressive. That was important in choosing sites. As triumphant retrenchment reached across the waist of Britain, it had to make an obvious statement, be something seen by allcomers. *Gaze upon my works, ye mighty, and despair.* This was to be no fence in a wood.

From Limestone Corner moorland flattens and stretches away to the east but, after less than half an hour in the saddle, Hadrian will have caught his first glimpse of what his surveyors had been talking about, the feature which had drawn them to propose this line: the Whin Sill. It was perfect for what the Romans intended. Sheer cliffs to the north and a fairly gentle slope up over grassland to the south. Geology had been particularly helpful to Hadrian.

The Whin Sill is the result of an ancient collision. An unimaginably long time ago, around 420 million years BC, the crust of the Earth was moving, forming and reforming enormous continents, filling and draining vast oceans. What became southern Scotland lay on the edge of a huge landmass and, separated by a prehistoric sea, northern England lay on the rim of another. When these two continents collided, Scotland's harder rocks ground and scraped over England's leading edges, the crust of the Earth corrugated and buckled, the floor of the ancient sea was squeezed upwards, and the foundations of the landscape of Northumberland and Cumbria were laid down.

Like the wavelets of an indrawn tide, the folded ridges of the landscape north of the Hexham Gap supplied the raw materials for Hadrian's dramatic plans. Not only did the cliffs of the Whin Sill act as the foundation, one of the other results of that ancient collision was a profusion of outcrops, and they too were helpful. Quarries were found near the surface and often in vertical faces, and coal seams also peeped through in various places. These coal-heughs were to prove extremely useful sources of fuel in a treeless landscape.

The Whin Sill is broken by several steep-sided nicks. One of the most famous is at Sycamore Gap, and like the track of a fairground rollercoaster the Wall swoops down from the clifftops, sweeps through the Gap and up the other side. As much as anything these sections of Wall are examples of imperial single-mindedness and unflinching obedience. The legionaries no doubt cursed loudly and shook their heads as they built a stone wall up these near-vertical inclines – but they did it.

The cliffs end abruptly above Greenhead, and the Wall descends to the flatter ground of the Irthing Valley and the Solway Plain beyond it. From the crossing of the river at Willowford to its terminal at Bowness-on-Solway, turf was at first used instead of stone as a basic building material. The Wall must have run over grassland on this stretch. The change was not dictated by a lack of quarries and good stone. Later in the second century the turf was eventually set aside and replaced by stone. The initial difficulty had been a shortage of the limestone needed to make lime mortar.

Hadrian extended the run of the Wall to Bowness in order to cover all of the Solway fords then in regular use. But genuine sea traffic was also seen as requiring close control. Beyond the end of the land-wall, a sea-wall hugged the Cumbrian coastline, possibly reaching as far south as Ravenglass. Five major forts were built at regular intervals and forty-nine turrets and milefortlets have so far been plotted. There was no Wall as such, no need for one, but there was almost certainly a connecting road and possibly some ditching. This appears to have been slight, little more than 1.5 metres wide and 1 metre deep, and perhaps it was the boundary of a military zone. Elsewhere there are the faint shadows of parallel ditches.

Hadrian's Sea-Wall is often ignored or written off in a footnote, but it was clearly part of the original intention, and the fort at Maryport not only dates earlier, possibly built in AD 72, when Petilius Cerialis was at Carlisle, it was also put under the command of Maenius Agrippa, a friend of the Emperor and presumably a trusted senior officer. In all, from Wallsend to Ravenglass, the Wall ran more than 180 kilometres, an immense, complex and fascinating monument to the power and reach of Rome.

ANOTHER GREAT WALL

Stories of the Far East had filtered to Rome for generations. Trade brought spices, fine silks and tales of exotica. Hadrian himself had been to the Persian Gulf, perhaps a younger Trajan would have emulated Alexander the Great and led armies to India. Antoninus Pius is known to have received ambassadors from China, from the emperors of the Han dynasty. They too were interested in walls, and had been building them for some time. The Great Wall of China, with its broad walkways, crenellations and turrets dates very much later, having been built for the Ming dynasty in the sixteenth century. The wall that Hadrian and Antoninus may have heard about was in some ways more impressive. Built mostly of rammed earth and gravel, the walls raised to defend the northern borders of China had existed since *c.* 200 BC and the reign of the first emperor of all China, Qin Shi Huangdi. In all, these ran for an astounding 6,400 kilometres and are the largest man-made structures ever built. Perhaps Hadrian was impressed, even inspired.

The symbolism invested by Hadrian in his Wall was not the only reason for its construction. The great labour was undertaken for several practical purposes. As in the German forests, clear demarcation – something unmissable – was important. In the new world of consolidation, being either side of the Wall would have real meaning – in the Empire and outside it. The Wall's presence had military value (not as a fighting rampart: it was too narrow, not built to allow enfilading fire along its length and not meant to be defended like a medieval castle) in that it could prevent large numbers of enemy warriors from getting through it quickly. The *Historia Augusta* records a simple strategic rationale. The Wall was built *qui divideret Romanos barbarosque*. The sense of the verb, it has been persuasively argued, is stronger than merely to divide or separate. It really means 'to force apart' the Romans and the barbarians. And this reading becomes even more persuasive when the political landscape is looked at more closely.

The Brigantes, the largest native kingdom in Britain, appears to have been a federation including the Carvetii in the Eden Valley in the east, and the Textoverdi, the Lopocares and the Corionototae along the banks of the Tyne. When King Venutius attempted to defend his huge hillfort at Stanwick, he called on *help from outside*, that is, from the north. Agricola's lines of advance in AD 79 encircled the dangerous Selgovae, and the construction of the Sea-Wall down the Cumbrian shore clearly anticipated a threat from the Novantae in Galloway. By driving a concrete, heavily guarded and unmistakable frontier through the Hexham Gap, Hadrian forced apart this powerful alliance of the hill peoples of the north. Of course their kings could communicate, and it seems that sometimes they did succeed in inflicting damage, but the glowering presence of the Wall would prevent them from combining quickly and in force.

Economic imperatives rarely lagged far behind military objectives in the Roman Empire. Just as in Germany, those passing through the Wall probably paid *portaria*, a tax on movement and goods. Cattle and sheep rustling in the hills and upland valleys of the north Pennines and the Cheviots was not the invention of the Border Reivers of the sixteenth century. Its origins were ancient, and a useful economic effect of the Wall was to prevent cross-border raiding almost entirely (or at least without a considerable outlay in bribery). At the height of the lawlessness of the 1570s and 1580s Elizabeth I of England's council seriously considered rebuilding Hadrian's Wall, rejecting the idea only on the grounds of cost.

Much more danger appears to have lurked in the western districts around the Wall. There was thought to be no equivalent need for a Sea-Wall down the North Sea coast, and no outpost forts were built (at first) in the east. The Votadini were not only almost certainly friendly to Rome but also key providers of essential supplies to the large garrison. In the west it was different, and three forts were established in forward positions, at Birrens, Bewcastle and Netherby. The last was known as *Castra Exploratorum*, the Fort of the Scouts. Patrolling and intelligence gathering were clearly seen as necessary at that end of the Wall. If Hadrian hoped to force apart the barbarians, it seems that he meant to achieve it in the centre and the west. The balance of the garrison was weighted there. In the east, the Tyne was probably already a frontier between the Votadini and the peoples to the south.

Perhaps because it was more settled, building began from the eastern end. And work began everywhere at once. Or so it must have seemed to the native peoples. No doubt exhibiting the impatience characteristic of those in high office, Hadrian will have demanded immediate action, and in the late summer of 122 progress would have been rapid and dramatic.

SOUVENIRS

Not long after it was completed, the Wall appears to have become a tourist attraction in Britannia. The Rudge Cup, the Amiens Skillet and the Staffordshire Skillet all carry the names of forts inscribed on them, usually around the rim of the vessel. All have a sequence of forts at the western end, and not the entire run. Like mugs with Blackpool or Bournemouth painted on them, they seem to have been popular. The survival of three artefacts of such an individual type is surely significant. Discovered recently, in 2003, the Staffordshire Skillet, or *patera*, has a name inlaid: Aelius Draco. Perhaps he was a soldier who served out his time on the Wall and his messmates had a memento made for him.

Once the line of the Wall had been accurately surveyed and marked (the Roman military made extensive use of maps), the countryside burst into a frenzy of activity. Detachments of soldiers were despatched to quarries, woods, sandpits, rivers and streams to discover local suppliers of all manner of goods, to build limekilns, blacksmiths' forges and workshops. Smoke from thousands of fires plumed into the Northumberland skies. Not until the Industrial Revolution seventeen centuries later would the landscape of the lower Tyne see such toing and froing.

Three legions were commanded to build the Wall. The II Augusta, the VI Victrix and the XX Valeria Victrix represented a combined workforce of at least 7,000 men. Each legate will not have needed reminding that their men had been set to work in hostile country. Having left a cohort behind at their regional bases at York, Chester and Caerleon, the legions also required protection and their first action will have been to build secure quarters. In the midst of so much activity, it has been difficult to detect where they camped, but while use will have been made of existing forts, the construction of the Emperor's Wall was a field exercise and his soldiers will have pitched their leather tents behind a palisade. Scouts no doubt rode out on regular patrols to anticipate enemy activity. There had been war in the north only three years before and, as each man worked, his weapons were not far away.

The legions built the Wall because they had all the necessary skills. In addition to their primary role as heavy infantry, many men were also stonemasons, blacksmiths, carpenters and carters. And each legion was used to operating as a self-contained unit. Hadrian and Nepos decided to use this to advantage. Construction of the Wall was split up into legionary lengths of about eight kilometres, what was thought to amount to a season's work. And there would be productive rivalry between the men of the II, the VI and the XX.

Building was supervised by a Clerk of Works known as the *Praefectus Castrorum*. His first task was not to send gangs to the line of the Wall but to assemble all the logistical elements needed to make the project happen. It was very complex, and logistics were the key to success. As a general rule of thumb, for every one man building the Wall itself there were a further eight working to support him, supplying materials, digging ditches, watching the horizon for warbands of enemy horsemen.

Gangs worked ahead of each other in a clear sequence. After the turf was cut out and preserved for later use, a shallow trench was dug along a line pegged out with cord by the surveyors. Flags, boulders and other large loose stones were brought forward by oxcart (certainly at the east end of the Wall where the ground was not difficult) and bedded into the clay or earth, making as level a foundation as possible. Where the Tyne was navigable, the river will have been used to bring up materials. Barges and ships were the largest form of bulk transport available to the Romans. Meanwhile at the nearby quarries (the furthest from the Wall appears to have been Black Pasture, 1.3 kilometres from the fort at Chesters) men were clearing vegetation and throwing down bottoming to make hard standing so that they could get at the stone and get it out.

More stonemasons probably worked at the quarries than on the Wall itself. With difficult journeys by oxcart and pack-horse over rough country and often uphill, it was vital to keep carriage weight to a minimum. Once stone had been levered or cut out with wedges, it was roughly sized according to its use. Ordinary Wall stones were manageable and could be loaded onto a cart or a pack-saddle by one man, occasionally two. These blocks of what is known as squared rubble were cut flush at one end (the best end, according to the grain) usually with a scappling hammer rather than a chisel and mallet. The blocks were then tapered away from the cut face into a blunted pear-shape. This was done to make it easier for the less skilled men at the Wall, allowing them to bed stones quickly, only having to present a keyed course on the outside; what we see now. The tapered end was set to the inside so that it bonded better with the rubble and clay core, and also did not touch its neighbours at the sides and need to be cut to fit. This method of working made for rapid progress.

GANGS OF THE NEW WALL

Within the legionary lengths, there were sectors run by each centurion. These were worked by gangs with strictly organised roles. It is estimated that at the site there were 30 men working as a unit, 15 on the north side and 15 keeping pace with them on the south. In each gang, 3 men laid courses of stones and beds of mortar, 4 mixed, kept wet and brought forward mortar, 3 filled the core while 4 provided clay to bond it and there was 1 general labourer, probably the youngest – the lad who would have made the tea if they had had any. Down at the quarry 55 men worked. Of these the vast majority both quarried and roughed out stones, and 10 or so worked on the discarded rubble, breaking it down so that it could be used to fill the core. These numbers say nothing about transport, wood-felling and scaffold-work, sand-quarrying or any of the myriad other tasks. They are the estimates of an experienced modern mason.

The quarries mostly produced sandstone and gritstone, both sedimentary and easy to work. The whinstone from the Sill was usually too hard. Mortar was made from limestone and, happily, the eastern and central sectors appear to have a sufficient supply to hand. In the occasional slack moment, some of the masons at the quarries left inscriptions. At Haltwhistle Burn, the VI Legion made its mark, but nineteenth-century quarrying removed the lettering. North of Housesteads, at Queen's Crag, there is an undated inscription which is certainly Roman, and at other places men carved a phallus and testicles – a symbol of good luck and no doubt the subject of ribald comparison.

Up on the Wall the turrets and milecastles were built first. Perhaps this was decided because of the volatile nature of the area, perhaps it would also help with plotting the line of the Wall correctly. Archae-ologists have been able to demonstrate this order of building because the turrets and milecastles were left with projections designed to bond with the incoming stretch of connecting Wall. Like the irregular edges of an unfinished jigsaw, the courses of stone stick out on either side.

The most complex and difficult elements of each milecastle were the arched gateways. Teams of specialists quarried and assembled them. To cope with the additional structural stress, larger stones were needed for both the piers and the arches themselves. Some survivors have been found to weigh half a tonne. At the quarry, bursting hammers were used to shape the big blocks. With an axehead shape at one end and a flat sledgehammer face at the other, they could be worked quickly in the hands of an experienced man. Known as *voussoirs*, the wedge-shaped stones for the arch had to fit precisely, and a procedure called *setting-out* was used. Once all the faces had been cut roughly flush (finer work could be done at the site) the arch was, in essence, built lying on the ground with each stone set in its place and the necessary symmetry achieved. Good masons can judge these proportions by the eye. Once all was ready, the components of the arch were lifted onto a train of oxcarts. Much too heavy to be picked up by muscle-power, they were loaded by block-and-tackle hoists. These were sophisticated and took several forms. Most com-mon was probably a tripod with a pulley at its apex and strong flax ropes threaded through it. It was very dangerous work, and the velocity of a heavy stone block when a rope shears is startling.

For the highly skilled job of building the piers of an archway, the Romans' lifting technology was simple but ingenious. Once a large stone had been roughed out at the quarry, a mason took a punch and made a hole on each of the opposite sides. They had to be at exactly the same height and width, precisely opposite, otherwise the stone would rise out of balance and could slip. Then pincers, called *nippers* on British building sites, were held into each hole and the strain taken by men hauling on the pulley rope. The block was slowly hoisted and let gently down onto the cart bed. A centurion will have roared at anyone who slackened his grip too soon and splintered a cart.

Some examples of a different method of moving stones can still be seen by the observant along the Wall. Using a curved-end chisel, concave triangular holes were made in large blocks, like the basic shape of an isosceles triangle with its apex missing. Masons still use this ancient method and call the cuts *Lewis holes*. These allowed stones, such as voussoirs, and especially the keystones at the top of arches, to be lifted from their centre. Nippers got in the way of any attempt to slot shaped stones into the semi-circle of an arch. Lewis holes were based on a simple notion. Into the triangular hole a metal grip was inserted. Curved outwards so that its teeth gripped the undercut sides when tension was put on the pulley rope, they were immensely strong and immensely useful. Once a keystone was carefully lowered in, the grip was pulled out easily after the rope had slackened. At that moment the arch was formed and, provided it settled correctly after removal of the semi-circular wooden frame (called a *centre*) that it was assembled on, the gang moved on to the next milecastle.

TOOLKIT

Over 2,000 years, stone has not changed much and neither have the tools used by masons to cut and shape it. The Romans even had saws, although they ran on muscle-power rather than electricity. The ancient iron toolkit fell into two groups. Picks, walling hammers, axes and adzes were used directly on the stone and were preferred by the masons working at the quarries who roughed out what had just been pulled out of the strata. Experienced men take time to look at a stone before they lift up a hammer. Examining the grain, they select a weak point and can often lay open a big boulder with little more than a tap. Several sorts of chisels – claws, bullnoses, gouges, bent chisels, nickers and punches – were in common use for making holes and were all driven by mallets. The wooden version, sometimes called a mel, was used for planing and other less-skilled jobs. Finer judgement needed a metal-headed mallet with most of its weight at the top. These are known as Italian mallets. Working in Greenlaw, the old county town of Berwickshire, Dave Rumbles is a highly skilled mason able to carve lettering in the Roman manner. He works a blank stone with it canted at a 45-degree angle so that the dust and chippings fall away. Loosely gripping an Italian mallet (too tight and tiredness soon sets in with mistakes to follow) and a fine chisel, he can carve at a steady and rhythmic pace, never taking his eyes off the stone.

Transport logistics were the core of the huge operation begun in AD 122. A four-wheeled ox wagon pulled by as many as ten beasts could haul two tonnes of stone, about seventy normal Wall stones, or four or five pier stones or voussoirs. It has been estimated that an astonishing 30,000 vehicles of one sort or another were used in the three years the Wall probably took to complete. To pull them, around 6,000 oxen were yoked to the heaviest loads. Moving at 3 kilometres an hour, they were slow and ponderous, but steady and not excitable. Horses and mules were much quicker and more nimble-footed, important in difficult country, but had less muscle-power. Nevertheless, it is estimated that the Wall builders used more than 14,000.

The legions already had many pack-animals to carry their tents and other kit. Mules were generally preferred to horses because they were hardier and needed less fodder. On an x-frame pack-saddle, mules could carry as much as 200 kilograms and they could reach the less accessible areas of the Wall – as could men. It is important not to underestimate the amount carried by legionaries and other labourers. To a considerable extent, Hadrian's Wall is a monument to human sweat.

The Romans appear not to have been kind to their pack-animals, driving them beyond what was sensible, as observed in a decree of Constantine Augustus in AD 357: *very many persons by means of knotty and stout clubs force the public post animals . . . to use up whatever strength they have*. Feed must have been a substantial problem, especially in the difficult central sector of the Wall, and the legionary quartermasters had to have acquired a prodigious supply of hay after the first cut in late June, at the earliest. That implies a great deal of co-operation with native farmers. Twenty thousand draught animals, working hard, will have exhausted the available grazing very quickly.

The core of the Wall was filled by rubble, clay and soil laid in between two outer skins of masonry. Lime mortar was usually used for bonding, and its production was another major industrial operation. Some kilns for burning limestone already existed. The Vindolanda lists mentioned *men sent to the kilns* and the need *to burn stone*. But in 122 many more were urgently required. Always sited close to the limestone quarries, they burned for several days, consuming copious amounts of fuel (in itself another constant need), to produce the powdered lime essential for the masons. Sand was also needed.

Mortar was made with one part lime, three parts sand and water. At Fallowfield Fell, near Chesters, a very large sandpit was certainly excavated by the Romans, and there must have been many others.

Mortar was almost certainly mixed off-site, probably near the lime kilns, and then taken up to the Wall wet. Logistically very complex – and dangerous – this sort of awkward transfer had to be managed many times, even in very rough country. The problem was that the powdered lime is so acidic that it burns badly to the touch, lifting off skin in a moment. Loading needed tremendous care, especially when it was windy, and if any spilled during carriage then a pack-animal would have been seriously injured. Sand and lime were carefully turned and folded in volcano-like cones as water was added in stages (just as it is now by those without a mechanical mixer). Then the mixture was loaded into panniers slung on pack-saddles, and the mules were carefully led up to the building site. The mortar beds which can still be seen on the Wall are generally not thickly laid, unlike modern compo. This required real skill to keep the beds level and the outer face flush.

SOLDIERS AND SAILORS

Everybody who was at hand helped to build the Wall. Even the sailors of the British fleet were press-ganged into service. Tile-stamps, inscriptions and other scraps of evidence indicate that they were certainly at work at the eastern end. It may be that they organised and piloted barge traffic up the Tyne, much the best way to carry bulky and heavy building materials. But they will not have been Jolly Jack Tars giving their landlubber comrades a hand. The Classis Britannica contained many men who were as much soldiers as sailors, equipped more like modern marines. And they could have possessed many of the building skills needed to work just as effectively on land.

As the milecastles, turrets and the Wall itself rose ever higher, another element of planning came into play. The finished Wall was probably about four metres in height and, to lay the top courses of stone and fill in the core, scaffolding was needed. Even higher scaffolds were required at the milecastles and turrets. At any given time during the building season (this lasted about thirty-five weeks – working in the winter weather involved disabling difficulties) each legion had approximately five work-gangs taking the Wall to its full elevation, four specialist groups working at the milecastles and two completing the turrets. All of them needed scaffolding. Experts have reckoned that 150,000 metres of straight wooden poles were cut to provide it. This meant a massive sourcing and felling operation in AD 122 and 123.

Putlog holes, where scaffolding was wedged into existing courses of stonework for stability, have been found along the Wall, but it is likely that most frameworks were free-standing. This saved on wood, and the frameworks were easier to move on. Straight-sawn timber is a relatively modern invention, and the irregularities of natural tree growth will have made for some rickety and dangerous structures. Lifting up heavy Wall stones off a scaffold in a high wind was not something many men will have volunteered for.

Progress is likely to have been rapid, especially when the Emperor and his Governor were riding back and forth along the line. It is thought that Hadrian stayed in the north-east for three months, probably lodging at Vindolanda for part of the time. Nevertheless the whole area must have looked like a gigantic building site for a long time. At Highshields Crag, just to the north of Vindolanda, there is evidence to show that, after the foundations were dug, no further work took place for a long enough time to allow soil to blow over the site and cover it. Birdoswald Fort was begun and then abandoned. Scrub grew up inside the half-built walls and had to be burned off before work could resume.

Inscriptions allow some secure dating for the construction of Hadrian's Wall. In addition to that of the Emperor, the name of Aulus Platorius Nepos is found in several places. And since no other Governor is commemorated anywhere, it seems likely that the project was completed, with some omissions, during his tenure of office. Nepos probably left Britannia in 125, 126 at the latest.

That end date was only made possible because the scale of what he and Hadrian had planned was reduced, almost at the outset. The original Wall foundations were nearly 3 metres in width and probably calculated to carry a very high and impressive superstructure. This was quickly modified and a new width of 2.1 metres specified. Along much of the line the masonry is offset at the bottom courses where the narrower wall sits on top of broad foundations. This was almost certainly done to save time and materials.

THE NAMES OF THE FORTS

If Ravenglass is included, and the forts that were off the line of the Wall, like Vindolanda, are not, what follows is a list of the names given to the Wall forts, with their meanings. Most are Celtic; there are only two in Latin:

Wallsend – Segedunum – The Strong Fort
Newcastle – Pons Aelius – Hadrian's Bridge
Benwell – Condercum – Viewpoint Fort
Rudchester – Vindobala – White Peak Fort
Halton Chesters – Onnum – Waterfort
Chesters – Cilurnum – Riverpoolfort
Carrawburgh – Brocolitia – Heatherfort
Housesteads – Vercovicium – The Fort of the Good Fighters
Great Chesters – Aesica – Fort of the God
Carvoran – Magnis – Rockfort
Birdoswald – Banna – Promontory Fort
Castlesteads – Camboglanna – Fort on the Curved Bank
Stanwix – Uxelodunum – Highfort
Burgh-by-Sands – Aballava – Appletreefort
Drumburgh – Concavata – Hollow Fort (Latin)
Bowness-on-Solway – Maia – Greatfort
Beckfoot – Bibra – Beaver Fort
Maryport – Alauna – Rockyriverfort
Burrow Walls – Magis – Plainsfort
Moresby – Gabrosentum – Goatspathfort
Ravenglass – Glannoventa – Beachmarketfort

There was much more to Hadrian's Wall than just a wall. After it was more or less complete, work-gangs began to dig a defensive ditch on the north side. It was deep and wide. At a depth of 2.5 to 3 metres with 33 per cent sloping sides, the ditch presented a real barrier and, because the whole excavated area was between 9 and 12 metres wide, it could not easily be bridged. The spoil was piled up on the north side to make the ditch seem even deeper, and it was probably revetted with the turf removed at the beginning of building work. Roman soldiers were used to ditch-digging; they did it routinely while overnighting on campaign. And it was thought to be a vital skill. The great first century

AD general Domitius Corbulo once remarked that *the pick was the weapon with which to defeat the enemy*. The *dolabra*, an entrenching tool carried by legionaries, no doubt swung hard and often on the northern flank of Hadrian's Wall, but the work was unusually difficult. When modern-day volunteers at Vindolanda imitated the work done between 122 and 126, they found ditch-digging much harder than wall-building.

The reason for this was not only to be found in differences in fitness and toughness; it also related to the nature of the ground. At Limestone Corner the hard rock immediately in front of the Wall simply could not be removed to make a clean ditch, and the vain efforts of the soldiers can still be seen. One huge boulder still carries the slots cut into it for wedges. These were no doubt hit hard with bursting hammers under the critical eye of a centurion, but the great boulder would not split and had to be left where it was: a monument to Roman frustration.

Limestone Corner was not unusual in presenting difficulties. Much of the ditch had to be dug out of clay deposits and this was what exhausted the modern-day Vindolanda diggers. When dry the clay was almost rock-hard and when wet it turned to putty, sticking to the blades of shovels and very heavy to lift. When it rained, as it will have done often on the work-gangs at the Wall, the ditch simply filled up, did not drain and had to be bailed before any more excavation could be done. Then there was the problem of spoil removal. In such a deep and wide ditch, triple shovelling was necessary as it got near the required depth. One labourer at the bottom hacked out as much spoil as they could lift, brought it up to shoulder height and deposited it about halfway up the slope. Then a second person picked it up and lifted it to the top. There a third mounded the spoil on the northern bank and smoothed it off. If baskets or stretchers were used, the work might have been easier, but much slower.

More satisfying than all that slog must have been the building of the Wall's four bridges across the Tyne, the North Tyne, the Irthing and the Eden. For it seems that they were things of beauty. All are long gone now, but traces of the bridge at Chesters, where the Wall crossed the North Tyne, are eloquent. Probably one of the earliest structures to be completed, it was carried on eight hexagonal piers which supported small arches of about 4 metres in width. Cutwaters divided the current of the river and, for symmetry and strength, they seem to have been built both upstream and downstream.

DAM DIFFICULT

Like Trajan's great bridge over the Danube, all of the four Wall bridges were built with the same basic technique. A cofferdam was driven into the river-bed where each of the stone piers was designed to sit. The most difficult of the four would have been the Pons Aelius. The Gateshead Gorge canalised the sprawling Tyne into a strong current between two areas of high ground. In essence a cofferdam was a watertight box constructed from piles banged into the river-bed. Always larger than any of the bridge's piers, its purpose was to expose the bed so that it could be built on. Iron-tipped oak piles were first hammered in by a pile-driver lashed to a barge anchored at the site. This was a large and heavy stone hoisted by block and tackle on a frame and then dropped. It must often have hit the pile off-centre. Once an oblong had been completed, engineers set to, driving in an inner skin of more piles and then gradually sealing the joins with clay. Using a waterscrew (invented by Archimedes of Syracuse) turned from barges, or from the banks if the river was not wide, water was lifted out. On the North Tyne and certainly on the Irthing, it would have been possible to bail each cofferdam with large buckets and a hoist. When the river-bed was at last exposed, tar-covered piles were hammered into it and building began on top of them. Pre-cut stone was laid with a rubble core and bound together with pozzolana cement. Roman bridges were famously elegant.

Although it made no sense to carry the Wall across a bridge, it seems that the Romans did exactly that. The platform was the same width as the broad wall foundations – and what does make sense is a walkway from one bank to the other. Perhaps there was a boom chain suspended above the water level to inhibit those who fancied rowing under the Emperor's Wall. In 207 to 208, the Hadrianic bridge was replaced by a grander three-arched version, which had impressive two-storey abutments at either end.

Cawfields milecastle lies near the western edge of the Whin Sill, not far from where the Wall drops down to Greenhead. In a good state of preservation, it is much visited – and marvelled at by some. Like the entire Wall, it displays a certain bloody-mindedness, even an unbending rigidity of thought. Up on the Sill, Cawfields commands long views to the north, but the gate on that side opens onto a sheer drop. Only 30 metres to the west is a much better and flatter site, one of the nicks in the Whin Sill (the route taken by visitors), and it would have allowed access through both of the milecastle's gates. But the milecastle had to be a mile, exactly a mile, from the next one, so that was where it had to go.

GARRISONS

Many languages were heard along the Wall in the 120s. Forts were garrisoned from all over the Empire, from Spain, France, Belgium, Holland, Switzerland, Syria, Hungary, Greece, Romania and Germany. Troop dispositions are also informative. They show where the Romans expected trouble and what kind. Inscriptions are handy guides to who was where – but there are still some question marks along the line:

Wallsend	Cohors quingenaria equitata [?]
Benwell	Ala quingenaria [?]
Rudchester	Cohors quingenaria equitata
Halton Chesters	Cohors quingenaria equitata
Chesters	Ala Augusta ob virtutem appellata
Carrawburgh	Cohors quingenaria equitata
Housesteads	Cohors milliaria peditata
Great Chesters	Cohors VI Nerviorum quingenaria peditata [?]
Carvoran	Cohors I Hamiorum quingenaria peditata
Birdoswald	Cohors I Tungrorum milliaria peditata
Castlesteads	Cohors quingenaria peditata
Stanwix	Ala Petriana milliaria
Burgh-by-Sands	Cohors quingenaria equitata [?]
Drumburgh	[?]
Bowness-on-Solway	Cohors milliaria equitata
Beckfoot	Cohors quingenaria peditata
Maryport	Cohors I Hispanorum milliaria equitata
Moresby	Cohors quingenaria equitata [?]

The first phase of building work showed much more general inflexibility. When the Wall was connected to its turrets and mile-

Chesters Fort (copyright © Liz Hanson)

The remains of the *vicus* at Vindolanda (copyright © Liz Hanson)

How the Wall might have looked – the reconstruction at Vindolanda (copyright © Liz Hanson)

Barcombe Hill behind Vindolanda (copyright © Liz Hanson)

Above. Housesteads Fort
(copyright © Liz Hanson)

Left. The south-west corner of
Housesteads Fort, rebuilt in part
by John Clayton's masons
(copyright © Liz Hanson)

Buildings beyond Housesteads Fort (copyright © Liz Hanson)

The only section of the Wall where walking is permitted, west of Housesteads Fort
(copyright © Liz Hanson)

Sycamore Gap (copyright © Liz Hanson)

Part of the central section looking towards Crag Lough and Hotbank Farm
(copyright © Liz Hanson)

Left. Stones for the arch at milecastle 37 (copyright © Liz Hanson)

Below. The Whin Sill and the central section (copyright © Liz Hanson)

Right. Wall foundations with a dyke built from Roman stone in the central section (copyright © Liz Hanson)

Below. A detail of the Wall (copyright © Liz Hanson)

The steep gradient on the Whin Sill (copyright © Liz Hanson)

Detail of the Wall near Housesteads (copyright © Liz Hanson)

Above. The quarry at Walltown, which took a bite out of the Wall (copyright © Liz Hanson)

Left. The rubble core of the Wall at Walltown (copyright © Liz Hanson)

The early turret at Walltown Crags (copyright © Liz Hanson)

Milecastle, near Birdoswald (copyright © Liz Hanson)

An impressive run of Wall east of Birdoswald (copyright © Liz Hanson)

Birdoswald Fort. The timber posts mark the location of the post-Roman hall (copyright © Liz Hanson)

Turret at Birdoswald (copyright © Liz Hanson)

Poltross Burn milecastle, near Birdoswald. The railway runs very close (on the left-hand side). (copyright © Liz Hanson)

Massive defences were a common feature throughout the Roman Empire. Linear barriers such as Hadrian's Wall, however, were not typical, although remains in Roman Syria, at Rasafa and Halabiya for example, give a good impression of how the Wall might have appeared in its heyday. The following pictures illustrate a number of features which would have formed part of Hadrian's Wall but which are better preserved elsewhere, including the inevitable back-up systems such as roads and garrison towns that were integral to the maintenance of frontier defences.

Right. Dura Europos was a garrison city, originally settled by veterans of Alexander the Great's army, and shares many characteristics with the Northumberland garrisons: barracks, a *praetorium*, a *Mithraeum* and – like Vindolanda – preserved documents (Copyright © Warwick Ball)

Gonio, on the Black Sea coast in Georgia, boasts probably the most intact legionary fort in the entire Empire, where it is still possible to walk the entire circuit of the parapet (Copyright © Warwick Ball)

A better impression of how Hadrian's Wall might have appeared in its heyday is given by the massive frontier defences along the Euphrates frontier in Syria, such as Halabiya, part of a hugely elaborate – and expensive – system of military works built mainly in the later empire to defend against the Persians (Copyright © Warwick Ball)

At Halabiya on the Euphrates, the superbly built stone *praetorium* is still preserved to a height of three storeys (Copyright © Warwick Ball)

A combination of desert conditions and superb masonry has also meant that the deserts of Syria and Jordan are still littered with well-preserved Roman frontier forts, such as that at Hallabat in Jordan (Copyright © Warwick Ball)

Relatively modest frontier baths such as those at Chesters or South Shields would hardly have resembled the huge elaborate multi-sports complexes found in the cities, but more the smaller ones such as the Hunting Baths at Leptis Magna in Libya, wonderfully preserved right up to roof level by sand dunes (Copyright © Warwick Ball)

Left. In the drier conditions of the East grain was more usually stored in underground silos. The most impressive underground storage facilities were the immense cisterns such as Rasafa, resembling the nave of an underground cathedral (Copyright © Warwick Ball)

Below. The defence of the frontiers depended as much upon the rapid deployment of troops as the fortifications themselves, hence good quality military roads were essential – built, maintained and used almost solely by the army. A magnificent stretch of Roman road sweeps across the hills for miles behind Tarsus in Turkey (Copyright © Warwick Ball)

castles, it restricted Roman as well as native freedom of movement. The garrison was initially very small, on paper only 1,000 to 1,500 men and, if the Tungrian strength report from Vindolanda is any guide, probably many fewer in practice. All that these men could do was observe and patrol. A much larger concentration of troops was stationed at each of the forts along the Stanegate Road, sometimes 2 or 3 kilometres south of the Wall. If an emergency sparked, they had some distance to go to deal with it. And when detachments of soldiers reached a milecastle, they could only funnel through its gates slowly. It was all very unsatisfactory. Roman armies always instinctively sought the open ground and – perversely – their own Wall was preventing them from reaching it quickly.

Not long after work began in 122, a decision was taken to move forts up to the line of the Wall. And, so that access to the north, the likely source of most trouble, could be much more immediate, gates were sited beyond the Wall line. At Chesters, where a cavalry regiment was based, three of the four fort gates allowed troopers to ride directly out, without having to pass through the Wall. The original plan was a monumental mistake, producing the obvious effect of penning in the garrisons, but the decision to change appears to have been taken quickly.

One of the results of this early blunder and its remedy is spectacular. Housesteads is probably the most beautifully situated of all the Wall's forts, and because of its location in the central sector, remote until the road-building of the mid eighteenth century, it has survived remarkably. The Border Reivers also helped preserve the old Roman fort during the fourteenth to sixteenth centuries. Using the ready-made cut stone which lay everywhere to hand, they built a longhouse and at least two bastle houses on the site. These were heavily defended, thick-walled structures designed to frustrate rather than repel attackers. The remains of one can clearly be seen outside the southern gate at Housesteads.

A ground floor, or pend, was built without windows and it was intended to keep safe a farmer's beasts during a raid. They were driven in, packed tight, bellowing with fear, and the stout door barred shut from the inside.In the roof of the pend there was sometimes a trapdoor to the first floor. This was more easily and more usually accessed by an outside

ROMAN WALL BLUES

Service in the frontier garrison may have had its bleak moments, but it surely cannot have been as bad as it was painted by W.H. Auden in 'Roman Wall Blues':

> Over the heather the wet wind blows,
> I've lice in my tunic and a cold in my nose.
>
> The rain comes pattering out of the sky,
> I'm a Wall soldier, I don't know why.
>
> The mist creeps over the hard grey stone,
> my girl's in Tungria; I sleep alone.
>
> Aulus goes hanging around her place
> I don't like his manners, I don't like his face.
>
> Piso's a Christian; he worships a fish;
> There'd be no kissing if he had his wish.
>
> She gave me a ring but I diced it away;
> I want my girl and I want my pay.
>
> When I'm a veteran with only one eye
> I shall do nothing but look at the sky.

(from *W.H. Auden. Collected Poems*, Faber and Faber)

When W.H. Auden lived in America, he had a map of the North Pennines pinned up, from Swaledale in the south up to the line of Hadrian's Wall. He described it as his 'great good place'. In 1937 Auden wrote a radio play about the Wall which was broadcast live from Newcastle on 25th November. Its framework was a family day out at Housesteads Fort and it incorporated what Auden imagined were Roman voices. His friend, Benjamin Britten, composed and conducted the incidental music, including a setting for 'Roman Wall Blues'. The score was thought to be lost but in 2005 a copy resurfaced. It belonged to a 99-year-old member of the choir brought in by the BBC to sing it. In the event they were not used, and in his diary Benjamin Britten wrote that the play had gone 'fearfully badly'.

stair or ladder, and out of its tiny windows defenders hurled abuse and anything else they could find at the horsemen circling below. Bastle houses were primitive but effective, a poor man's peel tower. To the Armstrongs of Gandy's Knowe, a branch of one of the most notorious of all the reiving surnames, the irony of rebuilding a much lesser defensive structure on the fringe of one so sophisticated might not have been lost. They were ferocious, ruthless thieves, but not usually ignorant. The perimeter of the fort itself was probably barricaded into use as a cattle corral, often somebody else's cattle, as the Armstrongs rode the moonlight and raided in the Tyne Valley and to the north.

At the time of the Border Reivers, William Camden compiled his great antiquarian history *Britannia* (published in 1586). He rode along the line of the Wall, a countryside he thought *lean, hungry and waste*. Hadrian's Wall amazed him: *Verily I have seen the tract of it over the high pitches and steep descent of hills, wonderfully rising and falling*. Camden knew of Housesteads Fort, understood that there was much to see but, to his intense frustration, he could not get near it: *I could not safely take the full survey of it for the rank robbers thereabouts*. Bandit country.

Considering how the climate had *hardened the carcases* of Borderers, he observed how the descendants of the horsemen in the Vindolanda letters lived:

> In the wastes . . . you may see it as were the ancient nomads, a martial kind of men who, from the month of April into August, lie out scattering and summering with their cattle, in little cottages here and there, which they call shiels and shielings.

It may have been the sort of conservation unknown to English Heritage, but the reivers' occupation of the old fort and their lack of any architectural ambition kept the circuit of walls intact and the *steading full of houses*, as they knew it, relatively undisturbed. James VI and I of Great Britain eventually began the process of bringing Housesteads to the notice of a wider world. After his brutal but effective police action of 1603 to 1610 against the Border Reivers, the by-then-redundant frontier began to settle down. The bandits retreated further and further into the hills and, by the end of the seventeenth century, the first visitors were coming.

In 1725, the antiquarian William Stukely made an early drawing of the site. It shows a farmstead built inside the walls, perhaps the successor of the longhouse, and a scattering of altars and inscribed stones over the slopes below the south gate. By 1751, the Military Road had been laid out, much of its length bottomed with Wall stone, and it passed only 500 metres south of the fort. Amongst those who left a record of what they saw was William Hutton, who arrived in 1802 full of enthusiasm:

> I retreated next morning over a moss to my favourite pursuit, which brought me to Housesteads, the grandest station on the whole line. In some stations the antiquary feeds upon shells, but here upon kernels. Here lies the ancient splendour in bold characters.

Archaeologists have pieced together the story of Housesteads. It appears always to have been something of a showpiece. As one of the forts integrated into the line from the outset, it occupied a central place in the central sector, perched high and visible on the cliffs of the Whin Sill. It is impressive even when only glimpsed out of a car window from the road below. The site is sloping, although not as extreme as at Cawfields, and it seems to present Housesteads to the south for all to gaze upon it. The outlook on every side is absolutely commanding.

The forts and milecastles of the central sector struggled to find reliable and substantial sources of water, despite the rain. Below Housesteads the Knag Burn runs through a nick lying to the east. It penetrates the Wall through a culvert built at its foot. Flanked by small guardhouses there is also a rare gateway (cut in the early fourth century) directly through the Wall. Inside the fort stand the remains of cisterns probably used to collect rainwater off the roofs. Other garrisons were served by simple aqueducts, occasionally from the north, clay lined and cleverly sited.

Despite its elevated position, Housesteads seems to shelter in the lee of the Whin Sill, and it is less buffeted by the winter winds than other forts on the Wall. The free-draining farmland around the fort has historically been cultivated rather than grazed. Aerial photographs show not only the contours of Roman terracing but also the remains of small medieval rig-systems. When John Clayton of Chesters bought the farm so that he could preserve and investigate the fort, he faced stiff competition from bidders anxious to keep tilling such good land.

THE WORK OF GIANTS

By the eighth century the Roman Wall and the towns of the south of Britain had ceased to function as large communities. Some towns were on sites continuously inhabited by smaller populations whose own buildings eroded and even erased what had stood there before. A ready re-use for quarried, squared-off and handily sized building stone could always be found. Roman altars were incorporated into the structure of Jedburgh Abbey, and in Carlisle Cathedral the facades are speckled with stone robbed from Hadrian's Wall and nearby Stanwix Fort.

The English and the native British were not contemptuous of Roman architecture. They simply had little use for it as it stood because their social structures were different, smaller in eighth century betrays a sense of awe, and even regret at what time and disuse had done to the old cities:

The Ruin

Splendid this rampart is, though fate destroyed it,
The city buildings fell apart, the works
Of giants crumble. Tumbled are the towers,
Ruined are the roofs, and broken the barred gate,
Frost in the plaster, all the ceilings gape,
Torn and collapsed and eaten up by age.

The Romans called it Vercovicium, a place-name with a shadowy modern survival in nearby Barcombe Hill, the site of an ancient quarry above Vindolanda. Derived from Old Welsh roots, Housesteads' original name means something clumsier in English, the Fort of the Good Fighters. The earliest garrison was the I Cohort of Tungrians, posted to the fort from Vindolanda around AD 122/123. After their exploits in the front line at Mons Graupius under Agricola, they were certainly reckoned to be good fighters, and the name might simply reflect that reputation. Equally possible is a transfer. Slight traces of a native hillfort have been seen on Barcombe Hill and perhaps the old name travelled 2 kilometres to the north-east to settle on the new fort and its men. That would also explain the similarity between the two place-names. The modern name is certainly a reference to the remains of the Roman buildings: the houses inside what looked like a walled inbye enclosure, a steading.

The layout of Vercovicium is classic. Perhaps because of the very long tradition of success, rarely suffering more than temporary reverses over 500 years or so, the Roman army was very conservative in its thinking. For example, fort design was generally standard throughout the Empire, no matter how different the climate, the geography or the political context and its requirements. From Inchtuthil in the Perthshire woods to the vastness of the Persian desert, the same playing-card shape and internal design was built again and again.

Any innovations were minor. Unlike African or Asian forts, Housesteads had a coal-house. Near the east gate, it was filled with what local people used to call *craw coal*, the coal that could be quarried and carried away from coal-heughs such as Shawhead Drift, south-west of Vindolanda. There was almost a tonne of it, and at Risingham and Corbridge evidence of more coal storage has been found.

Up until the early nineteenth century two collieries at the foot of Barcombe Hill were still being worked, and over at Ramshawfield coal mining on some scale continued for longer. The ready availability of coal in a landscape with few sources of wood was a boon to the soldiers who shivered in the winter at Housesteads. The bath house, the hypocaust heating system under the commanding officer's house and wherever the garrison would light a fire or a brazier to keep warm – all of these will have benefited from the supply of Tyne Valley coal.

The Romans' dogged conservatism is surprising given their un-hesitating ruthlessness when making decisions, such as the movement of the forts up to the line of the Wall. At Housesteads and elsewhere, places where permanent garrisons were settling down, a more obviously defensive military architecture might have developed. But there is no evidence for emplacements for artillery, for example, or for projecting gatehouses and towers (like those of medieval castles) which would allow enfilading fire to rake along the length of the fort walls, severely hampering any attempt to break through.

However all that may be, a certain aspect of domestic life is splendidly illustrated amongst the ruined buildings of Housesteads. Tucked into the south-east corner of the fort, the latrines are well preserved. They are surrounded by cisterns, festooned with drains – and communal! No cubicles. This has caught the public's attention like few other details of Roman army life. Communal, sit-down toilets? The very idea!

Guides to the site delight in explaining that there was seating for about twenty men, a surprisingly small capacity for a garrison of 800 soldiers who regularly consumed a good deal of roughage. A well-drawn coloured reconstruction of men using the latrines, their under-garments around their ankles, adorns the guidebook. It must be one of the more unexpected illustrations in British historiography. But worse is to come. In their hands the soldiers are shown holding sticks with something attached to the end. Much worse. In a small concession to seemliness, the soldier furthest away appears to have used the stick and he leans forward towards a water-filled drain which runs around the middle of the floor.

What, exactly, is going on? The caption for the illustration is vague. It should read: *How Roman soldiers wiped their backsides.* At the end of each stick, it was said that a small sponge was attached. Having completed the first part of their business, the soldiers were believed to wipe their backsides by scrubbing vigorously back and forth – and then rinsing the sponge in the drain on the floor.

At least two thoughts occur. Did each soldier have his own stick and sponge? And how securely were the sponges attached? Very, it is to be hoped.

The problem with this bizarre scene is the sponges. Well, one of the problems. Although their use in latrines is attested by two Roman writers, Martial and Seneca, it is often forgotten that they were describing an aspect of everyday life around the shores of the Mediterranean, where sponges grow naturally and are harvested by divers. There are none in the North Sea, or the Solway Firth. And it is highly unlikely that sponges were imported in bulk to be used for such an – everyday – purpose by ordinary soldiers. Amidst all the grunting, farting and exhaling, to say nothing of any comments, moss was probably used. And not rinsed.

Perhaps it was sold to soldiers in some quantity in the streets and shops of the *vicus*, the civil settlement which huddled around the walls of Housesteads. Despite the relatively remote location, the settlement was large with buildings to the south and east of the fort. Two discoveries are particularly vivid.

In the backlands of one of the houses, which sat gable-end on to the main street, a small shrine was found. It housed a well-preserved piece of relief sculpture. Three small figures stand in a line and are more or less identical. Wearing the *byrrus Britannicus*, a hooded cloak which fastened at the front and was a well-known export to European markets, they stand passive and enigmatic. They represent the *Genii Cucullati*, the Hooded Gods, and were given offerings as the protectors of the household.

On Chapel Hill, a ridge south of the *vicus*, altars have been found dedicated to gods native to Frisia in western Holland. They were raised up by units of Germanic warriors hired as irregular troops. The Cuneus Frisiorum, who may have been cavalry troopers, worshipped Mars Thincsus and the Aliagasai. A dedication mentions Numerus Hnaudufridi, another band of soldiers from beyond the Rhine. The translation is 'Notfried's Own' and they sound like a prince and his warband. Whatever their origins and their beliefs, their presence in the north was not decorative. Trouble still broke out on the frontier.

The dates attached to these inscriptions are later, before AD 235. When the Wall was still young, a century before, Rome could garrison the frontier without recourse to barbarian mercenaries. The most prestigious regiment stationed on Hadrian's Wall also occupied by far the largest fort. Virtually no trace can now be seen of it. At Stanwix, on the eastern banks of the Eden, opposite the centre of Carlisle, a fort of nearly 10 acres was built to house the Ala Petriana. This was the only milliary cavalry cohort in Britannia, a force of around 800 troopers and commanded by a Prefect, the most senior officer anywhere on the Wall.

The suburbs of modern Carlisle have obliterated any remains left by the stone robbers, and the only hint of Uxellodunum, the High Fort, is a pathetic plaque mounted high on a house wall on a street corner and some coloured bricks laid along the line of the fort's south wall in a car park behind the Cumbria Park Hotel. Some fragments of the original masonry could once be seen under a window of thick bottle glass laid into the tarmac, but the elements have clouded it so much that nothing can now be made out. Compared with the ruined glories of Housesteads, Stanwix' fate is sad, if inevitable. Perhaps its obliteration is the reason why its pivotal role is sometimes ignored.

RENDER UNTO CEASAR?

The Romans plastered everything, generalised one eminent historian. He was writing about the buildings inside their forts at the time but his assertion is a reminder that the white marble, the naked sandstone and the monochrome appearance of much of antiquity and its remains were not what the Romans – or the Greeks – saw. They had their sculpture painted, the friezes on their buildings were often highly coloured and the interior walls of quite modest structures sometimes had frescos. Floors were tiled with coloured mosaics where they could be afforded. Plaster, or render, on the outside had a practical function in that it kept out the worst of the weather as well as brightening up the environment by making the most of the light. Plastering, like painting kerbstones in a modern army camp, was a good way to keep soldiers busy and out of mischief.

Hadrian's Wall was probably rendered, at least parts of it. At Castle Nick, Denton and elsewhere traces of render or whitewash have been found. One Wall expert believes that not only was the face of the Wall plastered white, but it was also scribed with false joints. What an arresting sight! A white wall snaking through the green and brown countryside, stark, unmissable, dominating.

The crack troopers of the Ala Petriana were stationed near Carlisle because it was seen as the hinge of the Wall, not merely its western terminal. The Cumbrian Sea-Wall stretched far to the south and all indications point to the Roman strategists' view that the west was the critical sector of the frontier region. In contemporary Celtic society a cavalry force of 800 well-armed and -horsed men represented a small army, and when the Petriana clattered out of the gates at Stanwix, their standards glinting and fluttering, it will have been an impressive sight. What is unclear is the wider role of their Prefect. As the most senior officer on the Wall, did he have jurisdiction over others? Or did orders come directly from York?

Also buried, but less mysterious than Stanwix, the fort at Maryport was a vital link in the military chain which held the north. Sited up on the Sea Brows, high above the Cumbrian shore, the fort has not been smothered in housing or any other modern development. It lies quiet under a grass field, used for pasture and not ploughed, its characteristic shape visible on the ground and especially clearly from the air. Beside it stands a fascinating building, now the Senhouse Roman Museum. Housed in a silent battery used for training gunners in the Royal Naval Volunteer Reserve (guns which did not fire were a condition of the gift of the land by Mrs Senhouse), the collection of objects is startling, better than any on the Wall, with the possible exception of Vindolanda.

In 1870, in the corner of a farm field to the north of the fort site, a cache of seventeen Roman altars was found. Deliberately buried some time in the late second or early third centuries, they tell a clear and continuous story. The altars are in such excellent condition that, not only is the lettering crisp and easily legible, traces of paint can still be seen on them. It was the greatest single find of Roman inscriptions ever made in Britain. In addition to these, there is a great deal of sculpture, some of it native, some of it unique. And yet the fort has never been excavated, nor has the *vicus*, and the Senhouse Museum is far too little visited. Maryport is not generally seen as an integral part of the story of Hadrian's Wall. But of course it is and, when the archaeologists finally arrive, treasures are likely to come out of the ground.

Maryport was a sea-fort. From the Sea Brows almost all of the Galloway coast can be seen and, even on dull days, the grey hump of the Isle of Man darkens the western horizon. The fort's strategic role was primarily defensive from the outset as its lookouts watched for trouble sailing across the Solway Firth. It also turned inland, acting as key link in the encirclement of the Lake District, probably as much a source of opposition to Rome as the North Pennines.

The fort prompted the development of a large *vicus* which straddled the road leading out of the north gate. A detailed geophysical survey has discovered a long ribbon of buildings, stretching for more than 350 metres and including some very large structures. Some are thought to be industrial or used for storage. Associated coal and iron debris has been found. In the lee of the fort, the smoke and fumes from all that work will have blown away from the garrison. The commanding officer in post in 122, Maenius Agrippa, was probably an aristocratic figure with even more high-tone tastes than the Batavians at Vindolanda. Coal smoke is not something he will have wished to sniff as he was entertaining guests.

MASTERS AND COMMANDERS

The surviving Roman records of Britannia appear detailed when compared with historical periods at either end of the life of the province. But they are in fact patchy: the sequence of governors, for example, is far from complete. One of the joys of the finds at Maryport is the quality of the inscribed records. Here is a complete list of the first six commanders of the I Cohort of Spaniards based at the fort.

Marcus Maenius Agrippa – Tribune
from Camerinum in Italy
Caius Caballius Priscus – Tribune
from Verona [?] in Italy
Marcus Censorius Cornelianus – Prefect
from Nimes in France
Lucius Cammius Maximus – Prefect
from Solva in Austria
Lucius Anstistius Lupus Verianus – Prefect
from Le Kef in Tunisia
Helstrius Novellus – Prefect
from Italy [?]

Some of Maryport's most fascinating sculpture was found in the area of the *vicus*. A Roman altar was cut down and reshaped into a large phallus. On one side a serpent wearing a torc slithers up to the head, while on the other a human head with a strange necklace of fish is carved. In the absence of anything comparative or any helpful texts, the iconography is impossible to read, but the use of the phallus as a defence against evil may be what was intended. The sculpture was found amongst several cremation burials and perhaps it was erected to protect them. There is also a wonderfully well-preserved Epona, a Celtic goddess of fertility, who takes the form of a mare. Her name is probably not the derivation of the word pony. She is known from many European sites but the Maryport piece is the only complete representation yet found in Britain. Also recognisable is Cernunnos, a horned god often linked with the Brigantes.

Worship of these deities was not confined to the Celtic population. The Romans often incorporated local cults into their pantheon and sometimes created hybrids, twinning classical gods with Celtic counterparts. Not far away, across the Solway, near Gretna, there was a famous shrine to Apollo Maponus. The name of the latter, a native deity, is still heard in the Dumfriesshire place-name of Lochmaben.

SKY-GODS

The Roman pantheon survives overhead. The planets of our solar system are mostly named after gods venerated in Britannia and some have aspects of their ancient attributes:

Mercury is the smallest planet and is named after the wing-footed messenger of the gods.

Venus is seen as the Earth's sister planet and is named after the goddess of love and beauty.

Mars is the red, or angry, planet and is named after the god of war, the soldiers' god.

Jupiter is the largest planet in the solar system and is named after the king of the gods.

Saturn is almost as big and is named after the father of Jupiter and the god of agriculture.

Uranus was a late discovery (1787) and is named after a Graeco-Roman god of the sky.

Neptune has the strongest winds and is named after the god of rivers and, later, of the sea.

After the forts had been brought up to the line of the Wall and the ditch in front of it completed, Roman planners turned their minds to the problem of the south. If part of Hadrian's intention had been to force apart a tight network of allies, then his dispositions at Stanwix, down the Cumbrian coast, at the western outpost forts, and the general focus of the Wall system appeared to cope with the threats rumbling in the north. But, to its rear, the barrier must have felt exposed. Another momentous decision was taken.

In order to create a clearly defined military zone, a wide ditch would be dug in the area immediately to the south of the Wall. The Romans did not call the ditch the Vallum. This mistaken label was first attached by the normally meticulous Bede of Jarrow, the great eighth-century historian of the English, a man who knew the Wall well. Vallum may be the accepted name for the vast ditch system dug behind Hadrian's Wall but, in the second century AD, it was the Latin word for a palisaded rampart. And it is the derivation of the English 'wall'. *Fossa* is a ditch or trench, not Vallum. But the original misleading label has stuck.

It was a remarkable feat of military engineering. So that it could present a really formidable barrier, the whole entrenchment measures 37 metres across: impossible to bridge and very difficult to traverse on foot. And it ran behind the entire length of the Land-Wall, from the Tyne to Bowness-on-Solway without interruption. In many places where there is no trace of any masonry and even the cleft of the Wall ditch has gone, the Vallum is still visible. Arrow-straight, much larger than any other element of the frontier works, it is perhaps the most enduring mark made by Hadrian on the British landscape.

The line was chosen where the ground allowed a deep ditch to be dug, and occasionally that pulled the Vallum well to the south of the Wall. Between 5.4 to 5.9 metres across the top, it was excavated to a depth of 2.6 to 2.9 metres and, unlike the Wall ditch in the north, which had only a narrow bottom (known as an ankle-breaker), the Vallum was 2.1 metres across at its foot. This made for much steeper sides, a 60 per cent slope – very difficult to climb in and out of. All of the spoil was probably hacked out by gangs of auxiliary troops, rather than legionaries, and they piled it up in mounds on either side. These were separated from the edges of the steep-sided ditch by broad berms 9 to 12 metres in width. This much clearance was needed to avoid the danger of infill or subsidence. The spoil heaps were then revetted with turf to stop them crumbling. Anyone who approached the Vallum had to climb these banks and had no choice but to make themselves very visible to soldiers on the Wall.

The Vallum was a very substantial obstacle. Over time the Romans allowed it to become even more of an obstacle as water pooled in the bottom of the ditch (there is no evidence of any drains) and were probably happy to see thorns and other scrub grow – except on the berms and mounds.

The most telling effects of the creation of the Vallum were twofold. Most dramatically, it cut the number of crossing-points through the Wall from seventy-nine gateways through the milecastles to fourteen.

These arched gateways, so painstakingly constructed only a short time before, became secondary as the focus of movement shifted to a series of causeways thrown across the Vallum near the forts. One of the most surprising and quirky sites along the Wall is a Vallum crossing just to the south of Benwell Fort. Half covered by a reservoir and a main road, and drowned by the redbrick suburbs of west Newcastle, the fort has completely disappeared. But at the bottom of a terrace of semi-detached houses behind the local Social Security offices, the causeway over the Vallum has miraculously survived. Protected by iron railings and stout gates, the ditch has been restored to something approaching its original depth. But most impressive is the causeway itself. The bottom stones of one of the piers of its massive gatehouse perch precariously right on the edge. They supported a free-standing massive structure, like a small triumphal arch, which had stout, iron-studded doors and was manned day and night. Behind it rise the cobblestones of several layers of the roadway which led to the vanished fort.

The overall effect of the Vallum was to create a military zone which ribboned through the countryside, with such tightly and clearly controlled access that it was the ultimate *authorised persons only* area. It protected the forts from damage and theft (a good deal of gear, such as carts, and stock will have been left outside the walls of milecastles, turrets and even forts) and allowed much more secure and unhampered movement between the garrisons. Supply traffic must have been constant and, before the creation of the military zone, quartermasters will have had to secure their valuable goods every night, perhaps behind palisades, certainly under close guard. By excluding the native peoples so completely, this irritant diminished.

What undoubtedly increased was frustration on the far side of the Vallum. One example will suffice. For millennia the stock farmers of the Tyne and Irthing Valleys had driven their flocks and herds up the hill trails on the ancient journey of transhumance. Summering out on the fells, their beasts grazing the upland pasture, shepherds and farm laddies had lived in shielings described by William Camden. North of the Tyne, the Wall and its Vallum stopped this time-honoured traffic in its tracks. The new zone had simply removed a wide swathe of land from the native agricultural economy, and made it extremely difficult for farmers to use land to the north of it. It is unthinkable that commanding officers would allow herdsmen to drive their beasts across one of the fourteen causeways, along the streets of a fort, through the northern gates and out onto the commons beyond. At milecastles it might have been easier, but since the Wall ditch shows no sign of having had solid crossings, it is hard to see how cattle and sheep might have been safely prodded and whacked across narrow wooden bridges – if there were any.

VALLUMS GALORE

Ditches and dykes were used to demarcate bits of Britain long before and long after the construction of Hadrian's Wall. Offa's Dyke (or Dike) is the most famous. King of Mercia from 757 to 796, Offa fought fierce campaigns against the invading Welsh princes and, to show where their territory ended and his began, he had a *vallum magnum* built from sea to sea. Stretching 220 kilometres, much longer than Hadrian's and Antonine's walls put together, it runs from the Severn to the Dee estuary. The largest earthwork ever dug in Europe, at any time, it is an extraordinary – and far from well understood – monument. Offa called on his people to give military service and work in gangs to dig a 2-metre ditch and build up a 7-metre rampart to the east of it. The whole layout is more than 20 metres across. Its sheer mass and height made it very difficult for the horse-riding Welsh warbands to cross, and near impossible for them to raid cattle and drive them back. In the north, Wat's Dyke completed the line and its terminal is at Basingwerk on the Dee. Unlike the Roman walls, Offa's Dyke appears to have contained the Welsh, and the modern border runs close by.

As the great Wall project neared completion, the standard of mason work began to deteriorate markedly. It is as though there was a scramble to the finish line, perhaps a mad dash to complete before the departure of the Governor of the province, Aulus Platorius Nepos. At Housesteads, Birdoswald and Chesters, the piers and voussoirs at several gateways show poor craftsmanship. There is evidence of more than just hints of great haste. At Housesteads the lower piers of one gate are tidily enough finished but the capstones, where the arch springs, have scarcely been worked at all. In several milecastles some of the massive stonework is not so much badly finished as abandoned *in situ*. It seems that as long as the arches and gateways stayed up, at least for the moment, that was fine.

PLANETREES

Someone changed minds near the farm of Planetrees, not far north of Hexham. As it marched westwards from Wallsend and New-castle, the Wall was built ten Roman feet wide. But at Planetrees, a decision was taken to carry on eastwards at only eight Roman feet in width. Perhaps construction had simply been over-engineered or was taking too long. Seventeen centuries later, William Hutton, a far travelled antiquarian of the early nineteenth century, arrived at the place where the Broad Wall became the Narrow Wall. Mistakenly ascribing its construction to Septimius Severus, he was appalled at its destruction by a Mr Tulip and took it as a personal affront.

> At the twentieth-mile stone, I should have seen a piece of Severus's Wall seven feet and a half high, and two hundred and twenty-four yards long: a sight not to be found in the whole line. But the proprietor, Henry Tulip, Esq. is now taking it down, to erect a farm-house with the materials. Ninety-five yards are already destroyed, and the stones, fit for building removed. . . . I desired the servant with whom I conversed, 'to give my compliments to Mr. Tulip, and request him to desist, or he would wound the whole body of Antiquaries'. As he was putting an end to the most noble monument of Antiquity in the whole Island, they would feel every stroke. If the Wall was of no estimation, he must have a mean opinion of me, who would travel six hundred miles to see it; and if it was, he could never merit my thanks for destroying it.

Perhaps fighting broke out during the final phases of construction and, in the way that things often happen, the unfinished stonework was simply left in place. With the eventual departure of the legions, most of the really skilled masons in their ranks went too. It may well be that there were too few with sufficient skill to tidy up stonework that had been thrown up.

Once the forts had been more or less completed (the work at Birdoswald seems to have been disrupted more than once), their garrisons moved in. The most common type of auxiliary cohort on the Wall was a mix between infantry and cavalry, the *cohors quingenaria equitata*. Many of these soldiers had marched north from their postings on the Welsh border and in the South Pennines, where it was hoped that the situation was stable. Not including the Sea-Wall, that added up to a total garrison of 9,090 auxiliaries, on paper.

In the central sector, at Housesteads, Great Chesters, Carvoran and Birdoswald, all units were *peditata*, or foot soldiers. Why pure infantry should have been preferred in the countryside so well understood and beloved later by the horse-riding Border Reivers is not clear. If their ancestors had similar equestrian skills – and it is highly likely that their *very many cavalry* did – detachments of foot soldiers chasing them up hill and down dale sounds like a laughable tactical mismatch. The traditional raiding methods of hit and run will have worked every time. But the Romans were usually very astute – and there may well have been a clear but now lost justification for those dispositions up on the Whin Sill.

In any case, the reach of cavalry was long and rapid. Reckoning that the link between the infantry of Housesteads and the troopers stationed at Chesters down in the valley of the North Tyne was not close enough, another fort was built between them. At Carrawburgh, surely the bleakest location on the Wall, Brocolitia was established. Brocolitia means the Heathery Fort, and it still is. Before the masons could begin, the Vallum had to be filled in, and that fact dates the new fort as an afterthought. A cohort of mixed cavalry and infantry appears to have been inserted in the gap.

On the northern bank of the Tyne the original eastern terminal of the Wall may have been the fort at Newcastle, at the Pons Aelius. Under the medieval castle, the site of the *New*castle (and a later Roman fort whose traces have been found under the arches of the Victorian railway viaduct which slashes right through the precinct, separating the keep from the main gatehouse), a modern hotel, the Moot Hall and a pub, the remains of the Hadrianic fort may lie undisturbed for a long time. Little trace of the Wall has been found immediately to the east, but what there is suggests another afterthought. No broad Wall foundations, only narrow Wall building, probably means that the stretch leading out to Wallsend was begun after the drive westwards. It may be that the broad barrier of the lower Tyne was more porous than anticipated.

The course of the Tyne was much wider and meandering in 122. The river had not been dredged and was not as deep as it is now. Perhaps the native peoples were simply ignoring all that impressive stonework upriver at Newcastle, going around the eastern end of the Wall by taking to their boats or wading across at low tide at fording places.

The site chosen for the fort at Wallsend sits on the crown of a long and lazy bend in the Tyne with clear views both upriver and down. The Wall arrived at its north-western corner and then, adopting the fort's ramparts, turned through 90 degrees to emerge as what is known as the Branch Wall. It ran south down to the riverbank and continued out into the current. And there Hadrian's Wall terminated (or began) – but not before a final imperial flourish.

Across the Tyne stands the ancient church of St Paul at Jarrow. Once it was part of a monastery (twinned with Monkwearmouth) which was home to Bede, one of Britain's earliest and very greatest historians. When the first Abbot, Benedict Biscop, founded these communities, he was anxious to build *in the Roman manner* and brought masons from Europe with the necessary skills. Plenty of authentic Roman building materials were lying about near Jarrow, only a boat trip across the Tyne. Ready-cut stones from both the fort at Wallsend and the Wall itself can still be seen at St Paul's, especially amongst the monastic ruins to the east of the church. In 1783 stonemasons were beginning to restore the fabric of the old church when they came upon two fragments of a Latin inscription. The lettering was very large and the panel it had been cut into must have been huge. Here is a translation:

> Son of all deified emperors, the Emperor Caesar Trajan Hadrian Augustus, after the necessity of keeping the Empire within its limits had been laid on him by divine command . . . once the barbarians had been scattered and the province of Britannia recovered, added a frontier between either shore of Ocean for 80 miles. The army of the province built the wall under the direction of Aulus Platorius Nepos, Pro-Praetorian Legate of Augustus.

Several historians have convincingly conjectured that these words were carved on the plinth of a massive statue, one which stood somewhere near Jarrow. Hundreds of kilometres away, at the southern end of Britannia, is a clue as to what the statue might have been. At Richborough, the massive triumphal arch erected during the reign of the Emperor Domitian was an imposing memorial to earlier conquests and an impressive welcome to the province. It seems that Hadrian planned an equally impressive goodbye. He was later to make a boastful but probably accurate claim: *I have achieved more by peace than others [have] by war.* More than the hated Domitian! At the end of the Branch Wall, where it had been built out into the midstream of the River Tyne, there probably stood a huge statue of Hadrian, the Emperor who had commanded a Wall to be built across Britain. For all who saw it, and especially those who sailed under its stern gaze, it must have been an awesome sight.

As with every sensible and successful Emperor of Rome, Hadrian's focus was on the army. Without its loyalty and discipline, he could not survive and nothing could be achieved. If the Wall was principally intended as a symbol, its message to the native peoples was incidental. Whatever they thought, the legions would crush them. Much more important was the army, its morale, the support of its senior officers. By erecting a colossus on the northern frontier of Britannia, subduing

---

COLOSSI

Massive statues of gods and emperors were not uncommon in the Roman Empire, but the most famous was probably the Colossus of Rhodes. A huge bronze representation of the sun-god Helios was created by Chares around 280 BC and was said to stand more than 30 metres high. Set up at the harbour, the great statue may have stood astride its entrance with ships passing between its legs. But more likely it did not. The Colossus was toppled in AD 224 in an earthquake, but Hadrian would certainly have seen it on his travels. The other famous Colossus of the ancient world has also gone, but its name survives. A huge statue of the Emperor Nero stood near the Via Sacra in Rome but, after Nero's suicide, it too crashed to the ground. When Vespasian began to build a great amphitheatre on the site, the name stuck and it is still called the Colosseum.

the landscape to his will, defeating and containing the barbarians, and having his policy inscribed beneath for all to read, Hadrian was reinforcing the radical strategic changes which he made during his reign. The age of an empire without limit was over, there would be no more conquest for the sake of it. But it would be a triumphant limit. The Roman army would now assume a defensive role, become the keepers of the peace rather than the makers of war.

7

Abandonment, Invasion and Desertion

So that it would be instantaneous, or at worst very rapid, Hadrian drew a coloured line on the left-hand side of his chest, exactly in the place his doctor had shown him. Then he commanded Mastor, his huntsman, to stab him, to drive the blade deep and hard between his ribs, straight into his heart and put him out of what seemed like an eternity of misery. With promises of great riches, of piles of gold and silver coins, and threats of dire consequences if he did not do what his Emperor instructed, Hadrian had brought his huntsman armed to his bedside. He begged for death. There would be no retribution, no prosecution, Mastor would be immune – if only he would do this last, desperate service for Hadrian. He *bitterly lamented the state to which his illness and his helplessness had reduced him – notwithstanding that it was still within his power, even when on the brink of death, to destroy anyone else.*

No doubt terrified, Mastor lost what nerve he had and refused to kill the Emperor. He was not an aristocrat, not a Roman, but a tribesman from the Iazyges, from the Danube, a nobody who would probably be killed in the first frantic hours after Hadrian's death. Wise to refuse his master's pleadings, Mastor reported what had taken place.

The pain must have been very hard to bear. It seems that by the early summer of AD 138 the Emperor was passing into the terminal stages of heart disease, suffering from increasingly severe haemorrhages, his arteries hardening and preventing proper circulation. It had begun as nose-bleeds and was quickly developing into something very much worse. Hadrian also had what was known as dropsy, a painful build-up of fluid in his body.

After the failed attempt to persuade and coerce Mastor, Hadrian's adopted successor came to see the dying Emperor. Here is the passage from the *Historia Augusta*:

Antoninus and the Prefects went in to see Hadrian and begged him to endure the necessity of the disease with equanimity. Antoninus told him that he would be a parricide if, after being adopted, he allowed him to be killed. Hadrian was angry and ordered the person who had informed them to be killed – he was, however, saved by Antoninus. He at once wrote his will. But he did not lay aside the business of state . . . He did in fact try to kill himself again; when the dagger was taken from him he became more violent. He asked his doctor for poison, who killed himself rather than comply.

Hadrian was sixty-two. Worn out after a reign of more than twenty years, eleven of them spent travelling around his vast domain, he had become increasingly unwell. And just as insidious, he began to attack, dismiss and even dispose of those who had been friends and companions, who had given solace and support through the loneliness of absolute power. Aulus Platorius Nepos, former Governor of Britainnia and builder of the Wall, had been very close and at one time a candidate for the succession. So confident was he in Hadrian's favour that he dared to send the Emperor away when he had had the decency to come to Nepos' house and enquire after his health. No one, anywhere, was ever too sick to see an Emperor – but there appear to have been no immediate repercussions. *Led on by suspicions* and listening to *whatever was whispered about his friends*, Hadrian cast Nepos out from his inner circle, calling his old comrade an enemy.

It could have been worse. Two senators, Polyaenus and Neratius Marcellus, *were compelled to suicide* and two men of equestrian rank who had been imperial staff members and advisors were dismissed; Valerius Eudaemon was *reduced to poverty* and Avidius Heliodorus' services were no longer required.

Hadrian continued to be obsessed by the death of Antinous: the boy was deified and his worship formalised into a cult. Twinned with the goddess of the hunt, Diana, Antinous was to have a temple dedicated to him in a town near Rome. And in the gardens of the imperial palace on the Palatine Hill, there was a further public commemoration, a series of sculptured reliefs of Hadrian and his young lover hunting. In his temple Antinous was shown as the god Silvanus, the patron of huntsmen. Perhaps that connection supplied the tortured reason for Hadrian's selection of Mastor as the agent of his own death. In any case it seems like a rather grandiose celebration of nothing more than happy times, of the Emperor doing what he loved best with the person he loved most alongside him.

After his return to Rome in the mid 130s, Hadrian indulged his other passion: architecture. Building work on several imperial projects was coming to an end. In 121 the Emperor had sanctioned a temple to Venus and Rome, as usual taking a meddling hand in the design himself. There was a basic flaw. Inside, the massive colossi of the goddess and Rome were seated on thrones of some sort, but the roof over their heads was much too low. Trajan's architect, Apollodorus, made the great mistake of pointing this out: *for now, if the goddesses want to stand up and go out, they will be unable to do so.* Hadrian was embarrassed at something so basic – and enraged. One historian recorded Apollodorus' murder and, given the Emperor's unhesitating ruthlessness with others, it may be an accurate report.

Perhaps the grandest, most emblematic architectural project was Hadrian's own villa. Built in the countryside around Rome, near the town of Tivoli, from which it took its name, it was both vast in scale and in conception. More than a kilometre from one sprawling end to another, Tivoli compassed the Empire, with Greek, Egyptian and Italian motifs. There was an amphitheatre, a canal, sculpture galleries, baths, an outlook tower and at its centre, at the Teatro Marittimo, a private retreat for the Emperor. Surrounded by a moat, this self-conscious symphony of curves and innovative design was supposedly where Hadrian could spend time in contemplation.

The impression is of an epic emptiness, a show of power and patronage for its own sake, a monument rather than a pleasure palace or an idiosyncratic expression of character. As Hadrian rattled around the cavernous halls of Tivoli, becoming more and more unwell, growing increasingly embittered, loathed and lonely, he trailed a gathering cloud of misery and frustration behind him.

Little had worked out as the Emperor had planned it. His first choice as heir, Lucius Verus, had tuberculosis. *He frequently coughed up blood*, but Hadrian had had the Senate confirm his adoption anyway. It seems that the Emperor's real preference was for a boy just a shade too young to succeed to the purple. Marcus Annius Verus was only fifteen, but if Lucius Verus could stagger on for a few more years, then he would at least have had this bright young man beside him looking and learning as the throne was kept warm. But Hadrian's extended family, not suprisingly, grew resentful and in 137 there was an attempted coup. Led by Pedianus Fuscus, the Emperor's grand-nephew, it probably did not progress beyond a plot, and it failed completely. Retribution followed swiftly as Fuscus was executed, and his grandfather, Servianus, thought to be implicated or at least a potential danger, was driven to suicide. Even though he was close to ninety years old, he was seen by Hadrian as someone who might outlive him and take the throne. Servianus made his preparations, burning incense and praying to the gods: *That I am guilty of no wrong, you gods are well aware. As for Hadrian, this is my only prayer: may he long for death but be unable to die.*

Servianus' curse came to pass. As Hadrian lay in agony, his groans echoing around the marble corridors of Tivoli, the plans for the succession unravelled. On the first day of 138, the consumptive Verus died and the future of the Empire was clouded with uncertainty. But, while he still breathed, Hadrian politicked. Having chosen a replacement, a respected and even well-liked senator in the shape of Antoninus Pius, he insisted that the boy he attached to Verus, the bright boy who would become Marcus Aurelius, be confirmed at the same time. In this way the Empire would be in safe hands for two reigns. Here are Hadrian's thoughts, expressed in a speech to the Senate, probably embellished by Dio Cassius:

> But since Heaven has taken [Lucius Verus] from me, I have found as emperor for you in his place the man I now give to you, one who is noble, mild, passionate and prudent. He is neither young enough to do anything rash nor old enough to be neglectful. He has exercised authority in accordance with our ancestral customs, so that he is not ignorant of any matters which concern the imperial power, but can deal with them all. I am speaking of Aurelius Antoninus here. I know that he is not in the least inclined to be involved in affairs and is far from desiring such power, but still, I do not think that he will deliberately disregard either me or you, but will accept the rule, even against his will.

Antoninus appears to have been less than enthusiastic. The wealthy owner of large estates in Italy, he was fifty-one when Hadrian adopted him – and he could see at first hand what the pressures of high office had done. His calm and common sense seems to have had an effect. After the episode with Mastor and the suicide of his doctor, Hadrian wrote to Antoninus with what, from an emperor, amounted to an apology:

Above all I want you to know that I am being released from life neither prematurely nor unreasonably; I am not full of self-pity, nor am I surprised and my faculties are unimpaired – even though I may almost appear, as I have realised, to do injury to you when you are at my side, whenever I am in need of attendance, consoling me and encouraging me to rest. This why I am impelled to write to you, not – by Zeus – as one who subtly devises a tedious account contrary to the truth, but rather making a simple and accurate record of the facts themselves.

The day finally came. On 10th July 138 Hadrian was released, it seemed, from Servianus' curse. At the desperate last, he had aggressively disregarded medical advice and, eating and drinking whatever he pleased, the Emperor appears to have hastened his end. Without fuss or political difficulty, Antoninus became Emperor. According to the *Historia Augusta*, Hadrian was first buried at Cicero's old villa at Puteoli and, in a withering final comment, the author added *invisus omnium* or 'hated by all'.

BLACK AND WHITE

We live in a world lit by bright colours. Two thousand years ago the world was less obviously vivid – and yet the sophistication of the ancient language of colour was much greater. Perhaps this was because of the wide spectrum of subtle hues seen in nature, and the fact that more precision is required to describe it. In Latin, for example, black and white were not just black and white. *Candidus* meant gleaming or shiny white, and St Ninian's Candida Casa for his very early church at Whithorn attached a more spiritual quality than a mere 'White House'. *Albus* meant matt white or chalky white, as in the White Cliffs of Dover, and the adjective must be related to *Albion*. By contrast *ater* was matt black or dead black, like a moonless night, and it had overtones of gloom or even malice. *Niger* was glossy black, like the fur of a sable or lustrous like the skin of a black person. Celtic languages were equally nuanced. The Gaelic adjectives *odhar* and *lachdann* describe points in the spectrum somewhere between a parchmenty sort of beige and porridge – but have no satisfactory equivalent in English.

Whatever judgement contemporaries offered, or subsequent historians made, there can be no doubt that Hadrian possessed a towering
intelligence and tireless energy. Perhaps he saw something similar in
Marcus Aurelius. Despite Hadrian's cruelties and obstinacies, there
was a cultured sensitivity in his nature. While he lay dying, enduring
the long hours of pain, Hadrian must have thought on all that he had
seen in his vast empire. From the Persian Gulf to the Strait of
Gibraltar, from the Danube to the German forests and the ancient
grandeur of Athens and Egypt, he had travelled more widely than any
who had held his office. Perhaps in the heat of July 138, in his last
days, he thought of the windy hills of northern Britannia, the place
where he had planned and built the great Wall. At least that would
endure, outlasting him and all who followed. His travels seemed to be
much on Hadrian's mind when he composed a remarkable and brief
epitaph in a few moments when the pain had receded and he was calm.
It seemed at last that he was ready to die.

> Little soul, little wanderer, little charmer,
> body's guest and companion,
> to what places will you set out for now?
> To darkling, cold and gloomy ones –
> and you won't make your usual jokes.

The Senate was not amused. So powerful was their hatred for Hadrian
that they at first refused to vote for his deification, an honour which
had previously been automatic. When they attempted also to annul his
acts, Antoninus intervened. If the Senate persisted with this, then it
should realise that one of those acts was Antoninus' own adoption as
heir. Was that what the Senate wanted to see annulled? The argument
was as much about respect for the authority of emperors, the integrity
of the office itself, and Antoninus was sufficiently astute to suffer no
challenge to that, even for someone as loathed as Hadrian.

Where he did play to patrician sentiment was in the matter of
Britain. Antoninus planned to repudiate the policy of triumphant
retrenchment where it had been most emphatically made manifest.
The great Wall in Britannia would become irrelevant. Exposed for
what it was, a *folie de grandeur* like the absurd villa at Tivoli, it would
be bypassed as Rome moved beyond the constraints placed on her by
Hadrian. There would be conquest once more! The legions would

march and the old glories (and, of course, opportunities for ambitious aristocrats) would unfurl and the eagle standards gleam again.

As Claudius did in 43, and other emperors since, Antoninus also needed an opening blaze of prestige. Having no experience himself as a soldier, he would nevertheless bathe his reign in the glow of immediate military success. Britain was a low-risk option. Literally insulated from the European Empire and the Mediterranean, any failure there could be contained, and if there was success then remoteness could only enhance it.

All of this was well received in Rome and, early in his principate, Antoninus acquired the honorific *Pius*. It means 'faithful' or 'loyal' and could have had several applications. By reviving the tradition of conquest, Antoninus Pius was being faithful to the spirit and history of Rome. A new and more harmonious relationship with the Senate, the Conscript Fathers, showed loyalty to old Republican institutions. Some might have seen Antoninus' defence of Hadrian, his adoptive father, as filial piety of an attractively old-fashioned – if misguided – sort.

MAGICAL MYSTERIES

The otherwise sober-sided Antoninus Pius and his empress were both members of the eastern mystery cult of Cybele. It involved self-flagellation, frenzied dancing – and self-castration. Here is the poet Juvenal's description of their rites: 'And now comes in procession / Devotees of the frenzied Bellona, and Cybele, Mother of Gods / Led by a giant eunuch, the idol of his lesser / Companions in obscenity. Long ago with a sherd / He sliced off his genitals: now neither the howling rabble / Nor the kettledrums outshriek him.' Evidence of the worship of Cybele has been found in northern Britannia. Digging at Catterick in 2005, archaeologists came across the grave of a transvestite priest. He or she castrated himself in a gruesome religious ceremony. Using a clamp, similar to one found in the Thames, he had cut off his testicles in imitation of Cybele's lover, Attis, who had made himself a eunuch as a punishment for an extramarital affair. Mystical eastern religions were popular in the Roman north, and temples to Mithras, an eastern god much favoured by soldiers, can be found along the line of the Wall.

Whatever the calculation and the cold reality behind all that spin, Antoninus seemed a canny political operator. While repudiating Hadrian's wrongheaded imperial legacy, he appeared to act like a faithful son. And, while ordering the legions to march against the barbarians, he seemed to be leading Rome into a fresh, new era. In fact history turned out differently. Far from harking back to the triumphs of Trajan, Antoninus never left Italy during a long reign of twenty-three years, and never once set eyes on an army or a frontier. Unlike Hadrian, freezing in the forests of Scythia or tramping around Britain, he stayed in Rome, kept the Senate and the mob happy and never went to war unless he absolutely had to.

Contemporary commentators had the delicate task of reconciling the competing images of a powerful war leader at the head of his legions, in spirit if not quite in body, with that of an Emperor who had decided to stay in Rome. In 142, the year of his consulship and the successful conclusion of the war in Britain, Cornelius Fronto managed this awkwardness very adroitly. Here is part of his speech to the Senate:

> Although he [Antoninus] had committed the conduct of the campaign to others, while sitting at home himself in the Imperial Palace in Rome, yet like the helmsman at the tiller of a ship of war, the glory of the whole navigation and voyage belonged to him.

Amongst Antoninus Pius' earliest acts was the appointment of Lollius Urbicus to the governorship of Britannia. In 139 Urbicus was at Corbridge, rebuilding the military depot, no doubt inspecting the Wall garrison, gathering intelligence, making his plans. Dere Street, the old invasion road, crossed the Tyne nearby and the legions would soon be marching north. It seems that there had been war in Britain. The Greek writer Pausanias reported it in this enigmatic passage:

> Also he [Antoninus Pius] deprived the Brigantes in Britannia of most of their territory because they had taken up arms and invaded the Genounian district of which the people are subject to the Romans.

Genounia is a mystery (it may be a garbled rendering of an Old Welsh place-name cognate to *gwyn* or even *Guotodin*, but it seems unlikely) and its inclusion in a notice of what was happening in Britain may simply have been a blunder. There was a district known as Genaunia in the province of Raetia, modern Switzerland. The use of Brigantes looks like a catch-all for northern British barbarians much in the way that Siberia came to stand for a vast tract of the north-east of the old Soviet Union even though the name originally referred only to the lands immediately to the east of the Urals. Brigantes probably included the Selgovae of the Southern Uplands and the Ettrick Forest, the Anavionenses of Annandale and the Novantae of Galloway. They were, in any case, allies of the Brigantes, part of the great federation of northern hill peoples. The later dispositions of forts in southern Scotland also strongly suggest that the Damnonii of the Clyde basin had sent warbands to attack the Romans.

In the second century AD the kingdoms of lowland Scotland were vigorous. Archaeology has revealed an expanding population and a growing density of settlement. It may be that the kings in the west and the south had turned on the Votadini of the Lothians and the Tweed basin. They had been Roman allies and suppliers, if not exactly subjects, but probably bound to them by treaty. One interpretation of Genounian district holds that it refers to the territory of the Votadini and their cousins across the Forth in Fife, the Venicones. Not part of the Empire in 139, they had briefly been subjects of Rome when Agricola was provincial Governor. Perhaps Antoninus Pius and Lollius Urbicus planned to bring them back into the fold after Hadrian's badly sited Wall had excluded them, leaving them to the mercy of their covetous neighbours.

In the summer of 140, the new Governor at last rode at the head of an invading army. Their route or routes to the north are not known for certain but they may have followed Agricola's lines of advance up Dere Street in the east and the modern A74 in the west. Forts were built and rebuilt along these approaches. Three legions were stationed in Britannia in 140, and later inscriptions suggest that the VI Victrix based in York and the XX Valeria Victrix at Chester sent only detachments. Only the II Augusta came in its entirety from Caerleon on the Welsh border, probably leaving behind only a skeleton garrison. This at first glance appears perverse – most men travelling the longest distance, but it probably reflects the pattern of unrest in Britannia at the time. The south was sufficiently secure and quiet to allow all of the II to march north, while the

Pennines and the territories either side of them needed watching. Enough legionaries to deal with an emergency had to be left at Chester and York.

Of the auxiliary regiments, the Batavians were serving in Europe, but the feared Tungrians almost certainly formed part of Urbicus' strike force. Others, such as the Hamian Archers from Carvoran and the cavalry, the Ala Augusta, from Chesters had raised their banners and were going to war.

In two years of campaigning, perhaps less, that war had been won. No details survive but in AD 142 coins were minted to commemorate a great victory. And in Rome Antoninus Pius was acclaimed Imperator, the first and only time this happened. Job done.

Or it seemed to be done. The frontier of the Empire had been successfully extended by 150 kilometres, a victory gained and new territory subdued. But some in the imperial administration sniffed. Here are the comments of a Greek civil servant, Appianus:

> The Romans have aimed to preserve their empire by the exercise of prudence rather than to extend their sway indefinitely over poverty-stricken and profitless barbarian peoples. I have seen embassies from some of these in Rome offering themselves as subjects, and the Emperor refusing them, on the grounds that they would be of no use to him. For other peoples, limitless in number, the Emperors appoint the kings, not requiring them for the Empire . . . They surround the Empire with a circle of great camps and guard so great an area of the land and sea like an estate.

And later, Appianus offered his own interpretation of imperial attitudes to the province first conquered by the armies of Claudius:

> They have occupied the better and greater part of it [Britannia] but they do not care for the rest. For even the part they do occupy is not very profitable to them.

Others saw it differently and, paradoxically, were more pragmatic about the political wisdom of spending money and resources on invading bits of territory of little economic value. Here Hadrian's friend, the poet, Annaeus Florus, is talking about two remote provinces, Britannia and mountainous Armenia:

It was fine and glorious to have acquired them, not for any value, but for the great reputation they brought to the magnificence of the Empire.

In Britain the job was done efficiently. Over a wide swathe of southern Scotland Urbicus set his victorious soldiers to the tedious task of consolidation. Roads were refurbished and new stretches constructed. Forts were dug. From Glenlochar, near Castle Douglas, and from what is now Gatehouse of Fleet to Castledykes and Bothwellhaugh in Clydesdale, garrisons showed the flag and began to patrol and gather intelligence. Roads struck directly through the heart of dangerous hill country, nowhere more so than the dramatic Dalveen Pass between Upper Nithsdale and the upper reaches of the Clyde. There was an unmistakable sense in the 140s of the beginnings of provincial government.

The hub of the occupation of the south was at Newstead on the banks of the Tweed, in the lee of the Eildon Hills, the place called Trimontium. Close to Dere Street, which probably bridged the Tweed nearby, at Leaderfoot, Trimontium was the largest fort north of Hadrian's Wall. With several substantial annexes (fenced and guarded enclosures) around it, Newstead was a supply depot as well as important tactically. Brilliantly excavated by a Melrose solicitor, James Curle, before the First World War, it has given up one grisly memory of warfare in southern Scotland. Buried with a good deal of military rubbish, several skulls were found in a series of pits. Roman burials always took place well away from human habitation, often on roadsides, and in any case the skulls had no associated skeletons. They had not been interred. On Trajan's Column soldiers are shown raising up the severed heads of Dacians and, at the gates of a camp, two have been impaled on poles and stuck into the ground. At Vindolanda Andrew Birley's team have recently found a skull which had been stuck on a pole in exactly the same way. DNA analysis has demonstrated that the dead man was probably a native warrior from the kingdom of the Anavionenses. It seems certain that the Newstead skulls were those of captured or killed Selgovan soldiers whose severed heads were spitted on poles and set up at the fort gates in a gruesome display of Roman ruthlessness. We are inclined to see the legionaries and auxiliaries are clinical and efficient killers. This shows an atavistic savagery – something surely worthy of a barbarian.

After the native kings had been defeated and their lands brought under control, something extraordinary then took place. Here is the entry in the *Historia Augusta*:

[Antoninus Pius] conquered the Britons through the agency of the Governor, Lollius Urbicus, and having driven off the barbarians built another wall in turf.

Another wall! Twenty years after Hadrian commanded his vast project to commence and perhaps fifteen years after its completion, the Roman army built another wall across Britain. The same legions were involved and many of the same soldiers are likely to have started work on a second wall. While they are often stoic about the insanities of army life, soldiers are not immune automata. Many of the older men must have shaken their heads when the orders were given. What was wrong with the first wall?

Nothing at all. Except that it had been built on the orders of Hadrian. His name was inextricably attached to it, and if Antoninus wished to be seen actively repudiating his policies then one of their greatest monuments needed to be abandoned. Immediately. But this extraordinary decision has another fascinating aspect. It was not extraordinary to the Romans. We see these massive works differently, as expressions of vast expense, resources, will and effort. To abandon something like Hadrian's Wall as soon as it was completed would have been a profligate waste.

Antoninus and his generals did not see the decision in this light. At their command was a large, versatile and highly skilled army which would need to be paid and fed whatever happened. The abandonment of Hadrian's Wall was not a disaster or a waste, just a matter of strategy. Because they had the army, as much a huge and relatively well-disciplined labour force as a fighting machine, the Romans thought on a different scale. They were masters of the world and it was for them to order it as they saw fit.

These were pervasive attitudes. If their officers thought like this, so did the men and, while the prospect of building another wall will have raised the eyebrows of more than a few centurions, there was no hesitation in setting about the task. In any case, this wall would be easier: half the length and built out of turf, not stone: no problem.

As with Hadrian's Wall, the western kings appear to have given more cause for concern and, before any soldier began work on the Wall, it seems that forts were built to hold down the lower Clyde basin. The line chosen was indeed much shorter at 59 kilometres compared with 120 kilometres. It was to run from Bridgeness on the Firth of Forth in the east to Old Kilpatrick on the bank of the Clyde in the west, across the narrow waist of Scotland. Crucially, there was to be no Vallum, a tremendous saving of labour and time, and, while a short sequence of forts was planned at either end, nothing on the scale of the Cumbrian Sea-Wall would be needed.

TURF WARRIORS

The garrison of the Antonine Wall is less well attested than that of Hadrian's Wall and only those forts with named units are listed below.

Mumrills	– Ala I Tungrorum
	– Cohors II Thracum
Rough Castle	– part of Cohors VI Nerviorum quingenaria peditata
Castlecary	– part of Cohors Tungrorum milliaria peditata
	– part of Cohors I Vardullorum milliaria equitata
	– vexilations from II Legion and VI Legion
Bar Hill	– Cohors Baetasiorum quingenaria peditata
	– Cohors Hamiorum quingenaria
Cadder	– Cohors quingenaria peditata
Balmuildy	– Cohors quingenaria peditata
Castlehill	– Cohors IV Gallorum quingenaria peditata
Old Kilpatrick	– Cohors I Baetasiorum quingenaria peditata

The Antonine Wall straddled more than the shortest distance between the North Sea and the Atlantic sea-lochs of the west; it was also a man-made recognition of one of Scotland's most profound geographical divisions. To the south lay Clydesdale and Ayrshire, the fertile Lothians, the gentle slopes of the Southern Uplands and Galloway, and the rich farmland of the Tweed basin. In the north were the mountains and the islands, the formidable rampart of the Highland Line visible for many miles. There was Fife to the north-east, and beyond it the coastlands of Angus and Tayside, and while these places had powerful links with the south they were nevertheless culturally distinct. What is now Scotland used to be split into two, and Tacitus thought that the north was like *a different island*.

And it was. Motorways and modern drainage have erased this ancient frontier. Two thousand years ago, landward communications were much more difficult. At the western end of the line of the Antonine Wall, the Highlands rise up abruptly. In the central section, overland travel to the north was made circuitous and even dangerous by the Flanders Moss. A wide tract of treacherous marshland, it made much of the valley of the meandering River Forth impassable in winter and very awkward in summer. Drainage had to wait until the eighteenth and nineteenth centuries. Only in the east, through the Stirling Gap, was there firm passage. Funnelling under the glowering crag of the great castle, armies intent on the conquest of all of Scotland were forced to march that route. For this now-lost reason of geography, Stirling held the key to the whole kingdom for many centuries.

With no emperor to interfere, Lollius Urbicus and his surveyors rode from the Forth to the Clyde pegging out the line of the new Wall. They made good decisions. Even though the geography is much less dramatic than the Whin Sill, the Antonine Wall nevertheless commands the ground emphatically. Rising up from the coastal plain at Bo'ness, it quickly finds the high country to the south of the valley of the River Carron. From there long vistas stretch out over west Fife and as far as the Ochil Hills. In contrast with the bleak prospects from the high parts of Hadrian's Wall, these are views of heavily populated areas, fertile flatlands bordering the Forth and the better-drained terrain towards Alva and Dollar. In the central section, the Wall hops from one vantage point to the next, is by no means straight, and at Croy Hill and Bar Hill it climbs to its highest point above sea-level. The valley of the little River Kelvin provides a handy southern slope where the garrison could look out over the Campsie Fells and the threatening mass of the Drumalban Mountains behind them. At Balmuildy the line turns sharply north-west for a few hundred metres and then strikes through what is now the well-set Glasgow suburb of Bearsden before reaching its terminus at Old Kilpatrick on the northern bank of the Clyde. Only the ford at Bowling lay beyond the end of the Wall; all of the others were upstream.

Outlier forts and fortlets were built across the river at Bishopton and even further west at Lurg Moor and Outerwards. More substantial were the forts beyond the eastern terminal. Cramond stood on the Forth shore, at the outfall of the River Almond, and, 18 kilometres further east, Inveresk was built near another river-mouth. From these, soldiers could watch the Fife shoreline, probably not fearing attack from that quarter but, rather, attacks on it. The corn-growing Venicones were likely Roman clients, well within the protective compass of the new Wall, and the lookouts at Cramond and Inveresk will have watched for suspicious movement on the northern shore. Further help for native farmers lay beyond. Lollius Urbicus reactivated part of the old Gask Ridge system and there were outpost forts once more at Ardoch, Strageath and north-west of Perth. This was a comprehensive pattern of occupation and an entirely unmissable show of strength. The Empire had come back north.

Work began on the new Wall. Probably in the summer of 142 the three legions dug the first of their temporary labour camps. The outlines of eighteen of these have been detected, mostly from the air. As at Hadrian's Wall, construction was organised in legionary lengths and also appears to have begun in the east. Following the line laid out by the surveyors, the gangs first dug a shallow foundation trench. Stone footings were tapped in, made as level as possible and the edges set out with large kerbstones finished only on the outside face. Even though it was to be a turf wall, a great deal of stone was quarried. The building principle was simple: to build a flat and stable foundation, and border it with kerbstones which would keep the width of the Wall consistent and help prevent spreading.

Culverts were let into the foundations at frequent intervals so that, in winter, or after heavy rain, there would be no ponding behind the rampart. There had been too few culverts on Hadrian's Wall, and it seemed that the legionary builders were learning.

Since the basic building material, turf, lay around the line of the Wall and did not need to be quarried, the logistical support for the men working at the site was much less extended and much less complex. Once the stone founds had been laid, virtually every soldier could be involved in construction because they undoubtedly possessed the skills required. On the march, most nights, the Roman army dug temporary camps which used exactly the same methods. Despite the fact that some learned opinion now believes that the Antonine Wall took several years to build, in fact it rose quickly.

Each legionary was issued with a crescent-shaped turf cutter, something like the tool now used to straighten up the edges of perfect suburban lawns. With it, soldiers expertly sliced out large rectangular pieces of turf. And, as with almost everything they built, the Romans specified a standard size, in this case 45 centimetres by 30 centimetres by 15 centimetres. That is large, and if taken from damp ground, a single turf might have weighed 30 kilograms. One of the advantages of using them was that one man could carry a single piece but, at that weight and bulk, it might easily have disintegrated. If the ground was dry, it would be even more difficult to keep a large piece of turf together. On Trajan's Column there is an illustration of turf cutting and it shows one soldier loading a large piece onto another man's back with the help of a rope sling. That seems a lot of handling for a simple job, but it may well have been standard procedure.

Perhaps ground conditions varied more than they do now. The point of turf as a building material is the grass on top of it. Its roots knit the earth together sufficiently for it to keep its basic shape when lifted out of the ground. These were not the tidy squares of turf delivered by today's garden centres. Natural pasture in AD 122 had much longer and stronger roots than the wispy stuff grown by farmers and horticulturalists today. If the work on the Antonine Wall was done in the spring and summer when the grass and all the other herbage and the weeds that grew in it were tall, then not only would cutting be awkward, the roots in the ground would have been more vigorous and binding – and in some cases very much longer and tougher.

Whatever their size, the turfs were laid like stone with each course's joints bonding as neatly as possible with the middle of the one below. On a base of 4.2 metres, the Wall was able to rise safely to 2.5 metres. For stability the sides sloped, narrowing to a 1.8 metre top. This was not like stone in that sense, and there could be no vertical faces. In any case the profile and possibly the height of the Wall would have altered quite quickly as the turf settled and moisture drained downwards.

As with Hadrian's Wall, there is much debate about what the top of the Antonine Wall looked like. Was there a walkway? Was there a wooden breastwork with crenellations? The answer is probably yes to all of these. A sloping turf surface is much easier and quicker to climb than a vertical stone wall, especially one which had been rendered. It seems inconceivable that the soldiers on watch would not have had access to the top of their Wall, or indeed a breastwork to shield them – from the weather if nothing else. And one with crenellations will have made the rampart look higher and more formidable.

What also made the Wall look taller was the forward ditch. North of the Wall, work-gangs dug down to 3.5 metres and piled the upcast on the northern flank to make the downslope even deeper (the Antonine Wall used much less turf than the original western end of Hadrian's Wall, between the Irthing and Carlisle, but the ditch was significantly deeper, again giving an impression of greater height). The whole earthwork was 12 metres across. The ditch is the most visible relic of the Wall, there being very little to see of the turf rampart, and surprisingly at its most impressive in Falkirk, at Watling Lodge. Between it and the Wall a substantial berm was left. And behind both, the legionaries laid down a military road which ran the entire length, from Bridgeness to Old Kilpatrick.

One particular element of the building programme is eloquent. On Hadrian's Wall the soldiers dug pits known as *lilia* on the north side. Remains of them have been found at Byker and Throckley in New-castle. Filled with sharpened stakes and then covered over with leaves and twigs, they were the Roman equivalent of barbed wire, intended to break up an assault. On the Antonine Wall the builders appear to have expected attacks and there are examples of extensive fields of *lilia*. At Rough Castle, near Falkirk, there are no less than ten rows of pits offset like the black squares of a chessboard, and in each row there are twenty pits. This sort of added defence took a good deal of effort and some maintenance – but it was obviously thought necessary.

The organisation of the garrison on the Antonine Wall was differ-ent. And, as in the south, there were changes of plan. At first, forts were to be arranged in a similar order with one every 12 kilometres or so. There were to be seven in all, with fortlets interspersed and, at Camelon, one fort forward of the rampart. And then the plan suddenly changed. As the work-gangs reached the stretch between Bearsden and Duntocher, not far from the Clyde and the end of the line, it was decided to add no less than ten new forts to the Wall. Now there was to be a garrison (of differing sizes) every 3.5 kilometres. What prompted this radical change in plan is not recorded – but it must surely have been something dramatic. Perhaps there was hostile action against the Wall and its soldiers during construction. It lay close to the Highlands, difficult country to patrol, and perhaps warbands erupted out of their glens without any warning and launched themselves at this extraordinary structure and the men who were daring to make it.

BLOCKED IN BEARSDEN

Property prices in the genteel Glasgow suburb of Bearsden might be thought to benefit from the presence of Roman remains. History on a doorstep adds a certain cachet. Less appealing to estate agents might be the fact that one of the most interesting finds at the fort was the effluent from a latrine. Like the famous example at Housesteads, it was communal. The sewage drained into the ditches beyond the rampart where it was covered with water – and therefore probably did not smell. Analysis has revealed a largely vegetarian diet for the average soldier: cereals supplemented by wild fruits and nuts, such as raspberries, brambles and hazelnuts. Food was not as fresh or as hygienically prepared as it is now and some of the men suffered from roundworm and whipworm. Too much information? Less worryingly, bits of ancient moss were found in the ditches and absolutely no trace whatsoever of sponges and sticks.

The native kings knew of the great stone Wall in the south and it may be that some of their warriors had joined their allies, the Brigantes, and fought in the countryside around it. When a second Wall began to slice through their own territory, it is not likely that they were content to sit quietly and watch. And as Roman soldiers worked, they were more vulnerable to surprise.

Meanwhile Hadrian's Wall appears to have been all but deserted. To allow easier access, the gates were removed from the milecastles, and every 40 or 50 metres some of the upcast was backfilled into the Vallum to make causeways. Garrisons fell back to the old Stanegate forts of Corbridge, Vindolanda and Carlisle. The focus was now firmly in the north as the turf Wall took shape.

The density of the Antonine Wall defences is very striking. The garrisons were stationed very close to one another. Admittedly they varied in size from the small detachment which fitted into the tiny fort at Duntocher to the much larger units based at Balmuildy, for example. Most of the soldiers were infantrymen and there was cavalry only at Mumrills in the east (the Tungrians) and probably at Bearsden in the west. Given the boggy and difficult nature of the ground immediately to the north of the Wall, infantry may have been a better option. The Roman army always preferred to fight in formation, using well-rehearsed tactics. By contrast, native horsemen were raiders and skirmishers, like the Border Reivers long after them, with sure-footed ponies able to move quickly through uncertain ground. This seems like a mis-match but, in reality, it was probably not sensible for the Romans to pursue but rather to police effectively those places they could reach on foot. As ever they were determined to fight only on their own terms.

ANTONINE NAMES

Perhaps because the Antonine Wall was in operation for such a comparatively short time, we do not have a complete list of well-understood names for the forts along it. Some are entirely unknown, others wildly speculative. However, place-names sprinkled on either side of the Wall are interesting. 'Medionemeton' means Middle Shrine and it might have two references. The less likely location is a Roman monument known as Arthur's O'en. Looking a bit like a huge oven or a giant beehive, it stood 3 kilometres north of the Antonine Wall, near the River Carron. It was probably dedicated to the goddess Victory, perhaps in thanks and celebration for the defeat of the northern kings in the campaign of AD 139–142. A large, circular and domed structure, it was demolished in 1743 and its dressed stones used to build a mill dam for the Carron Ironworks. The other, more likely, location of the Middle Shrine is Cairnpapple Hill near Linlithgow. An elaborate prehistoric temple and burial site for millennia, it seems to stand on a Scottish meridian with clear and long views in every direction. The Highland Line, the Forth, the Southern Uplands and the Firth of Clyde can all be seen from its summit, and the name means the Stone of the Priests in early Gaelic.

At Newstead, the conditions were different. The well-drained rolling farmland of the central Borders was good cavalry country. In addition to two cohorts of the XX Legion, a full regiment of troopers

was stationed on the banks of the Tweed. The Ala Augusta Vocontiorum had the hitting power and the speed to confront the fast-
moving warbands of the Selgovae. Horses for courses.

At Newstead, and outside the walls of most of the forts on the
Antonine Wall, the soldiers built annexes. In part these enclosures
were a quicker and more economical solution to the problem solved
by the Vallum dug so laboriously to the south of Hadrian's Wall.
Instead of all that sweat spilt to create a secure military zone behind
the entire length of the Wall, Lollius Urbicus' planners decided to
localise it. At the flanks of the Antonine forts, annexes could be used to
house additional troops, enclose stock or provide a well-guarded
cordon around goods, which might otherwise have disappeared during the night.

The date of the completion of the Antonine Wall is nowhere
recorded, but the finishing of its legionary lengths is. A set of unique
stone plaques, known as distance slabs, has been found, which carry
the names of the legions who did the work, commemorating who did
what. Set up on both the northern and southern faces of the Wall at
the end of each length, some are very ornate – and informative. Not
surprisingly the mascot animals of the legions appear: a charging boar
for the XX, and a goat and Pegasus, the winged horse, for the II.
Various representations of the goddess of Victory are also carved.

The story of the War for the Wall is told in two of the most
interesting slabs. Set up by the II Legion, one of these carries a central
inscription, which is mostly taken up with the many names of the
Emperor Antoninus Pius. Reading from the left, there is a panel
showing a Roman cavalryman riding over four naked barbarians,
clearly vanquishing them. Or him. The four figures may represent one
warrior being attacked, knocked to the ground and wounded, and
perhaps begging for mercy, his weapons cast away. No mercy was
given, for at the bottom of the panel he has been decapitated. The
sculptor was no great artist, but he has tried hard to impart a sense of
movement to the cavalryman and his pony. Its tail is up, its forelegs
leaping into the gallop, and its rider's cloak flies out behind as he
thrusts downwards with his spear.

On the right of the inscription there is a religious scene. Under the
banner of the II Legion, a priest, probably the commander, Aulus
Claudius Charax, pours out a libation onto an altar. Wearing what is
probably a senatorial toga, he is surrounded by his fellow officers.

Some are bearded, like both Hadrian and Antoninus, while others are clean-shaven, and it may be that these are rough portraits. A figure plays the pipes and another kneels beside three animals: a bull, a sheep and a pig. Soon these poor creatures will have their throats cut in sacrifice, and the strong impression is that this ceremony is a dedication to celebrate the completion of the Wall, or at any rate the section at Bridgeness. It may also be a thanksgiving for the victorious outcome of the war being fought on the other side of the panel.

A distance slab was found at the western end of the Wall, at Hutcheson Hill, which shows another legion celebrating. In a central panel this time, the goddess of Victory awards a wreath to the XX Legion. As she places it on the beak of one of their eagle standards, two kneeling, naked and bound captives watch from the side panels. There can be no doubt about who is who and what is what. Rome has not just won but triumphed over the miserable, naked barbarians of the north.

Nakedness on the distance slabs was clearly the condition of defeat and enslavement but, as noted earlier, when one of the Vindolanda letters observes that the natives were *naked*, it meant that *they are unprotected by armour*. This was something the Romans not only sneered at but found difficult to understand. But in reality the sort of well-made and effective protection worn by legionaries and auxiliaries was unusual in the ancient world. Because the Roman army was professional and the deposit of a great deal of investment in training and pay, it made sense for soldiers to be well protected and for them to survive as long as possible. Dead soldiers were simply a waste. In the main, native warbands were not professional and did not wear armour. Their cavalry did not resemble the helmeted trooper riding across the Bridgeness slab.

The Antonine reoccupation of Scotland and discoveries at Corbridge have contributed a great deal to an understanding of this crucial Roman advantage. At the site of Newstead Fort the remains of a *lorica segmentata* were found by James Curle in 1906. This was the most common type of body armour worn in the western Empire from the late first century AD on into the middle of the second. Designed like a set of wide, overlapping metal ribs, it fitted around the abdomen and was flexible, allowing a soldier to move without much constraint. In combat an ability to move freely and quickly could be a matter of life or death. The Newstead type, and also a damaged lorica found at Corbridge, had heavy protection on the shoulders. Sword strokes over the top of a shield were obviously common and the overlapping shoulder plates are also fitted together like scales, both to protect and make it possible for a fighting soldier to raise his arm unhindered.

These cuirasses must have been very expensive, but it seems that soldiers bought them, either second-hand or direct from the manufacturer. Factories must have existed all over the western Empire, for, over the period of their use, hundreds of thousands of loricas were worn. The process of manufacture was all manual. Plates were hammered into shape, not produced by rolling mills. Roman armour lasted a long time and was passed on by fathers to sons; some examples are known to have survived in use long after the Empire in the west had disappeared.

Chain mail was more expensive, but more flexible. It took around 180 hours to make the most rudimentary shirt because it had at least 22,000 rings. Officers wore them, and often scales were latched onto the rings to make an even tougher piece of armour. The surprise is that mail was worn by auxiliaries. How did they afford it?

Parts of helmets have been found along Hadrian's Wall and they all appear to have followed the same basic design. A skull cap or *pot* had three elements added. At the back there was a wide neck-guard, to the sides hinged cheek-pieces, and a thick brow-band was fitted at the front to deflect downward blows. Most distinctive, at least in Hollywood epics, were the red horsehair cockades worn like a brush on the top. An example was preserved in the anaerobic mud of Vindolanda and in the main such decorations were the prerogative of senior officers. It should perhaps be expected that cavalry helmets had a little more dash. Often heavily decorated, some had a plume-tube fitted so that when the horses galloped whatever they had attached would stream out behind. The trooper on the Bridgeness slab wears a fine example, shaped like a pony tail. At Newstead a splendid metal cavalry mask was found. Not a piece of armour, it was used only for display on the parade ground. The comments of the infantry can easily be imagined.

The Antonine Wall showed every sign of permanence. A large garrison had been concentrated in a small, well-placed and heavily defended area – in fact it was only slightly smaller than that of Hadrian's Wall, which was of course twice the length. There were between 6,000 and 7,000 soldiers in seventeen forts, compared with a

ROMAN SPORRANS

The *lorica segmentata*, a mail shirt, could only reach down so far, and Roman soldiers were unable to protect what many men reckon to be the most vital part of their anatomy. The Roman solution was a kind of sporran. A few leather straps were sewn onto a belt and had metal studs hammered into them. This was flexible enough to allow free movement and it did offer some protection – although not much. Like a heavy sporran, it could probably have been uncomfortable while running or even walking quickly. Perhaps most Roman soldiers relied on their long shields and a sporting respect from the similarly vulnerable warriors they fought against. But then again, perhaps not.

total of around 8,000 on the stone wall in the south. Such large numbers suggest a large native population. Most of their duties were more like modern police work: the pursuit, trying and punishment of criminals (with commanding officers as magistrates), the escort of important people and a general effort to keep order. During the reign of Marcus Aurelius' son, Commodus (AD 180–192), forts and towers were built along the banks of the Danube *to prevent the secret crossings of petty raiders.*

The Antonine system seems also to have been much more clearly thought out, more integrated. All the forts faced north and formed part of the rampart, while the road behind them linked them all very closely. The Antonine Wall was perhaps the most advanced example of a Roman linear frontier.

There was no sense that it would be a short-lived expedient. *Vici*, the familiar civil settlements, quickly grew up and, beside the walls of the fort at Carriden, the inhabitants seem to have been particularly independent-minded. Having organised themselves into some sort of self-governing entity, they set up an altar, dedicated to Jupiter Best and Greatest. It also named Aelius Mansuetus on it, possibly a civil official or leader.

A pottery workshop was established at Bearsden by a man called Sarrius. It was part of a chain. He already had factories near Leicester and Doncaster, and, as the north opened up, Sarrius could clearly recognise a business opportunity when he saw one. It appears to have been successful: several sherds have been found with the firm's name on them.

Despite all this activity and all the effort expended to build a new northern frontier, it was abandoned after only fifteen years' occupation. It was Antoninus Pius who made the final decision. Probably in 157, he and his council in Rome decided to pull the frontier back to Hadrian's Wall. Lollius Urbicus, the former Governor of Britannia and builder of the new Wall, was instrumental. By 157 he was almost certainly Prefect of the City of Rome and a key member of the imperial council. Knowing the situation in Britain better than anyone else, he may have advocated the pull-back himself. The invasion and holding of the north had long since served its purpose and after twenty years on the throne Antoninus no longer needed to be associated with any fading glory. And, with legionaries certainly included in the Antonine garrisons (usually this sort of frontier posting was given to auxiliaries), there is a hint of overstretch.

The Wall was not demolished nor the ditch backfilled. It stood high enough to be clearly visible to the surveyor, William Roy, in the middle of the eighteenth century, and the ditch has survived well in places

---

TAGINES

Archaeologists digging at Bearsden Fort came across pottery made for cooking in an African style. Large pots were produced to sit directly on top of a brazier. How did they get there? There are no records of units from North Africa posted on the Antonine Wall – but there was a war in the province of Mauretania (part of modern Algeria) during the reign of Antoninus Pius. It began in 145 and ended five years later, and it may be that units were sent from the frontier in central Scotland on an immense journey to the frontier in North Africa to fight against more barbarians. There they appeared to have enjoyed the local cuisine and, when they arrived back in Bearsden, they had the right sort of pot fired in a kiln and made a brazier to hold it. The pots sound very much like tagines, heavy earthenware pots used by North African nomads to cook on charcoal braziers. They have conical lids which ensure that none of the condensation caused by cooking escapes, and this enrichs the stew or whatever else is being cooked. Cosmopolitan indeed.

even now. Forts and their buildings were slighted or burned, and the distance slabs carefully buried. Having military honours for the legions inscribed on them, they were semi-sacred objects, and no barbarian, naked or otherwise, would be allowed to deface them.

As the Antonine Wall passed into history, misconceptions and myths began to gather around it. The normally scrupulous Bede of Jarrow got it wrong when he reported that it had been built in the fifth century when a Roman army returned to southern Scotland. Having helped the locals repel an invasion of Picts and Scots (some whispers of genuine history here), the Romans advised them to build a wall to keep marauders at bay. By the eighth century, when Bede was writing at Jarrow, *building in the Roman manner* meant stonework. Turf had to be the work of the primitive British:

> The islanders built this wall as they had been instructed, but having no engineers capable of so great an undertaking, they built it of turf and not stone, so that it was of small value. However they built it for many miles between the two estuaries, hoping that where the sea provided no protection, they might use the rampart to preserve their borders from hostile attack. Clear traces of this wide and lofty earthwork can be seen to this day. It begins about two miles west of the monastery of Abercorn at a place which the Picts call Peanfahel and the English Penneltun, and runs westward to the city of Dumbarton.

By the fourteenth century bad history had turned into myth-history. The Scottish chronicler John of Fordun reckoned that the Wall had been cast down (perhaps it was in a ruinous state by his time) by Gryme, the son of King Eugenius. Writing in the sixteenth century, George Buchanan thought that Graeme, a leader of the Picts, had broken through it. King Graeme? In any event the local name for the Antonine Wall was the Grimsdyke and it lives on in modern street-names. In Bo'ness there is a Grahamsdyke Road and a Grahamsdyke Lane, while in Laurieston there is a Grahamsdyke Street. If Gryme and the very unlikely Graeme are set aside, what did the name mean? There is an intriguing old Scots expression, a Grime's Dyke, which means a ditch made by magic. The Old English *grim* originally meant fierce or aggressive. Either interpretation could work.

There are powerful archaeological arguments that the withdrawal from the Antonine Wall was gradual, managed in stages over four or five years. Dating after 158, signs of rebuilding have been detected at Chesters, Corbridge and Vindolanda, and redeployment for some units may have had to wait until the old Wall had been repaired and made habitable. The turf section in the west was replaced with stone during this period.

Most important, there seems to have been trouble in Britain. Around 155 the Brigantes may have risen in rebellion and the depleted legionary garrisons at Chester and York may have been unable to contain them. Coins were issued with the image of Britannia subdued, usually a sign that a war had been won, and troop movements are also suggestive of trouble in the Pennines. An inscription pulled out of the River Tyne records the arrival of reinforcements for all three legions in Britannia. But, in the nature of fragmentary evidence, it is possible to interpret it in the opposite direction. Soldiers may have been sailing down the Tyne to reinforce comrades in Germany. What is certain is the arrival of another experienced and talented general as Governor. Julius Verus is recorded ordering building work at Birrens Fort, just to the north of Hadrian's Wall and at Brough, at the southern end of the Pennines, in Derbyshire. Despite the ambiguities around the question of reinforcements, it looks as though the Brigantes once again forced a change in Roman policy. After almost a century of occupation, their kings were still powerful. The simple cause and effect may be that Lollius Urbicus advised his Emperor to withdraw elements of the Antonine garrison to suppress revolt in the Pennines.

After a long reign, from 138 to 161, longer than any emperor since the first two, Augustus and Tiberius, Antoninus Pius died. He was seventy, and the succession followed on untroubled. Marcus Aurelius had been nominated by Hadrian and in the last years of Antoninus he was closely involved in government. In turn, his reign was to bring to an end what the great historian of Rome, Edward Gibbon, called a Golden Age:

> If a man were called to fix the period in the history of the world, during which the condition of the human race was most happy and prosperous, he would, without hesitation, name that which elapsed from the death of Domitian to the accession of Commodus.

It is doubtful if the kings of the Brigantes would have seen their world in quite the same roseate glow. Gibbon's estimate of the reign of Antoninus is in the same vein:

> His reign is marked by the rare advantage of furnishing very few materials for history, which is, indeed, little more than the register of the crimes, follies, and misfortunes of mankind.

Despite this sense of Britannia dozing contentedly in the high summer of imperial Rome, the south was threatened again in 161, and another good soldier, Calpurnius Agricola, was despatched to deal with it. His governorship is well recorded in a series of inscriptions set up on Hadrian's Wall as it was being recommissioned, and also elsewhere in the north. Newstead continued to be held, well forward of the Wall, and other outpost forts were maintained in the meantime.

In the Senate, Marcus Aurelius had insisted that Lucius Verus, long seen as the spare rather than the heir, be confirmed as co-emperor, the first time this had happened. It appeared that Marcus was the senior partner and Verus was given rein to campaign abroad in the eastern provinces. After an expedition to Parthia, in the Middle East, the *Historia Augusta* was not impressed:

> He had brought with him [on his return] both minstrels and pipers, actors, pantomime jesters and jugglers, and all kinds of slaves in which Syria and Alexandria take pleasure, to such an extent that he seemed to have finished not a Parthian war but an actors' war.

Verus died of apoplexy in 168, probably a suffering a stroke (*he lived on speechless for three days*) before expiring and Marcus was left to govern unhindered. Hadrian was enormously fond of him, and his judgement of Marcus Aurelius' abilities seems to have been sound. While forced to campaign almost ceaselessly on Rome's frontiers, especially the Danube, and endure the same sort of rigours Hadrian relished, he showed himself a true philosopher-king. What impressed Gibbon (and indeed anyone who reads them) was a series of writings, *To Myself*, which survived as Marcus Aurelius' *Meditations*. They are the deposit of a tremendous intelligence:

What peculiar distinction remains for a wise and good man, but to be easy and contented under every event of human life . . . ? Not to offend the divine Principle that resides in his soul, nor to disturb the tranquility of his mind by a variety of fantastical pursuits . . . To observe a strict regard to truth in his words and justice in his actions; and though all mankind should conspire to question his integrity and modesty . . . he is not offended at their incredulity, nor yet deviates from the path which leads him to the true end of life, at which everyone should endeavour to arrive with a clear conscience, undaunted and prepared for his dissolution, resigned to his fate without murmuring or reluctance.

Marcus' equanimity was tested in 168 when German barbarians burst through the Danube frontier and reached northern Italy before being caught and defeated. This scare must have had a profound impact in Rome. The Emperor was on the Danube in the late 170s, fighting, amongst others, the Sarmatians and their heavy cavalry. At the same time, Avidius Cassius rose in rebellion in the east, claiming the imperial throne. To buy a hasty peace, Marcus accepted 8,000 Sarmatian cavalry into the Roman army and, in AD 175, 5,500 of them arrived in Britannia. The culture shock on both sides must have been considerable. Marcus' rationale was probably very simple: a continental European posting for these horse-riding soldiers might see them slip away and ride home to the Danube shore, but escape from the island of Britannia might prove a little more tricky. Some time later, Sarmatian veterans settled at Ribchester in Lancashire, and there are traces of them at Chesters Fort on Hadrian's Wall. It may be that they were used in the war in the Pennines against the Brigantes.

Gibbon's Golden Age ended abruptly in 180 when Commodus Antoninus succeeded his father. Assassination attempts were made almost immediately, and it must be a testament to his ingenuity, strength of will and good fortune that he survived for twelve years. He was probably the most dissolute and chaotic emperor since Nero.

During the 180s war erupted again in Britain, and this time it threatened the whole province. Dio Cassius reported that native armies crossed the Wall that separated them from the Roman garrison, had killed a general (probably the Governor) and massacred his army. Evidence of destruction has been found along the eastern section, at the neighbouring forts of Halton Chesters, Rudchester and Corbridge.

A DRAGON ON A STICK

The Sarmatian heavy cavalry drafted into the Roman army by Marcus Aurelius wore armour and protection for their horses, but they held another innovation in their hands. They used a long cavalry lance, called a *contus* in Latin, perhaps 6 feet long and a deadly weapon with the momentum of a charging pony and rider behind it. The Romans adopted the *contus* quickly. Up to and including the Light and Heavy Brigades of Crimean fame, cavalry squadrons began their charge with the lance held upright and only levelled it at an enemy at the last moment. The Sarmatians attached flags and often a mythical beast to the end of them. The *draco* was a hollow, open-mouthed dragon's head with a long tube of red or white material flowing behind so that, when the horseman kicked his pony into a gallop, it would fill with air like a windsock. For extra effect, reeds were inserted into the dragon's mouth so that when air passed through, it seemed to scream. How this struck those hoping to repel a Sarmatian charge can only be imagined. Perhaps the dragons first hissed along Hadrian's Wall. By the fourth century many Roman cavalry regiments had adopted the *draco*. Britain's oldest national emblem, the red dragon of Wales, may well have come from the Sarmatians.

This suggests an invasion route down the Northumberland Plain and through the lower Tweed, sidestepping the garrisons at Newstead and the outpost forts on Dere Street.

Ulpius Marcellus was sent to replace the Governor and it took at least three campaigning seasons to restore some sort of order. But it seems that the forts to the north of the Wall were abandoned once more, presumably because their garrisons were needed to strengthen the south, and because Scotland could no longer be held. Birrens and Newstead were never again reoccupied, and on Dere Street, over the Cheviot watershed and down into Northumberland, High Rochester and Risingham were also given up. In spite of a coin issue in 184 to celebrate a victory, and the adoption of the title of Britannicus by Commodus, it sounds more like a stand-off than any clear-cut result. Native kings had seen a Roman retreat in the late 150s, and when a weak Emperor succeeded in 180 they hit hard and cleared his army out of all the territory occupied in 139 to 142. In the circle of firelight their bards would have sung of victory.

The invasion had a very visible impact in the south. Walls began to rise around towns. Before 180 only a few had protected themselves in this way but the shock of events in the north, the massacre of the army and the killing of the Governor, persuaded local authorities to spend a good deal of cash and effort to make their communities safer. Imperial permission was required for the building of town walls and it was not easy to obtain. Always suspicious of allowing independent strength of any kind, emperors were traditionally reluctant – but it seems that there was a general recognition that Britannia was now vulnerable.

The central difficulty for Rome was that the province was not very Roman. In Spain and France a thoroughly Romanised society had been created. Large cities had grown up and Latin widely adopted. In Britain it was very different. Out of a population of 2 or 3 million, only 10 per cent lived in the hundred or so small towns, and perhaps 50,000 on villa estates in the countryside. When the army and its dependants, and the villagers in the *vici*, are added, the total of those who might reasonably be called Romano-British makes up a fifth, or at best a quarter, of the whole population. The Celtic speech community was overwhelmingly dominant, and Latin remained the language of authority, the towns and the army – the apparatus of colonisation. In Britain Rome simply did not catch on.

Against a background of that sort of cultural arithmetic, the continuing struggles of native kings appear in a different light. Ulpius Marcellus and the other governors who dealt with regular British rebellions may well have believed that a densely populated and largely Celtic countryside would rise to support insurgents if they looked like succeeding.

Meanwhile Commodus became crazier and crazier. In 182 he appointed the Praetorian Prefect, Perennis, as, in effect, his prime minister, handing over government almost entirely so that he could concentrate on ever more exotic and cruel forms of debauchery. In an ill-judged attempt to widen political power beyond the Senate, Perennis decreed that legionary commanders would now be drawn from the equestrian order, one rank below. At a stroke he removed a key senatorial prerogative – the command of the army. There was uproar, especially in Britain. Led by young aristocrats who saw their careers thwarted, the army mutinied. The British legions wanted to protest directly against the changes and they sent a deputation of no less than 1,500 soldiers to Rome to put their case directly to Commodus. Astonishingly, they proved persuasive and Perennis was removed from office.

To try to settle Britain down, Commodus sent Helvetius Pertinax, a seasoned soldier who knew the province well, having served two tours of duty there. After some initial success in defusing more mutiny and squashing a plot to promote himself as a rival to Commodus, Pertinax found that the situation began to deteriorate. A legion rebelled and attacked Pertinax and his *amici*, his bodyguard. Only the Governor survived, having been left for dead. His revenge was swift and severe but it only served to foment further disaffection, and Pertinax was forced to ask Rome to relieve him of his command. The discipline considered so important by Hadrian was breaking down.

Commodus' behaviour did nothing to settle the gathering chaos. His madness, random cruelties and perversions were beginning to overwhelm the government of the Empire. Believing that he was the reincarnation of the god Hercules, he announced that he would appear publicly in the arena to demonstrate his divinity. As Consul and Hercules, at the same time, Commodus planned to fight as a gladiator and, of course, emerge entirely invincible. His assassination was arranged immediately.

Already Prefect of the City of Rome, Pertinax was proclaimed Emperor. But more chaos engulfed the Empire. When he attempted to bring the Praetorian Guard under closer and more direct control, Pertinax was murdered on the orders of the Prefect. The throne was then auctioned to the highest bidder and the Praetorians sold it to a fabulously wealthy and very foolish senator, Didius Julianus. No more durable than his predecessor, he was quickly removed as the frontier legions revolted, proclaiming no less than three candidates for the purple. Clodius Albinus, Governor of Britannia, claimed the throne at the same time as Septimius Severus in Pannonia (modern Hungary) and Niger Pescennius in Syria. A deadly game of deception and double-cross followed. Severus offered Albinus the title of Caesar, something reminiscent of Verus' role under Marcus Aurelius, while he marched east to confront Niger. After an emphatic victory in Syria (ending with the pursuit and murder of Niger), Severus then reneged on his promises to Albinus. A decisive battle became inevitable. With the British legions behind him and others from Spain and Gaul, Albinus met Severus' army at Lyons in 197. He lost.

How much of the British garrison also fought on the losing side that day is difficult to work out. Widespread changes of units in the auxiliary forts and on Hadrian's Wall have been taken to mean that the likes of the Tungrians followed Albinus on his European adventures and were removed after his defeat. But there is no certain information. What was definite was Severus' mastery of the Roman Empire, a mastery he would soon extend to the mutinous province of Britain.

He was the first African to sit on the imperial throne. Born in Lepcis Magna, now in modern Libya and one of the most substantial and impressive Roman sites anywhere, Severus was one of a growing number of powerful African senators. Clodius Albinus, from Tunisia, was another. Fertile, reliably productive and easily accessible by sea, the north African coastline had become wealthy and, by the end of the second century AD, its leading citizens were increasingly politically active. Severus' rise had been steady, unspectacular. By the time he defeated Albinus at Lyons, he was fifty-one and beginning to become what the *Historia Augusta* described as *crippled in the feet*. Towards the end of his life, his gout forced the Emperor into the indignity of being carried on a litter. It is said that the pain from gout is especially acute, and it cannot have made the already exhausting business of establishing his authority any easier for Severus. Thought harsh by the *Historia Augusta*, he was probably moved to irritation more often than most by the growing pain in his feet.

From the very outset of his reign the new Emperor carefully cultivated the loyalty of the army. He awarded soldiers their first pay rise since the days of Domitian – a long wait, almost exactly a century. Three new legions were recruited in the east, the I, II and III Parthicae. And, perhaps most popular, Severus at last permitted soldiers to marry legally.

Retaining a healthy suspicion of factionalism in Rome, he took immediate radical action. After removing the uncontrollable Praetorians entirely and replacing them with a much larger and much more loyal bodyguard drawn from the Danube legions, Severus also augmented the Vigiles, the urban cohorts who policed Rome. He stationed one of the new legions in Italy, treating it like any other province, and he further insisted that the II Parthica be based at

Albinum, only 30 kilometres from Rome. When he lay on his death bed in York in 212, the old emperor gave his sons some simple advice. Having risen and prospered with the support of the army, he told them *to give money to the soldiers and ignore the rest.*

Conquest also bound the legions to Severus and as soon as he had established himself, he led them on campaign in the east. The Parthian Empire was believed to be vulnerable, and by the end of 198 two new provinces had been created in Mesopotamia and Osrhoene, the first significant additions to the Empire since the time of Trajan. In North Africa an extensive frontier system of roads and forts pushed the barbarians further south and another new province was set up in Numidia, what is now eastern Algeria.

PARTHIA

Rome's greatest rivals in the east are usually treated much in the same way as the barbarians of the north. Given very little historical personality, they seem like a buffer, a monolithic enemy. The Parthians took over Iran and Mesopotamia in the first century BC, and in 53 BC delivered a massive blow by defeating and killing Crassus at Carrhae, massacring many legionaries. Parthia appears to have been a federation of vassal kingdoms governed by a dynasty which originated amongst the Parni, semi-nomads from the north. Their capital place was at Ctesiphon on the lower Tigris and their armies boasted a heavy, armoured cavalry and squadrons of deadly horse-archers. Zoroastrianism seems to have been the state religion, although there was widespread toleration of other cults. Modern Zoroastrians are known as Parsees. The frontier with Rome ebbed and flowed between the two rivers, the Euphrates and the Tigris, until a new dynasty, the Sassanids, pushed further west in the third century, humiliating the Empire with the capture of the Emperor Valerian in 260.

The focus on the Parthian campaigns called for holding action at the farthest end of the Empire, in Britannia. In 197 Virius Lupus, the Governor installed by Severus, was forced to buy peace in the north. A very large bribe was handed over to the kings of the Maeatae and the Caledonii, and in return some sort of treaty was agreed and Roman prisoners returned. These last were probably captured during raids into the province. If Severus wished to prosecute his war against the Parthians in the east, then he had little option but to buy time in the north-west of the Empire.

Dio Cassius had heard of these powerful native kingdoms:

> the two most important tribes of the Britons [in the north] are the Caledonians and the Maeatae; the names of all the tribes have been practically absorbed in these. The Maeatae dwell close to the Wall which divides the island into two parts and the Caledonians next to them. Each of the two inhabit rugged hills with swamps between, possessing neither walled places nor towns, but living by pastoral pursuits and by hunting.

The Antonine Wall is the more likely of the two and the Maeatae have left gossamer traces of their ancient name in the hills around it. Five kilometres to the north of Stirling rises the steep rampart of the Ochil Hills, and the most prominent part of the western ridge is known as Dumyat. It means Fort of the Maeatae. Near Denny, looking south at the central sector of the Antonine Wall, is Myot Hill, another stronghold. The name outlasted the Empire and in his *Life of Columba*, written in the seventh century, St Adomnan described *the war with the Maeatae*. It was fought by the Gaelic-speaking King of Argyll, Aedan macGabrain, and Adomnan remembered that Columba prayed hard for victory for his fellow Gael. His prayers may not have been answered because, in the event, two of Aedan's sons, Eochaid Find and Arthur, were killed. The same battle is recorded in the Irish Annals of Tighernach, but it is called *the battle of Circenn*. And Circenn was the name of the later Pictish province of Angus and the Mearns. All of which places the Maeatae where the place-names hint, just to the north of the Antonine Wall and in the Angus glens and coastal plain. The name itself is hard to parse – *Maeatae* may mean something routine like 'the Great Ones'. Certainly great enough to extract cash from the coffers of the Roman Empire.

Behind them or *next to them* was the territory of the Caledonii. The likelihood is that their kings ruled the lands to the north and west of their confederates. Unlike them, their name has endured, and expanded its meaning to include all Scots.

The treaty concluded by Virius Lupus did not last long. By 207 the warbands of the Maeatae and the Caledonii were mustering once more for raids to the south. The new Governor of Britannia, Alfenus Senecio, wrote an urgent despatch:

> ... the barbarians had risen and were overrunning the country, carrying off booty and causing great destruction ... for effective defence more troops or the presence of the Emperor was necessary.

This request was not made lightly. No governor wanted the massive burden of an imperial visit and all the disruption – and scrutiny – involved. The Maeatae and the Caledonii had probably made serious inroads; their hardy little ponies would have been capable of long distances and would have thought nothing of making 50 miles a day over difficult country. The warbands had probably penetrated deep into the richest part of the province, bypassing or overrunning Hadrian's Wall, staying clear of the main roads and the legionary fortresses.

Severus made immediate preparations for a campaign in Britain. Some historians have suggested that his main motive was the usual desire for prestige, but it was far too late in Severus' reign for him to bother about that. Britannia was probably in uproar, and Alfenus Senecio's request desperate.

The *imperial expedition* into Scotland and the heartlands of the insurgents was to be primarily focused on the east coast and heavily supported by sea. The fort at South Shields, at the mouth of the Tyne, was converted into a massive supply dump with no less than twenty-three granaries built to store food. It has been calculated that there was enough for an army of 40,000 men for three months in the field. Corbridge also saw new building, and at Cramond, west of Edinburgh, on the Forth shore, the old Antonine fort was refurbished.

The intended target was Tayside, the territory of the Maeatae. It seems likely that the German fleet, and perhaps even the Danube river flotilla, were brigaded with the Classis Britannica as transports and supply ships. And in 208 Septimius Severus, the imperial family, a senatorial council, most of the enlarged Praetorian Guard, detachments from several legions and the whole administrative apparatus of the Roman Empire arrived in Britain. And the dark and shifting shadows of palace intrigue came with it.

Based at the legionary fortress at York, Severus planned his campaign in the north. Contemporary historians recorded that part of the reason he came to fight in Britannia was to toughen up his sons, Caracalla and Geta, and to remove them from the fevered and unhealthy atmosphere of Rome. Probably because he did not trust him, the old Emperor decided to take Caracalla with him on campaign – where he could keep a wary eye on him. Severus' judgement turned out to be sound. Geta was set in charge of the province (what happened to Alfenus Senecio is not recorded) so that he could gain experience of government. The Empress, Julia Domna, was also at the fortress in York. Having regained her influence at court, she was to continue to play a motive role in imperial politics for the following two reigns.

When the huge Roman army rumbled northward, most of them marching up Dere Street, some on transports, all of them supplied and shadowed by the fleet, the kings of the Maeatae and the Caledonii will have shuddered. Severus' sprawling strike force was strung out on the metalled road for at least 8 kilometres, well screened by cavalry, the eagles flashing in the summer sun, the menacing thud of marching feet and rattling carts audible for miles. The army was so huge that it took four days to cover the 60 kilometres between Newstead and Inveresk on the Forth. When the *mensores* were pegging out the ramparts of the next camp, soldiers had only just passed through the gates of the one before. As they halted each afternoon, enormous temporary camps were dug, the largest at 165 acres. Thousands of cooking fires will have lit the night sky. Scouts no doubt reported back and the native kings sent envoys to offer peace. The Emperor brushed them aside, and the might of Rome swept on into Scotland.

At Carpow, on the southern shore of the upper Tay estuary, probably in the territory of the friendly Venicones, Severus' legions built a base. It could be supplied and reinforced by sea, and it looked west into the glens of the Maeatae; Strathearn, Strathtay and Glenalmond all lay within marching distance. Across the estuary the fertile fields of the Carse of Gowrie and Strathmore to the north may also have been readily reached. A coin minted in 208 shows troops crossing a bridge, and the historian Herodian had heard of plans made by Severus' commanders which anticipated water barriers to the advance. Perhaps the Tay was crossed by a bridge of pontoons from Carpow.

HILLMEN AND PLOUGHMEN

The archaeologist and historian Walter Elliot has walked much of the length of the great north road known as Dere Street (its name derives from the Anglian kingdom of Deira in Yorkshire, where it begins) and he has come to see it as more than a road. It strikes boldly north through Redesdale and up into the watershed ridge of the Cheviot ranges. It is difficult territory, full of steep inclines, and hard work for not only marching men but also oxen and horses. The logical route would have been the coast road, the line of what is now called the Devil's Causeway, which runs from Corbridge to Berwick-upon-Tweed and north into Berwickshire. Columns on this road could have been supplied by sea, whereas those taking the route of Dere Street through the hills needed to take everything with them and sweat as they carried it. Walter Elliot's years of study of the hill road has turned up a long string of fortlets, forts and temporary camps. There are the outlines of 38 fortlets placed at intervals along the road, about one to two kilometres apart. Each has a four-post watchtower, or signal station, on the nearest high place. And all had a clear line of sight to the west and visual contact with the fortlets immediately to the north or to the south. According to Elliot, this arrangement has all the lineaments of a limes or frontier road system of the sort found in Germany, or indeed on the Gask Ridge in Perthshire and the Stanegate road that predated Hadrian's Wall. Is Dere Street a frontier that mirrors an existing divide between native kindreds? The Votadini were ploughmen of the Tweed Basin and the Lothians, and they and their cousin-kindred of the Venicones in Fife were almost certainly allies of Rome and suppliers of corn for their armies. And the hillmen to the west, the Selgovae, were almost certainly the enemies of Rome. It is tempting to read history backwards and see boundaries running from east to west, like Hadrian's Wall. But perhaps this one ran south to north.

In any event no pitched battles or decisive victories were recorded for the great army. Archaeologists believe that they penetrated far to the north, to the Moray coastlands, maybe as far as Agricola, but it seems that the Maeatae and the Caledonii would not be drawn into a set-piece. They probably scorched the earth and forced Severus and Caracalla to rely completely on their fleet. In turn that shortened any campaigning season. Instead of glory in battle, the emphasis may have to have been on great engineering projects – like a bridge across the Tay – how the Roman army could tame the landscape, and its inhabitants, with technology. A treaty appears to have been made and territory ceded. In 210 more coins were struck and victory in Britain was celebrated.

PALATINE PALACE

The English word 'palace' derives from the name of the hill in Rome where the emperors had theirs. Originally the location of Augustus' house, it developed quickly into a large imperial compound. Domitian greatly enlarged the Palatine and by the time Septimius Severus became emperor, he was forced to have a platform built on the flanks of the hill and his residence plonked on top. To hide it, Septimius' architects built an ornamental screen which came to be known as the Septizonium. On another platform, this time on the north-western side, Elagabalus had his temple to the Syrian sun-god erected. The Palatine was not defended by walls but closely patrolled by the fearsome Praetorians. And it was handy for the Circus Maximus, the arena used for chariot racing. There was a passageway from the palace leading directly to the imperial box.

The treaties held for a year. In the summer of 211 the kings of the Maeatae and the Caledonii mustered their warriors once more and attacked the Roman garrisons. Severus was too ill to lead the legions north, and Caracalla went in his place. This time the strategy was brutally single-minded, nothing less than the annihilation of the warbands and the society which sustained them. But bloodshed seems to have been prevented by a single death. In the fortress at York, Septimius Severus died and Caracalla seems to have broken off his campaign to turn his immediate attention to the succession. In addition to paying the army, the old Emperor had exhorted his sons to act together. But his judgement of Caracalla was good. Seeing his chance with the army under his command on Tayside, he tried to persuade his senior staff to use their men to acclaim him as sole emperor. They would not, and Caracalla was forced to hurry south to York, or possibly London, to confer with his brother, Geta, and his mother, Julia Domna. There might be other claimants from outside the imperial family and it was best to present a united front, for the moment. Severus had intended his sons to succeed him as joint emperors and that was the legal position. At Carpow, detachments of the II Augusta were left, probably a significant presence. They were certainly still on the Tay in 212. An undignified retreat, a complete abandonment of the war in the north, would have made Caracalla look weak.

By 212 he looked strong. Having disposed of his brother, Caracalla reigned as sole emperor and he quickly set about reorganising Britannia. In order to reduce the risk of governors making an attempt on the throne with the backing of the entire garrison of three legions, the province was divided in two. Because it lay further from Rome, the north was renamed Britannia Inferior, or Lower Britain. It included the VI Legion at York and probably the garrison of the Wall. Britannia Superior, or Upper Britain, comprised the south and the legions based at Chester and Caerleon.

Caracalla strengthened the frontier. The fabric of the Wall itself was altered slightly: some turrets in the central sector were abandoned, the curtain repaired, and new, grander bridges crossed the North Tyne at Chesters and the Irthing at Willowford. At milecastles the double gateways to the north had probably been little used by carts and horsemen and they were blocked up and replaced by small postern gates. Elsewehere many forts saw refurbishment and even some new building.

The most striking aspect of Caracalla's frontier strategy could be seen forward of the Wall. In the west, two outpost forts were reinforced. Netherby, in the Esk Valley north of Carlisle, was known as Castra Exploratorum, the Fort of the Scouts. And it seems that the new emphasis was on patrolling and intelligence gathering. At Bewcastle, north of the Wall at Birdoswald, the fort was essentially better adapted to suit its site. Now it can only be reached by a single-track road and feels as though it stands in the middle of nowhere, with grey and dun-coloured moorland stretching away to the Bewcastle Fells. But in fact the fort lay astride a well-ridden route taken by raiders for millennia. In the sixteenth century Elizabeth I's government used Roman stone to rebuild what amounted to a small, squat castle to hold a troop of light cavalry. Their purpose was to police the hill trails followed by reivers from Liddesdale down into the Irthing Valley. The Romans probably built Bewcastle with a similar purpose in mind.

In the east, the fort at Bremenium, now High Rochester, commanded Dere Street as it climbed up towards the watershed at the Carter Bar. The reconstructed walls of the fort and three of the original gateways can be seen from considerable distances by those travelling along the line of the Roman road. Between it and the Wall, the fort at Habitancum, now Risingham, was really formidable. A milliary cohort of 1,000 mixed cavalry and infantry was based there along with a unit of scouts and a detachment of spearmen from Raetia, modern Switzerland. The fort is too small to accommodate all of these soldiers, even allowing for below-strength numbers, and it seems likely that some were either outposted elsewhere or that patrolling was constant and undertaken in force, or both. Traces of third-century Roman activity have been found at Jedburgh and at Tweedmouth, south of Berwick.

Caracalla's strategy worked. The evacuation of Scotland and the thickening of the frontier zone discouraged incursion, and for seventy years the Wall held firm. But successful Roman retrenchment would have been seen differently by the bards of the Maeatae, the Caledonii and the Selgovae. The great Empire had been driven back, the turf wall overrun, and even though they had the effrontery to patrol, the Roman scouts rode through a hostile land. Most of them cowered behind their Wall!

In the reign of Caracalla it became an even more meaningful divide. In 212 he proclaimed that all free men who lived within the bounds of the Empire would become citizens of Rome. *Cives* had real legal standing, rights which could offer protection and redress. If the miserable *Brittunculi* of Vindolanda lived on the right side of the Wall, they were now as Roman as the senators who strolled around the Forum. What this meant in practice is of course another matter, and social class and economic clout will have continued to outweigh all other considerations.

Caracalla was murdered in 217 by one of his bodyguards, evidently a man with a personal grievance to settle, and was succeeded by another African emperor, Macrinus, but he managed only a year. The

---

ROMAN AFRICA

Money brings power and, by the end of the second century, the economy of Roman North Africa was booming. Septimius Severus was the first – but by no means the last – African to come to great prominence in the Empire. The old Carthaginian empire had drawn its wealth from the fertile fields of what is now modern Tunisia and the green coastal strips to both east and west. Rainfall was regular and irrigation opened up new areas for the cultivation of olives and corn. Only Egypt produced more of the latter. The cities of North Africa prospered, and at El Djem stands a huge amphitheatre. Throughout the entire Empire only the Colosseum in Rome was larger. All of this abundance was protected by geography. In the Atlas Mountains and the Sahara Desert to the south, relatively few people lived and therefore the cost of defending the provincial frontier was nothing like as heavy as in Britain.

---

army intervened once more and, loyal to the family of Septimius Severus, the Syrian legions backed Elagabalus. He was only fourteen years old and the hereditary high priest of a local sun-god cult at Emesa. His unlikely promotion to the purple is explained by the shadowy machinations of the old Empress, Julia Domna. Before her marriage, she had been a Syrian princess, and Elagabalus was the son of her great-niece, and almost certainly her puppet.

The cult of Emesa, complete with its sacred black stone, was uplifted and relocated to a temple on the Palatine Hill in Rome. While Elagabalus celebrated strange and sexually exotic rituals in the worship of the sun-god, the Senate were at first puzzled, then embarrassed at the antics of the young Emperor, and finally hostile. He was insisting that his Syrian god be installed as the supreme god of the Empire. And then everyone would have to cavort around like Elagabalus. Symbolic marriages, divorces, remarriages and adoptions followed in rapid sequence, and the young Emperor was finally murdered in 222 and replaced by Severus Alexander. Although he lasted a good deal longer, until his assassination in 235, both his and succeeding emperors' total dependence on the support of the army began a damaging cycle. Between the death of Alexander and the end of the third century, there were fifteen emperors and many more candidates supported by various legions. The lowest point came in 260 when the Emperor Valerian was defeated and captured by the Persian king, Shapur I. Miserable and humiliated, he died a prisoner.

Insulated and remote, Britannia appeared to be little affected by the seething convulsions of imperial intrigue and infighting. The Wall garrison had been increased by a third, from just under 9,000 men in the reign of Hadrian to 12,000 under Caracalla. And the units began to settle, with few changes and almost certainly more and more local recruitment. After Septimius Severus permitted soldiers to marry, there seems to have been an attempt to house them differently inside the forts. Instead of the old barrack blocks with communal sleeping quarters for each platoon, or *contubernium*, new chalet-style rooms were built. At Vindolanda, Wallsend, Great Chesters, Risingham and High Rochester, this sort of accommodation has been detected, while at Housesteads the earth rampart backing onto the fort's walls was removed and new buildings erected.

The *vici*, the civil settlements, probably also expanded as a result of Severus' edict, and archaeologists see the third century as a period of some vigour along the Wall. But there appears to have been very little fighting. The continuing turmoil in Rome may have persuaded governors of Lower Britain to buy off the northern kings with more bribery.

Against a background of some security, Carlisle began to develop as an urban centre. Luguvalium, a name incorporating the Celtic god, Lugh, was little more than a fort built by Petilius Cerialis during his campaign of 71 to 74 in the north. After the establishment of the frontier along the line of the Wall, and the fort across the Eden at Stanwix was built, Carlisle slowly began to develop. Its site was attractive. Cerialis had had the fort built on the promontory where the castle now stands, and it was bounded on three sides by rivers and marshy ground but accessible from the south, up a gentle slope. That was where the *vicus* first developed, and keyhole archaeology has found early wooden buildings around the area of Blackfriars Street.

By the middle of the third century Carlisle had grown sufficiently to merit promotion. Named as the Civitas Carvetiorum, it became the principal urban centre in the lands of the Carvetii, the Deer People, what appears to have been the Eden Valley, North Cumbria and the lower Irthing Valley. Literally meaning a city-state, a *civitas* was run by the *ordo*, a council of *decuriones*, men of property drawn from the region as well as the town: more a county council than a town council. At full complement, the *ordo* of a *civitas* had 100 members with property over a certain value but in a relatively less wealthy part of Britannia; not all owned grand houses in Carlisle. Many probably had estates in the landward area.

Based on the ancestral lands of the Carvetii, the *civitas* was probably run by decurions who were mostly native aristocrats that had become partly Romanised, or at least wished to participate in Roman-style local government. They were expected to endow civic projects personally, just as Roman aristocrats were in the habit of doing, and also they probably paid a fee for the privilege of being a decurion. Two senior and two junior magistrates were elected to administer justice, oversee local tax-gathering and manage civic amenities such as the water supply, planning and road-building.

Most towns in Roman Britain had an engineered water supply, and Carlisle's must have been solidly built. As late as 685, it was still working. After the ambitious Northumbrian kings had brought the western end of the Wall and Galloway into their power in the seventh century, they appointed reeves to administer their growing royal estates. Carlisle was theirs, and when St Cuthbert came to visit, with the Northumbrian queen, in 685, Bede recorded remarkable Roman survival:

> Cuthbert, leaning on his staff, was listening to Wagga the Reeve of Carlisle explaining to the Queen the Roman wall of the city . . . the citizens conducted him around the city walls to see a remarkable Roman fountain that was built into them.

Wagga and his people (still called *citizens* by Bede) must have maintained whatever aqueduct or pumping or piping systems continued to bring water to this fountain. The walls were intact, and they enclosed a Roman street grid which was still being adhered to. Some time after 698 when a church dedicated to St Cuthbert was built in the city, the east–west alignment was altered so that it fronted onto a Roman street. Much later, a large arched stone building was still standing when the twelfth-century historian William of Malmesbury described its inscription to Mars and Venus.

Archaeologists have found grand relics under modern Carlisle. Stone columns and capitals are kept on display at Tullie House Museum, and hypocaust flooring used under the houses of wealthy citizens has been uncovered. They also displayed their wealth in death.

Since it was illegal to bury the dead inside the walls of Roman towns, the habit was to set up tombs by the roadside. Not only do these allow the line of the roads out of Carlisle to be plotted, but two in particular offer valuable information. A Greek merchant, probably with a specialised trade and who followed the Roman army as a supplier, died in the town. His wife, Septima, left a valedictory verse:

> To the spirits of the departed
> Flavius Antigonus Papias
> a citizen of Greece, lived
> 60 years more or less, and
> gave back to the Fates his
> soul lent for that time,
> Septima Do . . . set this up.

Later an elaborate tombstone with a sculpture of the deceased was found by the west road passing through Denton Holme. Wearing rich and expensive drapery, the lady sits on a high-backed armchair holding a circular fan and with a pet bird on her lap. A child stands beside her. It is a confident, stylish memorial to a luxurious way of life not seen again in Carlisle until the twentieth century.

It has been argued – convincingly – that Christianity was the only substantial historical legacy of the Roman occupation of southern Britain. One of our greatest saints almost certainly had his origins in the countryside around Hadrian's Wall and the *civitas* of Carlisle and its early Christian community. St Patrick was born in Britannia, not Ireland, and in his writings he left several tantalising snippets of information about himself and his early life. These have been brilliantly analysed by Professor Charles Thomas.

All of the episodes in Patrick's young life point to origins in the north-west of Britannia. He was abducted by Irish slavers and sold into captivity in Northern Ireland, becaming a shepherd for six years. When Patrick escaped, he eventually returned to Britannia to train as a priest before finally returning to Ireland to begin his great mission of conversion and thereby leave an indelible mark on history.

Patrick wrote that his father was Calpurnius, a deacon in the church and a decurion in the *ordo* of a *civitas*. He was wealthy enough to have both male and female servants and to own a *villula*, a small estate in the countryside. According to Patrick, it lay near *Vicus Bannavem Taberniae*, a place-name which appears slightly corrupted. *Vicus* is simple enough, a civil settlement outside the walls of a fort. But Calpurnius was also the decurion of a city – and where in Britannia was there a city close to forts with *vici*? If the text is taken to read *Vicus Bannaventa Berniae*, then the location comes slowly into focus. Banna is the distinctive name for the Wall fort at Birdoswald, and *venta* is a market, the market held at the *vicus*. So – was Calpurnius' small estate near Birdoswald? The last element in the puzzle of the place-name is *Berniae*, and that appears to be a transliteration of an Old Welsh word *bern* for a defile or a narrow pass. Near Birdoswald, there are several candidates. Perhaps the river-cliff at Greenhead, perhaps the steep banks of the burn at Poltross? In any event, the fort, and by extension the *villula*, are near Carlisle, the city where Calpurnius may have been a decurion.

Patrick also wrote that his grandfather, Potitus, was an ordained priest. This implies an organised church with a hierarchy (able to conduct ordinations) around 360, and this in turn strongly suggests links with a developed town. All of the elements seem to fit. Charles Thomas is certain that Patrick was born and raised in Carlisle and the countryside through which Hadrian's Wall runs. Perhaps the conversion of Ireland ought to be seen as part of the Wall's legacy.

Carlisle's new status as a *civitas* was first mentioned during the reign of the breakaway emperor, Postumus. After the shocking affront of Valerian's capture in the east, rebellions at the opposite end of the Empire saw the provinces of Spain, Gaul, Germany and Britain form what was known as the Gallic Empire. Under Postumus, it lasted little more than a decade before the Empire was put back together again by the energetic Aurelian. Britain appears to have been unaffected by these continental convulsions. But reform was in the air. After his accession in 285, Diocletian began the process of dividing the Empire in four. There were to be two senior emperors, the *Augusti*, including himself, and two junior figures, the *Caesares*. As Roman Europe settled down into this new pattern of power, Britain rebelled.

ZENOBIA

When the antiquary William Stukely first gazed upon Housesteads
Fort in 1775, he proclaimed it *the Tadmor of Britain*: a reference
which escapes most modern readers. Stukely used it as a comparison with the recent discovery of the magnificent city of Palmyra in
the Syrian desert. By 271 the Empire of this remarkable place had all
but eclipsed Rome in the east. Under their warrior-empress, Zenobia, the Palmyrenes had conquered Egypt, Arabia, Palestine, Syria,
Mesopotamia and much of Asia Minor. The *Historia Augusta* was
dazzled: . . . *in the manner of a Roman emperor, she came forth to
public assemblies, wearing a helmet and girt with a purple fillet . . .
Her face was dark . . . her eyes were black and powerful . . . her
spirit divinely great, her beauty incredible.* The oasis city of Palmyra
had ingathered fabulous wealth as a consequence of its position
astride several long-distance trade-routes from the east to the cities
of the Syrian coast. Zenobia's amazing empire lasted only a year.
The Emperor Aurelian defeated the Palmyrenes in three bloody
battles and successfully besieged the city. Caught while fleeing to
Persia, Zenobia was brought to Rome and rode a camel in Aurelian's triumph. Instead of the dark horrors of the Mamertine
Prison, she retired to a villa near the city – and no doubt thought
often on her year as Empress of the East.

The English Channel had become badly infested by pirates and
barbarian raiders. Having been successful against them, the admiral of
the Classis Britannica, Carausius, was thought to have done rather too
well out of the proceeds of captured booty. Diocletian's co-emperor,
Maximian, summarily condemned Carausius to death. With nothing
to lose, the admiral declared himself Emperor of Britain. Not as
overblown as it sounds, for the south of the main island had been
redivided into four provinces (from the Wall southwards, these were
Britannia Secunda, Flavia Caesariensis, Maxima Caesariensis in the
south-east and Britannia Prima in the south-west); Carausius also
controlled parts of northern Gaul. In 293 Maximian's junior imperial
partner, Constantius Chlorus, drove Carausius out of Gaul and,
crucially, retook the base of the Classis Britannica at Boulogne. A
secondary *coup d'état* then occurred when Carausius was assassinated

by the unlikely figure of his Financial Secretary, Allectus. Archaeologists have discovered the remains of an imperial palace he had time to
build in London before a Roman army invaded Britain. At a battle
near Silchester, Allectus was killed, and the short-lived British Empire
died with him.

Discord and weakness in Rome once again stirred predatory
instincts in the north. After four generations of peace, of generous
subsidies, of basking in ancient glories – what their kings probably
saw as a victory against the vast army of Severus and his son – the
Maeatae and the Caledonii once more talked of war and of great raids
in the south. In 296 warbands crossed the Wall, or sailed around it,
and they were recorded riding far to the south, even attacking the
legionary fortress at Chester. They must have been numerous, well
organised and confident. And they were given a new name. Writing of
the victories of Constantius Chlorus, a historian noted a fearsome
people he called the Picts.

Picti, meaning 'the painted or tattooed people', was probably a
soldiers' nickname, perhaps coined in 296 by those garrisons on
Hadrian's Wall who had not seen the northern warbands before. It
stands in a tradition of *noms de guerre* which called the *Saxons* after a
short-bladed knife they carried, the *Franks*, whose name means 'the
wreckers', or the *Vikings* who did exactly that, dodged in and out of
creeks, or *viks*.

The nickname stuck and almost certainly applied to a federation of
Maeatae, Caledonii, a people called the Verturiones (probably from
Strathearn and Menteith) and other groups. These came to include the
Scots from the Argyll coastlands and a people called the Atecotti. This
name translates simply as 'the Old Peoples' and they may have originated
from the Hebrides. St Jerome believed the Atecotti to be aboriginal
savages and claims to have witnessed them practicing cannibalism.

When the first raiders broke through into Britannia, they encountered much less resistance than in former times. By the beginning of the
fourth century the Roman army had reorganised. Gone were the old
distinctions between legions and auxiliaries. Now the frontier garrison
was known as the *limitanei*, and under imperial command was a
mobile field army called the *comitatenses*. Control over the men on the
Wall was removed from the Governor of Britannia and given to a
soldier known as the *Dux Britanniarum*, the Duke of the Britains
(meaning all four provinces).

The accent was firmly on defence in Britain, and while strong archaeological evidence found at Cramond and Carpow suggests that Constantius led an expedition to Scotland to quieten the Picts in 306, that was the exception. Numbers seem also to have declined markedly; units with the names of the old legions attached only had 1,000 or so, compared with 4,800 or 5,000, and cavalry troops were 150 rather than 460 or 500. And soldiers were conscripts, not volunteers, with the sons of veterans now being compelled to join the army. The decline was reflected in the occasional fraud, when commanders continued to claim dead men's pay by failing to report casualties in their units. On paper the Roman army sounded a great deal more formidable than it was in the field.

One solution was the co-option of mercenaries, and by the fourth century these were mainly German warriors. Some estimates put the proportion at a quarter of the total strength in the western Empire. When Constantius returned to York in 306, like Severus a century before, he died and was immediately succeeded by his son. Diocletian's power-sharing arrangement remained in force, but when Constantine was proclaimed at the legionary fortress, he needed solid support from his father's army, and prominent was a German mercenary king, Crocus. He commanded a band of Alemanni, men who had presumably fought against the Picts in Scotland.

Along the Wall repairs and refurbishment took place at the beginning of the fourth century. Work is recorded at both Birdoswald and Housesteads forts, and a new garrison arrived at South Shields. The *Numerus Barcariorum Tigrisensium*, or the Tigris Bargemen, originated in modern Iraq, but by the time they reached the mouth of the Tyne, they may have lost that specific function. But they probably still recruited in the Middle East because they gave the fort a new name. It was called *Arbeia*, the fort of the Arabs.

It took Constantine the Great until 324 to establish himself as sole emperor and his long reign produced two significant shifts of policy: the transfer of the focus of the Empire from Italy and Rome to the east and Constantinople, and the official adoption of Christianity as the state religion. The new religion had probably been imported into Britain by soldiers, and in the third century martyrs were killed at St Albans and at Caerleon. The beautiful church plate found at Water Newton was made in the early fourth century and Christian-inspired mosaics at the villas at Hinton St Mary and Frampton a little later.

These finds were made in the south, but on the Wall the signs of the new faith are sparse and of uncertain date. Chapel-like buildings have been identified at Vindolanda and Housesteads, but they were probably built after the end of Roman Britain.

FORGERIES

Clay moulds for making counterfeit Roman coins have been found both north and south of the Wall. This shady trade was made possible by the continuing debasement of the currency of the Empire. By the middle of the third century the imperial budget was running at 225 million denarii per annum and hundreds of millions of coins were being struck to feed it. There was not enough silver in the Empire to make what was needed and consequently coins were primarily minted from base metals. The Emperor Diocletian attempted to check the runaway inflation by issuing an Edict on Prices in 301. It listed cereals, beer, meat and other commodities and attached standard measures and prices to each, as well as the rates of pay for different sorts of worker. Like all attempts at a prices-and-incomes policy, it failed immediately. The market corrected the situation with characteristic crudeness. Exchange was based on bullion, silver or gold, no matter what form it came in. The Roman Empire ultimately fell because it ceased to produce sound money and became less and less able to pay for itself.

For the first half of the fourth century, the province appears to have been calm and prosperous. No raiding from the north is recorded for almost forty years after Constantine's accession at York. But in 342 the long period of peace was broken. The Emperor Constans arrived with detachments of the field army and immediately moved up to the Wall. It seems that Pictish warbands, perhaps in concert with their Scots allies, had attacked the outpost forts at High Rochester, Risingham and Bewcastle. All three were burned. Constans encouraged the *areani*, a new name for the scouts formerly called *exploratores*, to take a more actively defensive role, and the most northerly fort, at High Rochester, appears to have been abandoned. A treaty, and probably subsidies, were accepted by the northern kings.

By 360 these arrangements no longer held. The Pictish federation mustered and sent its warbands to raid an area north of the Wall, and perhaps behind it. Four regiments from the field army (including a unit of Batavians) in Europe were sent by the Emperor Julian to deal with the emergency. No details of the campaign have survived, but it was certainly not decisive. More attacks from the Picts, the Scots, the Atecotti – and a new group of barbarian raiders, the Saxons, came in in 365. Serious though they seem to have been, these assaults on Britain were only a prelude.

In 367 the province suffered as it had never done before – even during the rebellion of Boudicca. In a concerted series of incursions, coming from several directions, the Picts, the Scots, the Atecotti, the Franks and the Saxons descended on Britannia. Known as the *Conspiratio Barbarica*, the Barbarian Conspiracy, it saw the Pictish army pour through the Wall, the Scots and probably the Atecotti invade from the west, across the Irish Sea and the Solway, and the Franks and the Saxons attack the coasts of Gaul and perhaps the south of England. A pre-arranged plan was being put into action. Having communicated well in advance, raised the necessary forces, been in possession of good military intelligence, and worked out a timetable for invasion, the barbarian kings swept Britannia's defences aside and tore into the province. For two years they burned, looted and killed without check and over a wide area. It was a catastrophe, and a hammer-blow to an ever-weakening western Empire.

In the north there had been betrayal and collusion. The Pictish kings had bribed the Roman *areani*, the scouts operating forward of the Wall, to report nothing of the preparations for war, and probably to supply crucial intelligence on the state of the defences and troop dispositions. It seems likely that the great conspiracy was co-ordinated and planned in Pictland, an operation of considerable sophistication which modifies the usual image of screaming hordes, for once allowing that savagery could be accompanied by brains.

Once the Pictish army had broken through the Wall (they would not necessarily need the co-operation of the *areani* to sail around it), they sought out units probably deployed on the east coast, what was known as the Saxon Shore, and defeated them and killed their commander, Nectaridus. Then they turned on the *Dux Britanniarum*, Fullofaudes, and either killed or neutralised him. It was a triumph, a sweeping and comprehensive victory – complete mastery of the province. All the riches of Britannia, the villas and the prosperous towns, lay at the mercy of the fearsome barbarians.

Roman reaction was at first hesitant. The Frankish and Saxon attacks on the coast of Gaul were probably partly designed as a screen to prevent the continental field army from reaching Britain, and the two-year delay might simply be explained by difficulties in reaching the Channel. But by 369 a capable and experienced soldier arrived at last. Theodosius brought four regiments of the field army and his first action was to proclaim an amnesty for deserters (there had been many) from the *limitanei* and to swell his ranks with their numbers. Never intent on invasion, only interested in raiding, the barbarian army had broken down into small warbands. Theodosius was able to mop them up or chase them out of the province and restore some sort of order. Longer-term security depended on shoring up the northern frontier and, as soon as the south seemed more settled, Theodosius and his men set out for the Wall.

Because of the treachery of the *areani*, a new approach was needed. Two years before, in the North African provinces, Theodosius had dealt with the incursions of Berber tribesmen by creating alliances with buffer kingdoms between them and Roman territory. It looks as though he did something similar beyond the Wall.

The Picts, the Scots and the Atecotti all originated beyond the Firth of Forth and the Clyde Valley. Culturally distinct from the kingdoms between the two Walls, the Picts spoke a language which survives only in tiny scraps and elements of place-names. No one can now utter a sentence in Pictish, but philologists have deciphered enough to show that, while it formed part of the P-Celtic family of languages, it was different from the Old Welsh or Brittonic dialects spoken in the south of Scotland. The Scots talked to each other in Q-Celtic, the ancestor of modern Gaelic, and the Atecotti may have lived to the north of them, perhaps in the Hebrides. It is therefore likely that the Damnonii of the Clyde and the Votadini of the Lothians and the Tweed basin had more in common with the peoples who lived south of Hadrian's Wall than those beyond the Antonine.

The garrison of the Wall had probably relied on native recruitment for many generations. As early as *c.* 150 the tombstone of a Brigantian who fought in the Roman army was set up on the Antonine Wall. With all of this background in mind, it seems that Theodosius did indeed set up buffer kingdoms beyond Hadrian's Wall. To replace the duplicitous *areani* and the dangerously exposed outpost forts, the Britons would have to resist the ferocious Picts, and prevent them from overrunning their own territory in so doing.

The evidence for this change of policy is slight but very intriguing. The earliest genealogies, the kinglists, for the Votadini show strikingly exceptional names around the end of the fourth century. Amongst all of the early and clearly Celtic kings, Aetern, Tacit and Patern Pesrut stand out. All they require is the terminal *-us*. *Pesrut* is particularly telling: an Old Welsh epithet which means 'the man with the red cloak'. Was this a native Roman officer, perhaps from the Wall garrison, put in place by Theodosius? Or a native king given a Roman rank? Elsewhere there are more Celticised Roman names. Early rulers of the Damnonii are listed as *Cluim*, or *Clemens*, and *Cinhil*, or *Quintilius*, and in Galloway a powerful king was known as *Annwn Donadd*, or *Antonius Donatus*.

There was nothing unusual in this enlistment of barbarians in the defence of the Empire, it was happening all along the Rhine and Danube frontier. In return for settlement and a grant of land inside the Empire, and no doubt the payment of subsidies, new peoples and their kings pledged loyalty to the Emperor and helped turn back others who threatened from outside. Two further scraps of evidence suggest that this sort of transaction had been concluded by Theodosius for the territories beyond the Wall. On the summit of the Votadinian hillfort on Traprain Law, in East Lothian, a large hoard of late-fourth-century Roman silver was discovered. Much of it had been cut up from cups and bowls and folded over for easier handling and transport. Probably collected from wealthy Romano-British aristocrats, some of it carried Christian images and symbols. In an age when currency had become debased, and with a miniscule content of precious metals, the Traprain hoard looks like bullion. It may represent the fruits of a successful raid, but a much more likely explanation is that it was a payment, a Roman subsidy for an ally prepared to fight in defence of the Empire.

Theodosius may have been the creator of a fifth province in Britain. Named after the Emperor Valentinian, its location is uncertain – but what would have been the purpose of carving out yet another province from the four which already existed? *Valentia* was probably the new Roman name for southern Scotland, the territory between the two Walls controlled by the kingdoms of the Damnonii and the Votadini, and ruled by the likes of Cluim/Clemens and Paternus Pesrut. Its elevation was a way of bringing the northern allies inside the Empire, conferring *romanitas* (and perhaps their names) on them, and also incidentally celebrating a notable victory over the barbarians.

KING'S RANSOM

In a field near Kelso in the Scottish Borders hundreds of Roman coins have been found. Often ploughed, the King's Haugh reveals more each winter through careful metal detection. The coins seem to be scattered, not part of a hoard. But they do not amount to a King's ransom. Most are from the fourth century and are not silver-based, or gold, but small radiates struck from bronze. Far from being treasure, they are the small change of a money economy, only worth anything as a means of exchange. But Kelso is more than 70 kilometres north of Hadrian's Wall, in the centre of the ancient territory of the Votadini. Was the Tweed Valley briefly inside the bounds of the Empire, in the province of Valentia? Many of the bronze radiates come from the period after AD 369 and Theodosius' reorganisation of the north. The heaviest concentration is from the House of Valentinian (364–378) and there are more from the reigns of Arcadius and Honorius, shading into the fifth century. The find spot is very suggestive. At the confluence of the Teviot and the Tweed, the King's Haugh is commanded by the remarkable, and unexcavated, fortress of Roxburgh Castle. Famous in medieval times, it certainly had a longer history before then.

If the Picts and the Scots were discouraged by these new alliances, they had only to take to their ships to reach the tempting plunder of the south. But, despite their best efforts, they did not bring about the end of Roman Britain. Under pressure from the kingdoms to the east, especially the Huns, the Goths were pressing hard on the European frontier along the Danube. Valens, the eastern Emperor, allowed one group to settle in the province of Moesia, modern Bulgaria. But in 378 they rebelled after some harsh treatment and, at Adrianople, the Gothic army inflicted a crushing defeat and Valens was killed in the fighting. It was a turning moment. After Adrianople the Empire began to shudder and, in the west, to shake itself to pieces.

Meanwhile Britannia appeared to have rallied once Theodosius' measures had been put in place. The Pictish threat persisted, but it was contained by a dynamic new Duke of the Britains. A Spanish officer, known as Magnus Maximus, assembled an army and led it to victory in the north in 382. So successful was the campaign and so warm the glow of its prestige that Maximus was encouraged to make a bid for the Empire. Crossing into Europe, he took Spain and Gaul under his control and he ruled in the west until 388. Brought to battle at Aquileia in northern Italy by the legitimate emperor, Theodosius I (son of the saviour of Britain in 369), Maximus was defeated, captured and executed.

There were many usurpers at the end of the fourth century and their struggles for power weakened the Roman Empire just at the point when external pressures threatened as never before. But Magnus Maximus was remembered in Britain, and indeed his memory still lives. A sixth-century poem in Old Welsh, 'The Dream of Macsen Wledig', recalls his triumphs and it is likely to have been composed by the bards of the kingdoms of southern Scotland, known as *Yr Hen Ogledd*, the Old North; the courts of these kingdoms were the fount of much of the earliest Welsh literature. The survival of 'The Dream of Maximus the General' is perhaps understood by the success against the Picts of a native army raised in the Old North by a competent and

THE NOTITIA DIGNITATUM

Compiled during the fourth century, this fascinating document, loosely translated as 'The Ascertaining of Ranks', had as its primary purpose the setting down of the chain of military command in North Britain (and elsewhere) by listing officers, staffs and the units under their control. At face value it is impressive. Eleven regiments of cavalry and infantry appear to be based in Durham and Yorkshire and three others west of the Pennines, and then the entire garrison of Hadrian's Wall is set down with their forts in the correct geographical order. The overall impression is of continuity; some of the same units appear to have been soldiering on the Wall for almost three centuries. But what appears on paper almost certainly had no more than a nominal existence on the ground – no more than a shadow of ancient power.

ambitious Roman commander. Perhaps some of the warriors of the Damnonii and the Votadini went to Europe with Macsen on his quest for empire, to fulfil his dream.

Theodosius' young son and heir, Honorius, was nominally Emperor after 395, but his armies in the west in reality lay under the command of Stilicho the Vandal. The son of a barbarian soldier, he proved adroit in maintaining the balancing act which imperial government had become. Stilicho withdrew troops from the British garrison to plug gaps and shore up weaknesses in Europe, and it must be significant that the large-scale import of coins into Britain ceased in 402. This was likely cash to pay the army and the imperial administration, and after that date there may have been little left of either.

TUNGRIA NO MORE

Remembered in place names such as Tongeren, Tongerloo and Tongelre in Belgium, the Tungrians had a fearsome reputation and their prowess was instrumental in the conquest of Britannia. Cohorts of Tungrians spent a long time in Britain, and in the Notitia Dignitatum of the late fourth century, they are listed as I Tungrorum Milliaria (1,000 strong) stationed at Housesteads Fort. Four centuries in Britannia, a garrison on both the Antonine and Hadrian's Wall for their entire history, the Tungrians are unlikely to have retained much of a link to Tungria. In fact, if they intermarried with local women, they will have gradually assimilated. Sadly, attempts to trace their ancestral DNA are not likely to be helpful since there is and was a good deal of north-western European DNA already in Britain.

In the winter of 406 nature took a decisive hand. The Rhine froze over and many thousands of barbarians flooded into the Empire. Vandals, Alans and Suebi rampaged into the province of Gaul, looting, killing and causing chaos. Three years later their warbands crossed the Pyrenees into Spain and eventually the Strait of Gibraltar. After 429 the remarkable Vandal kingdom of North Africa came into being.

Britain found itself ever more embroiled in the ferment of imperial ambition. In 406 no fewer than three usurper emperors attempted coups with support from the province. In 407 more troops were withdrawn, and the following year, as if prompted, a series of serious barbarian attacks caused great damage. This time the Romano-British themselves, probably with the help of the kingdoms in the north, rebelled and expelled the representatives of the most recent usurper, Constantine III. Here is a concise account from the historian Zosimus:

> The barbarians across the Rhine attacked everywhere with all their power, and brought the inhabitants of Britain and some of the nations of Gaul to the point of revolting from Roman rule and living on their own, no longer obedient to Roman laws. The Britons took up arms and, braving danger for their own independence, freed their cities from the barbarians threatening them; and all Armorica and the other provinces of Gaul copied the British example and freed themselves in the same way, expelling their Roman governors and establishing their own administration as best they could.

Led by Romano-British aristocrats, backed by the warriors of the Old North and augmented by the Wall garrison (such as it was), the rebellion against the Empire appears to mark an end-point. The conventional signal for the passing of Britannia is usually seen as around 410 when a letter written by the chancery of Honorius advised the cities of the province to look to their own defences. It seems as though they were doing it anyway.

8

After Britannia

Nothing happened. At least, nothing much. Hadrian's Wall was not suddenly deserted, the gates of the forts left swinging in the wind. The money, the pay chests full of coins, stopped coming, and orders from any central Roman authority in Europe dried up. But after the troops were removed by Stilicho and Constantine III, no one else went anywhere. Along the Wall the garrisons, even the old units with fancy names from Syria and Spain, had long since been local, recruited on a hereditary basis, many of the soldiers following their fathers into what had become a family army. Others had been conscripted from the farms and villages round about. If the rank and file was hereditary and local, it is very likely that command was too. Over the last decades of the fourth century, as Roman control slackened all over the western Empire, the individual units probably more resembled the warbands from the north, their loyalty to their leaders outweighing any other. And if that loyalty was reinforced by a long Roman military tradition, perhaps with a set of standards preserved, old weapons and armour still in existence, then it would have been very strong.

In addition to cash and orders, what also came to an end was the wider role of the Wall. If Britannia had seceded from the Empire, then the meaning of the Wall was much diminished. No longer an international frontier, it retained only a regional significance. In essence the Wall garrison had lost its job.

It may well have gained another role. Written Roman records for the beginning of the fifth century in Britain are virtually non-existent. Historians have been forced to turn, often unwillingly, to the genealogies and traditions of the Old Welsh-speaking kingdoms of the North, Yr Hen Ogledd. Their stories survived because they were slowly transmitted to Wales and absorbed, especially in the kingdom of Gwynedd. Shadowy figures can sometimes be glimpsed flitting through the poems and the kinglists, men who may have had their origins in the lands between the two Walls.

Coelius, known as Coel Hen, or Old Cole, by the bards may have been the last Roman-appointed Duke of the Britains, based at the legionary fortress at York. In a bizarre historical memory, he is probably the figure behind the nursery rhyme, Old King Cole. At least eight dynasties list him either as a founder or an early king. The Welsh genealogies are heavily corrupted in places and Coel's wife is named as Stradwawl, which translates as 'Wall Road', and his daughter was Gwawl, or 'The Wall'. These sound like a confusion of areas of command with members of a family. The genealogies were transcribed by Welshmen distant in both time and space from the events after the end of Roman Britain. Coel's name lent credibility, his association with the power and legitimacy of the Empire added to the prestige of those dynasties who claimed him as an ancestor.

If he was indeed the last Duke of the Britains, then the commanders of Wall forts may have owed him allegiance. But, for that to be possible, evidence of continuity after the end of the province is needed. At Birdoswald just such evidence has been uncovered. After 395 a large timber building was erected on the foundations of the granaries near the west gate of the fort. It was then replaced by an even larger version. Archaeologists have been able to visualise a tall timber hall with a steep-pitched thatch roof and a porch-style door along one of the long sides. There was a hearth at one end, and finds have suggested that people of substance sat around it as the fire blazed, perhaps the commander of the fort of Banna and his captains. A good literary/historical analogy is the sort of hall immortalised in the great epic poem *Beowulf*. The seat of a king or a chieftain's power, it was where he and his warriors ate, talked, drank, celebrated, planned and governed the land around. *Beowulf* gives a pungent impression of what these halls were like, King Hrothgar's in particular, and here is part of Seamus Heaney's recent translation:

> . . . So his mind turned
> to hall-building: he handed down orders
> for men to work on a great mead-hall
> meant to be a wonder of the world for ever;
> it would be his throne-room and there he would dispense
> his God-given goods to young and old –

but not the common land or peoples' lives.
Far and wide through the world, I have heard,
orders for work to adorn that wallstead
were sent to many peoples. And soon it stood there,
finished and ready, in full view,
the hall of halls. Heorot was the name
he had settled on it, whose utterance was law.
Nor did he renege, but doled out rings
and torques at the table. The hall towered,
its gables wide and high.

The Roman masonry of the west gate lay immediately beside the great hall and, despite the stark differences in building styles, the continued passage of people, horses and carts under its arches underlined the legitimacy of whoever's utterance was law. There is more than a metaphor in this juxtaposition. A native structure built inside

---

ECHOES OF ROME

Until the early 1970s those who wished to matriculate at one of the four ancient Scottish universities required an Attestation of Fitness. Nothing to do with corporeal health, it was a document issued from Kinburn House in St Andrews which certified that applicants possessed O-Grade passes in Mathematics and Latin. Without it, not even the most brilliant could pass through the portals of Aberdeen, Edinburgh, Glasgow or St Andrews. When the certificate was abandoned, the teaching of Latin in schools suffered a steep decline. But in 2007 the rot appears to have stopped. Under the aegis of Project Iris, a revival programme run by Lorna Robinson, Latin is making a comeback. Twenty primary schools in London, and more in Oxfordshire, are introducing lessons in Latin. A Latin grammar was a recent bestseller. The revival will help with an understanding not only of Rome and its inheritors but also of language in general. And the latter can be profound precisely because Latin is a dead language. Its structure can be explored because none of that tedious business of learning how to ask where the bus station is or ordering lunch is involved. Perhaps once again intellectual fitness will be attested by a knowledge of Latin.

the rectilinear streets and walls of a Roman fort by men who probably spoke Old Welsh but regarded themselves as part of the armies of the Empire. Clearly life on the Wall had been changing long before the end of the province and the break with Rome.

The gifts given by kings like Hrothgar became even more important after the decade from 420 to 430. Around that time coinage ceased to circulate, and mass-produced pottery, whose production depended on a cash economy, also disappeared from the archaeological record. Along the central sector of the Wall, where the garrison could only be maintained by Rome or some other central authority with an interest in defending such a long frontier, the bustle and business of soldiering melted away quickly. At Housesteads the already diminished units were replaced by perhaps twenty or at most thirty people farming the field system beyond the walls, or tending their beasts inside the precinct. Nature began to reclaim the Wall, and wind-bent trees grew once more along the Whin Sill. Where the military zone had been cleared, scrub took root in the sheltered places, the ditches and in the Vallum, and grass crept over the metalled roads and streets. As each summer passed and leaves blew around the deserted milecastles and turrets, it looked less and less likely that Rome would return. Despite the victories of the consul, Aetius, and Syagrius in Gaul, barbarian kings ruled where once the Emperor's writ had run. Rome was fading. From his vantage point in Constantinople, the sixth-century writer Procopius observed:

> the Romans were never able to recover Britain, but from that time it remained on its own, under tyrants.

By *tyrants* he meant local kings, or usurpers of the imperial power.

By Procopius' time, the Celtic kingdoms of southern Scotland and northern England had formed and begun to flex their ancient power. In the west Rheged expanded around the shores of the Solway. Galloway, Dumfriesshire, Cumbria and perhaps the lands around Morecambe Bay were all ruled by its most famous king, Urien. Urien's name probably derives from *Urbgen*, which meant 'born in the city', probably the old *civitas* of Carlisle, what became the hinge of his kingdom. To the north the Damnonii developed into Strathclyde, with its capital place at the old fortress of Altclut, the Rock of the Clyde, at Dumbarton, which means the Fort of the British. And in the east the Votadini had become the Gododdin.

DUX BELLORUM

Fragments of a lost *North British Chronicle*, parts of it compiled by a monk called Nennius in the eighth century, spoke of a post-Roman *Dux Bellorum*, a War Leader. His name was Arthur, and the Nennius text recounts campaigns fought between the Christian British and pagan enemies. These may have been both Germanic and Pictish. Thirteen battles are listed, and toponymic research shows that nine were fought at places which lie between the Roman walls. Did Arthur lead the warbands of the vigorous British kingdoms of southern Scotland, the men of the Old North charged by Theodosius with the protection of the province of Britannia? Geography encourages this thought. History as well as tradition counts Arthur as a cavalry warrior, and his base of operations may have been at what is now known as Roxburgh Castle. The Old Welsh name was Marchidun, the Cavalry Fort.

By a traditional date of 547, a band of Germanic pirates had established themselves at the stronghold of Bamburgh on the Northumbrian coast. Led by a series of ambitious and dynamic kings, they carved out Bernicia, the territory at the eastern end of the Wall. There is a persistent tradition that the royal family and its warband occupied Arbeia, the fort at South Shields. Archaeologists confirmed the gist of this when they came upon traces of work done on the ditches and a gateway long after the Romans had gone. Sometime around 600, King Oswin of Bernicia was said to have been born within the walls of the fort.

The Northumbrian kings were anxious to buttress their authority by making clear connections with the Roman past. Its legacy lay all around, and it spoke of power and an ancient authority. Bede of Jarrow reckoned that Hadrian's Wall still stood close to its full height (and therefore presented an everyday barrier for farmers and travellers), and the forts along it would still have been impressive. Latin and the city of Rome and its papacy still lived in the work of the church. But Roman terminology was also attractive in the temporal world. During royal progresses the retinue of Northumbrian kings imitated Roman practices. Leading the procession into the king's estates, the *villa regia*, there was a standard-bearer carrying a Roman insignia called a *tufa*, a winged orb intended to add dignity to what followed. The royal warband became the *comitatus*, the royal chaplain the *pontifex*, and so on. Royal officials were known as *praefecti* and strongholds like Bamburgh were the *urbs regis*. All of this was intended to underpin the sense of the Northumbrian kings as inheritors of Rome. The memory of the Empire was still strong and still useful.

In a much more minor key, the parish structure began to develop as Christian conversion covered the land, and along the Wall it was adapted in a particular way. In the central sector the shape of each parish is oblong so that the lower-lying land near the Tyne formed the southern part and in the north it included a portion of the slopes reaching up to the Whin Sill. It was vital to include upland summer grazing, and the place-names along the Wall show where shepherds and herd-laddies built their temporary shelters. *Shield* or *shiel* is what these summer huts were called and, at Sewingshields, High Shield, Winshields and elsewhere they are remembered. The shepherds often used the angled walls of a milecastle or a turret as part of their shelter, and some were substantial as a result.

As the local economy developed, the plentiful dressed stone of the Wall became very attractive. Already quarried, its purpose long gone and forgotten, and free, all that it needed to become useful again was transport. In the early Middle Ages churches and monasteries were founded close to the Wall and, as they accumulated gifts and land, they began to build. At Tynemouth, Hexham and Carlisle courses of Roman stone can be seen in all of the early masonry. The northern boundary of Lanercost Priory, near Brampton, ran close to the line of the Wall. And after detailed examination of the remaining fabric, scholars have concluded that the magnificent church and its conventual buildings are constructed entirely from Roman stone. In two places Latin inscriptions can still be made out. One of them is upside down.

The western section of Hadrian's Wall, from around Birdoswald to the Solway coast at Bowness, has been heavily robbed out and much of it has entirely disappeared. In places even the Vallum is hard to make out. The central sector is much better preserved because of its relative remoteness, and also because of the presence of Border Reivers. An overwhelmingly pastoral and stock-rearing society, they had less interest in building and cultivation.

BRITANNIA PRIMA

Britain's westernmost Roman province lasted longest. As Anglo-Saxon kings and chieftains slowly extended their reach from the east, Britannia Prima appears to have maintained some sort of continuity. The towns at Wroxeter and Chester were not abandoned and may have been inhabited into the seventh century. Comprising Wales, the neighbouring part of the West Midlands, Gloucestershire, Devon and Cornwall, the old province may have sustained itself with the help of Germanic mercenaries. Pressure came not only from the east but also from across the Irish Sea. There was also a fleeting sense of the Empire and its citizens in the derivation of the Welsh word for Wales. Cymru comes from Combrogi (as does Cumbria and Cumberland) and it means 'Fellow Countrymen', literally, those who share a common border. And Wales and Cornwall survived long enough to preserve their versions of the P-Celtic language spoken in Britain before the Romans came. Only Breton and Basque outlasted the Empire and the all-pervasive influence of Latin in western Europe. When the old province at last fell to an invader in the 1280s, Edward I of England did two surprising things, both of which seemed to hark back to the days of Britannia Prima. Caernarfon Castle was built in imitation of the late Roman land-walls of Constantinople. And, more mysteriously, Edward had a body thought to be that of an emperor, Constantine II, brought to Wales for burial. Was he at last laying Rome in the west to rest?

The Wall survived well in the east, for the most part – until a substantial raid was mounted from Scotland, from the old territory of the Caledonii and the lands to the north. In 1745 what was known to his Gaelic-speaking soldiers as *Am Bliadhna Thearlaigh*, the Year of Charles, began. Invading England by the western route through Carlisle, the Jacobite generals wrongfooted the government armies marching against them. It proved impossible to get men and especially artillery from Newcastle to the west quickly, and, like the Romans, the Hanoverians decided that a road was needed. Commissioned by General Wade, it ran along the line of the Wall in the east for its first 48 kilometres. As a handy source of roadstone, much of the fabric was pulled down, pulverised and levelled. For long stretches the new road follows the course of the Wall exactly and the northern ditch lies immediately adjacent. Appropriately the B6318 is also known as the Military Road. Under the modern tarmac must lie a great deal of archaeology, not only the foundations of the Wall itself but also artefacts, coins, pottery and inscriptions associated with it.

The Military Road was never used in anger, and it did have the effect of making much of the remote central sector accessible to visitors. Historical interest grew and, with the establishment of the Society of Antiquaries in Newcastle in 1813, a forum for its formal expression came into being. Investigations, preservation and even some excavations began.

Many showed an interest in the antiquities on their doorstep, but none were as active or as determinant in the recent history of the Wall as John Clayton. Born in 1792, he was a lawyer by profession, a business-man by instinct and a passionate antiquarian. Between 1822 and 1887 he was Town Clerk of Newcastle, overseeing the spectacular expansion of the city. Working closely with the developer, Richard Grainger, he pushed through much of what became Georgian Newcastle. Clayton had the acumen to invest personally in Grainger's projects, something which has landed officials in Tyneside's local government in prison in the recent past. From the profits of development and from his huge legal practice, Clayton became wealthy and invested much of his money in actively preserving Hadrian's Wall. His house at Chesters had the fort of Cilurnum in its grounds, and by the time he was an old man four other forts and much of the central sector of the Wall were in his possession and under the protection of the Chesters Estate.

A biography of John Clayton summed up his thinking:

> To talk of preserving the Wall was useless as long as well-shaped, handy-sized stones lay ready to the hand of the farmer, and the carting away of its stones went forward merrily. The great pity of it was that it was the best portions of the Wall which were removed in this fashion, for the labourers naturally preferred to take the stones that were breast high in the standing wall to stooping and lifting them up from the ground into their carts.

Appalled at the continuing stone robbing, Clayton set his men on the huge task of preservation. Having bought the land across which the

Wall ran, gangs picked up the scatter of rubble and, with great care, rebuilt where they could. When the outer courses had been brought up to the same height, Clayton's men infilled the core with rubble, clay, mortar and earth. They then topped it off with turf to allow walking and to prevent too much rainwater from leaching into the fabric. So much of this sort of work was done in the central sector that it is sometimes known as Clayton's Wall.

Whatever modern archaeologists may think of his methods, John Clayton's role in the preservation of Hadrian's great project was absolutely critical. Using his financial muscle, he fended off almost all other interests. Without him there would now be a great deal less to see.

Anyone who doubts Clayton's pivotal role or sniffs at his methods should recall that threats to the Wall were not confined to the unenlightened nineteenth century. They continued well into the twentieth. At Cawfields and at Walltown, quarrying was still removing whole sections in the 1920s. But the greatest danger presented itself at a time when economic circumstances might easily have converted it into a reality. As coal mining in the Tyne Valley contracted, 800 men lost their jobs in the pits around Haltwhistle. For such a small community, it was a devastating blow, causing real hardship. But a saviour seemed to appear very quickly. Mr J. Wake of Darlington proposed to set up a new company in the area, Roman Stone Ltd, to begin quarrying along the Whin Sill. The stone lay near the surface, could easily be blasted out and freighted to market from Melkridge – and 500 new jobs would be created. The hungry families of Haltwhistle at last had some hope for a future. But there were protests from antiquarians, academics and others. Mr Wake compromised and promised to leave the Wall remains standing *where they were visible* on a sliver of whinstone. More protests claimed *that the Wall would be left on an unscalable knife-edge, with a 400 foot drop on either side*. After the likes of John Buchan and Rudyard Kipling became involved, the quarrying development was finally dropped. The Ancient Monuments Act was strengthened and the Wall was never again threatened in the same way.

Now, Hadrian's Wall is a World Heritage Site, one of only 800. A path has been created along its entire length, more and more people walk it each year, and facilities improve in step with them. More than a million people visited some part of the Wall in 2006. With the decline in agriculture, accelerated by outbreaks of foot-and-mouth disease (which in 2002 originated at Heddon on the Wall), tourism has become the biggest industry in north Northumberland and north Cumbria, especially in the central sector. Many farms now offer accommodation, pony-trekking, mountain-biking and much else. Almost two thousand years after his *mensores* pegged out the line of the Wall, the Emperor Hadrian has brought people back to gaze upon his works – and rejoice.

9

After Hadrian

Hadrian's Wall is the largest, most spectacular and one of the most enigmatic historical monuments in Britain. Nothing else approaches its vast scale: a land-wall 73 miles from east to west and a sea-wall stretching at least 26 and probably 50 miles down the Cumbrian coast. Many of its forts are as large as Britain's most formidable medieval castles, and the wide ditch dug to the south of the land-wall, the Vallum, is more monumental than any prehistoric earthwork.

And yet the story of the great Roman Wall, its builders and originators, was almost immediately misunderstood, confused or forgotten. Only five or six generations after the end of Roman Britain in the early fifth century the name of Hadrian had faded completely and been disconnected from his mighty creation, the dates of its construction had been got wildly wrong and the historical sequence of events had fallen badly out of kilter. The Wall still dominated the landscape, many thousands had lived along its length for three hundred years, a dozen great forts were still standing, inscriptions offering names and dates were everywhere – how did early historians fail to record even the rudiments of its story?

Gildas was probably a son of the Old Welsh-speaking kingdom of Strathclyde, born some time around AD 504 at Dumbarton on the Clyde. Having become a monk, he composed a fiery sermon *On the Ruin and Conquest of Britain*. Calling them ignorant tyrants, he raged against the corrupt and feckless contemporary British kings who were allowing the Picts and the Scots to raid from the north and pagan Germanic warriors from across the North Sea to settle large swathes of eastern and southern England. It is a splendid froth of invective probably composed in the 560s, and is one of the earliest written

British sources to survive in the post-Roman period. Interspersed amongst the insults are snippets of history, or at least tales which Gildas clearly believed were true. And some of them refer to Roman walls.

Magnus Maximus was an ambitious general in the late western Empire and in 383 he attempted to usurp the imperial throne. Having raised an army in Britain, he crossed the Channel to campaign in Europe, ultimately meeting defeat and execution at Aquileia in northern Italy. Gildas blamed Maximus for the troubles which then befell the old province of Britannia:

> After this, Britain is left deprived of all her soldiery and armed bands, of her cruel governors, and of the flower of her youth, who went with Maximus, but never again returned; and utterly ignorant as she was of the art of war, groaned in amazement for many years under the cruelty of two foreign nations – the Scots from the north-west, and the Picts from the north.

After tearful and piteous entreaties from an embassy of Britons, Rome sent a legion which promptly came into close conflict with the cruel enemies and slew great numbers of them. On the advice of their Roman rescuers, the British:

> now built a wall across the island from one sea to the other, which being manned with a proper force, might be a terror to the foes whom it was intended to repel, and a protection to their friends whom it covered. But this wall, being made of turf instead of stone, was of no use to that foolish people, who had no head to guide them.

Gildas was describing the Antonine Wall, built in turf between the Firths of Forth and Clyde on the orders of the Roman Emperor Antoninus Pius in the AD 140s. If he had been born in Dumbarton, very near the western terminal, Gildas would have known the old turf wall very well. His dating is badly wrong, reckoning its construction 250 years later, in the 390s. And Gildas also thought it the first great wall to be built in Britain, whereas it in fact postdates Hadrian's Wall. Perhaps the rapid abandonment of the Antonine Wall after 161 gave rise to the belief that it was of no use.

Another pathetic embassy to Rome, according to Gildas, produced a second expedition to Britain, and it was effective, *planting terrible swords upon the shoulders of their enemies, they mow them down like leaves which fall at the destined period*. This time the Romans set about building a second, much better, wall themselves.

> With the help of the miserable natives, [they] built a wall different from the former, by public and private contributions, and of the same structure as walls generally, extending in a straight line from sea to sea, between some cities, which, from fear of their enemies, had there by chance been built.

This seems like a description of Hadrian's Wall, with Roman Carlisle at the western end and perhaps Corbridge near the eastern. But it turned out to be no more effective than the turf wall, sighed Gildas. Once the Romans had departed, the assaults from the Picts and Scots resumed:

> To oppose them was placed on the heights a garrison equally slow to fight and ill adapted to run away, a useless and panic-struck company, who clambered away days and nights on their unprofitable watch. Meanwhile the hooked weapons of their enemies were not idle, and our countrymen were dragged from the wall and dashed against the ground.

Even allowing for the fact that he was writing an invective, Gildas' account is surprisingly poor. Only the persistent attacks of the Picts and the Scots appear to be historically accurate. Astonishingly, he believed that the construction of Hadrian's Wall was recent, not long before his own lifetime, 400 years later than its actual foundation in AD 122.

Gildas saw himself as a beacon of learning in the dimming days of the Dark Ages, in a post-Roman Britain which was sliding into anarchy: as a paragon of literacy, Latinity and a devout Christian aware of European as well as British history. How did he get it all so wrong?

A truly great historian, Bede of Jarrow, was similarly confused about who built what and when and why. He lived in the shadow of Hadrian's Wall; his monastery and his church of St Paul's were built with Roman stone robbed out of nearby forts and from the Wall itself, and, like the early church, the Northumbrian kings who were his patrons and protectors saw themselves in part as the heirs of Britannia, the Roman province which lasted almost 400 years. But in his *Ecclesiastical History of the English People*, completed in 731, Bede still gets it wrong, although not as badly as Gildas. A superb researcher, a genuine scholar who checked his facts, looked for more than one source, he adapted the BC/AD system of dating and made it a standard so that he could get the sequences of events in the right order and make all clearer. He understood that the stone wall north of the Tyne was built first, but he believed that it was done on the initiative of the Emperor Septimius Severus, and nowhere mentions Hadrian. That places its construction in the early third century not the early second. Also Bede insisted that it was an earthwork first, a wall of turf topped by a timber palisade. Then he adopts Gildas' version of events and adds some helpful personal observation:

> This famous and still conspicuous wall was built from public and private resources, with the Britons lending assistance. It is eight feet in breadth, and twelve in height; and, as can clearly be seen to this day, ran straight from east to west.

Bede had obviously seen the Wall for himself. In fact some scholars believe that he was born at a place called Ad Murum, literally 'At the Wall', a settlement on the site of what became the city of Newcastle. Bede was naturally curious, and it is surprising that he did not undertake research into a phenomenon which lay so close at hand – and that he was content to accept Gildas' garbled account.

After the eighth century the Wall seemed to pass out of knowledge, its mighty ruins mouldered in the landscape, overgrown and ignored. Medieval churches near the line used it as a quarry of dressed stone, and farmers made dykes for their inbye fields out of the tumbledown turrets and forts.

It would be many centuries before the story of Hadrian's Wall became clearer, before its context was understood and before archaeology could begin to reveal an astonishing wealth of information. The sixteenth-century antiquary William Camden was greatly impressed with the scale and sweep of the Roman Wall but unable to see as much of the magnificent central section as he would have liked. Border Reivers – *rank robbers* he called them – had occupied at least one of the major forts and made the countryside unsafe for travellers. The study of Hadrian's Wall developed real momentum in the eighteenth century when all things Roman and Greek were becoming generally fashionable. William Stukely and other scholars took a detailed interest and by the nineteenth century a formidable group of northern antiquaries at last began to uncover the real narrative behind this amazing monument.

10

Days on the Wall

Imagining the Wall as it was is almost impossible – especially in the east. With the constant hurtle and buzz of traffic, the sprawl of Newcastle and the confining canyons of the city centre, it is difficult to get even a sense of the rise and fall of the land. But at the Castle, what people often call the Castle Keep, in the heart of the city, it is possible to climb up and out of the noise and the river of people to see something of what the Romans saw. Wide stone stairs make for an easy ascent to the battlements and the flat roof. In both directions the view along the river is sweeping, and immediately to the south is the narrowing of the Gateshead Gorge. The Tyne is wide both upriver, particularly at the Dunston Coal Staithes, and downriver as it meanders towards the coast. But below the Castle Keep it is funnelled into the gorge where Hadrian had his engineers build the bridge named after him, approximately on the line of the Swing Bridge. It is the shortest crossing-point and no accident that the High Level, the Tyne Bridge and two others stand nearby. The ground falls away steeply from the Castle Keep down to the quayside, and opposite, on the Gateshead bank, the Hilton Hotel is perched on an equally steep slope.

To the north of the keep, the main railway line from Scotland crashes straight through to Newcastle Central Station. Bisecting the site of the castle with a black, smoke-stained viaduct, it is a piece of bloody-minded Victorian progress. Castle? Who cares? We need a railway and this is where it needs to go. Oddly, that sort of bloody-mindedness sits well on the line of Hadrian's Wall. He would not have hesitated either. Under the arches of the now-scruffy viaduct are two bits of exposed archaeology, the remains of a Roman fort built after AD 122. With no information boards to explain, overshadowed by Victorian progress, few people notice them.

Wallsend is the eastern terminal of the Wall, but the Castle Keep seems a good place to welcome the Emperor to Britannia. And, for some obscure reason, it is better to start an episodic journey along the Wall in the east. Most people who walk the new path start at Wallsend and finish up 135 kilometres later at Bowness-on-Solway. Perhaps their instincts tell them to follow the sun, rising behind them over the North Sea and setting beyond the Solway. Better than walking widdershins.

In the 1920s and 1930s the suburb of Benwell was built up along the West Road, and a reservoir flooded over most of the site of the fort of Condercum. Nevertheless two fascinating relics can still be seen, lying only a street or two apart. In what looks like someone's front garden, stand the foundations of a small temple. Dedicated to Antenociticus, a Celtic god, it is squat and surprisingly untouched, with no graffiti or vandalism. Perhaps the powerful spirit of Antenociticus is not entirely fled. One of his neighbours grows potatoes, double-digging in compost and horse-muck every winter. His collection of Roman artefacts covers every flat surface in the sitting room, and beautifully dressed stones line a short driveway.

Around the corner is something genuinely jaw-dropping. At the foot of a suburban crescent, there is a well-preserved section of the Vallum. Wide and deep, vastly out of proportion with its everyday surroundings, it has the monumental remains of a crossing and a gateway. Only the footing of the piers of the arch are left but they still somehow dwarf the houses, the parked cars and the garden sheds. The sheer incongruity is very attractive. The lady who lives in the house just to the north of the Vallum crossing has a key for the gate, and from her garden (with a Roman rockery) it is possible to see why the fort at Benwell was called Condercum, the Viewpoint Fort. Between the gable ends of the neighbours' houses and over their garage roofs, it is possible to see over to the Gateshead Fells and, dimly, make out the unmistakable shape of the Angel of the North. These two sites are badly signposted and seen only by the tenacious.

Back out on the West Road, which runs arrow-straight along the line of the Wall, more surprises wait. At the junction with the A1, a terrifying roundabout, stands Denton Turret and a 40-metre section of Wall. And on the far side of the maelstrom of cars and trucks thundering south, there is another run, two or three courses high this time.

Once on the B6318, the Military Road, the presence of the Wall becomes clearer. On the right, the northern ditch begins to appear and, as the housing thins out and farmland takes over, traces of the Vallum can sometimes be made out on the left. But the most obvious memory of Rome is the road itself. Straight and with commanding views on either side, it stretches westwards, looking for the high ground and the cliffs of the Whin Sill. At a much quieter roundabout, one with an old name, the Port Gate, it is worth making a detour, turning south off the Wall, down Dere Street, the A68, a few miles to Corbridge.

The Roman site (no one seems quite sure what to call it) west of Corbridge gives the first and only sense of something quintessentially Roman – town life. The site is arranged around the Stanegate, what seems in this context to be a main street. A good reconstruction drawing on the information board helps. On the left there is the hulking outline of a granary, and the stumps of columns outside its portals add to the atmosphere of Rome-on-Tyne. In the summertime English Heritage mounts Roman festivals at the weekends with re-enactors, Roman cookery, falconry, crafts and much else.

A few kilometres after the Port Gate, the Military Road begins to descend into the lovely valley of the North Tyne. At the crossroads with the A6079, it is rewarding to turn left and park at the sign for Brunton Turret. This is one of the first places where the Wall stands high. More than ten courses, well above head height, the turret is placed on a steep bank, no ditch needed in front. But its aspect to the north is completely blinded by a thick wood of mature trees. Nevertheless it is atmospheric, a place where it is possible to hear whispers of the long past, men soldiering, talking, complaining, stamping their feet in cold weather, looking up the valley in the summer sunshine. To the west, across the North Tyne, there is a good view of Chesters Fort and its impressive bath house. But a general sense of the first substantial fort on the Wall is made difficult by the way in which it has been excavated, with bits exposed in a version of keyhole archaeology and surrounded by fences.

Climbing up the steep hill at Walwick, the B6318 leads to suddenly higher ground and a very different landscape. After reaching its most elevated point at Limestone Corner, the Wall turns slightly to cross a long stretch of moorland. Perhaps the bleakest traverse in all its 135 kilometres, the path runs past the fort at Carrawburgh, the Mithraeum and Coventina's Well. In poor conditions it must be a long, head-down slog on foot.

The road swings abruptly away from the Wall ditch and crosses the Vallum at Archer's Wood. It is difficult to escape the sense that the modern road has taken a wrong turning and the grassed-over, ancient earthwork points the right way. The Wall at last makes its way up to Sewingshields Crag and begins its most dramatic run along the Whin Sill.

The fall of the ground cants the site of Housesteads Fort to the south and its impressive extent can easily be seen from the road below. Many travellers are tempted to stop and, even though the car park is some distance away – and followed by an uphill walk – Housesteads is the most visited fort on the Wall. From the gateway down at the Knag Burn, to the east, the fort looks commanding, even menacing. If anyone is seized with an urge to walk along a section of the Wall, Housesteads is a good place to begin. For almost 15 kilometres to the west, the Military Road is close and the Hadrian's Wall bus, the aptly named 122, can be picked up at frequent intervals to take walkers back to where they left their cars.

The glorious vistas of Hotbank Crags, Crag Lough, Sycamore Gap and Steel Rigg are all nearby and the thirsty may wish to break off at the car park near where the Wall dives down and up and round a corner. Only half a mile to the south, downhill, stands the Twice Brewed Inn, with one of the best selections of good beer anywhere. The food is wholesome and plentiful, the service excellent and the upholstery just comfortable enough to extend lunch on all but the sunniest days. The 122 stops outside.

The heartbeat of the Wall, the place where it comes most vividly to life, is near at hand. At Vindolanda, where Britain's greatest archaeological treasures, the lists and letters, were found, there is so much to see and understand that at least a day is needed – even for the most casual visitor. At the best of the Wall's other sites, history seems to have happened, all is well preserved but presented in a freeze-frame. Nothing more needs to be said. At Vindolanda it is different. History keeps happening as the excavation programme continues. Each summer season Andrew Birley and his team open up new areas, and visitors are invited to watch and ask questions. Frequently, objects are found, cleaned and discussed minutes after they come out of the ground. There is no anxious, academic guardedness, only a willingness to share in new knowledge.

The museum is excellent, the artefacts fresh and well displayed, and a well-made film runs on a loop to explain their context. All that is missing is a special exhibition telling the story of the lists and letters – and showing the best of them. Because of the need for and cost of preservation, the great treasures of Vindolanda are currently kept at the British Museum in London. They belong where they were written, in the north, and perhaps one day money will be found to bring them home.

At Cawfield milecastle quarrying has taken a great bite out of the Wall. It seems as though the milecastle just escaped, tottering on the edge of extinction. The northern gateway, leading over a precipice, is a wonderful, timeless example of military daftness, and the sloping site must have been a nightmare for its builders. To the south stretches one of the very best runs of the Vallum.

More quarrying at Walltown has removed another section, but up on the crags there is a turret which predated the arrival of Hadrian. Looking out over Thirlwall Common, the dark fringes of the great Kielder Forest can be made out, and away to the west the glint of the Solway. At the nearby Roman Army Museum at Carvoran, the centrepiece of an excellent display is an animated film, *Eagle's Eye*, and it offers a superb reconstruction of what the Wall and its garrison looked like.

The landscape shelves steeply down at Greenhead and undulates towards the valley of the River Irthing. At Gilsland, Poltross milecastle lies at the end of a winding path, half hidden by woods and immediately adjacent to the railway line connecting Carlisle and Newcastle. The walls still stand high but any sense of the past is instantly wiped when a train whooshes past, just across the fence.

The sector of the Wall between Poltross and Birdoswald Fort is less visited than it should be. In its way, with rollercoaster sweeps down to the site of the bridge over the Irthing at Willowford and, up the other side, it is just as spectacular as the Whin Sill. The section of the Wall leading from the milecastle above the river up to the fort is one of the longest and most substantial. Birdoswald is the last great site on the line. Excavated and exposed in only one corner, it nevertheless has high walls and massive gateways. Racing back across the centuries, a sense of what it was like comes quickly to mind at Birdoswald.

To the west, over towards Carlisle, the Wall quickly dwindles and even the Vallum is hard to see as it crosses fertile and frequently ploughed farmland on its way to the Eden Valley. Beyond it, walkers keep to the road leading from Carlisle to the Solway coast, and then follow the shoreline until the end of the path and the Land-Wall at Bowness-on-Solway. As they at last reach the village, those nearing journey's end are directed to a path offering good views across the firth to Annan and the Galloway hills. About halfway along they meet a wooden structure which marks the end of their marathon. More like a bus shelter than anything else, it is a little disappointing. In fact the Emperor Hadrian would have been appalled. Surely a triumphal arch would have been more fitting – for the reality is that, after two thousand years, the Wall remains triumphant.

Appendix 1

Significant Roman Emperors During the Time of Britannia

Claudius	AD 41 to AD 54
Nero	54 to 68
Vespasian	69 to 79
Titus	79 to 81
Domitian	81 to 96
Nerva	96 to 98
Trajan	98 to 117
Hadrian	117 to 138
Antoninus Pius	138 to 161
Marcus Aurelius	161 to 180
Commodus	180 to 192
Septimius Severus	193 to 211
Caracalla	211 to 217
Elagabalus	218 to 222
Severus Alexander	222 to 235
Maximinus	235 to 238
Gordian III	238 to 244
Philip the Arab	244 to 249
Diocletian	284 to 305
Carausius	286 to 293 (usurper emperor in Britain only)
Allectus	293 to 296 (succeeds Carausius only in Britain)
Constantine I	307 to 337
Valentinian	364 to 375
Theodosius	379 to 395
Magnus Maximus	383 to 388 (usurper in Britain and the West)
Honorius	393 to 408
Constantine III	407 to 411 (usurper in Britain only in the West)

Appendix 2

Significant Governors of Britannia

Aulus Plautius	43 to 47
Ostorius Scapula	47 to 52
Didius Gallus	52 to 57
Q. Verianus	57 to 58
Suetonius Paullinus	58 to 61
Petronius Turpilianus	61 to 63
Trebellius Maximus	63 to 69
Vettius Bolanus	69 to 71
Petilius Cerialis	71 to 73
Julius Frontinus	73 to 77
Julius Agricola	77 to 84
Unknown	
Sallustius Lucullus	84
Metilius Nepos	98
Avidius Quietus	98 to 103
Neratius Marcellus	103 to 108
Appius Bradua	108
Pompeius Falco	122
Platorius Nepos	122 to 127
Trebius Germanus	127 to 128
Julius Severus	128 to 132
Mummius Sisenna	135
Lollius Urbicus	139 to 142
Papirius Aelianus	146
Julius Verus	158
Statius Priscus	161 to 162
Calpurnius Agricola	163
Antistius Adventus	169
Ulpius Marcellus	178

Ulpius Marcellus again	184
Helvius Pertinax	185 to 187
Clodius Albinus	192 to 197
Virius Lupus	197
Valerius Pudens	205
Alfenus Senecio	205 to 207

After the division of Britannia into two provinces (and later four, and then five), its governors become less significant figures.

Bibliography

The Oxford World's Classics and the Penguin Classics series are indispensable, and both a joy and an adornment. I have used many of the translations over the years but the following were crucial in the research for this book.

Herodotus, *The Histories*, trans. Robin Waterfield, Oxford University Press, 1998

Pliny the Younger, *Complete Letters*, trans. P.G. Walsh, Oxford University Press, 2006

Plutarch, *Roman Lives*, trans. Robin Waterfield, Oxford Paperbacks, 1998

Lives of the Later Caesars, trans. A.R. Birley, Penguin Classics, 1976

Suetonius, *Lives of the Caesars*, trans. Catherine Edwards, Oxford Paperbacks, 2000

Tacitus, *Agricola, and Germany*, trans. A.R. Birley, Oxford Paperbacks, 1999

Tacitus, *Annals of Imperial Rome*, trans. Michael Grant, Penguin Classics, 1956

Secondary sources for a study of Hadrian's Wall are excellent; here are those which were most useful to me:

Bedoyere, de la, G., *Hadrian's Wall*, NPI Media Group, 1998

Birley, A.R., *Garrison Life at Vindolanda*, History Press, 2002

Birley, A.R., *Hadrian, the Restless Emperor*, Routledge, 1997

Bowman, A.K., *Life and Letters on the Roman Frontier*, British Museum Press, 1976

Breeze, D.J. and Dobson, B., *Hadrian's Wall*, Penguin, 1976

Breeze, D.J., *The Antonine Wall*, John Donald, 2006

Burton, A., *Hadrian's Wall Path*, Aurum Press, 2003
Crow, J., *Housesteads*, History Press, 1995
Davies, J., *A History of Wales*, Penguin, 1990
Davies, N., *Europe: A History*, Pimlico, 1996
Fraser, A.F., *The Native Horses of Scotland*, John Donald, 1987
Frere, S.S., *Britannia*, Pimlico, 1967
Goldsworthy, A., *Caesar*, Phoenix, 2000
Hill, P., *The Construction of Hadrian's Wall*, History Press, 2000
Johnson, S., *Hadrian's Wall*, Batsford, 1989
Moffat, A., *The Borders: A History from Earliest Times*, Birlinn, 2002
Morris, J., *The Age of Arthur*, Weidenfeld & Nicolson, 1973
Salway, P., *The Oxford Illustrated History of Roman Britain*, Oxford University Press, 1993
Scarre, C., *The Penguin Historical Atlas of Ancient Rome*, Penguin, 1995
Thomas, A.C., *Celtic Britain*, Thames & Hudson, 1986
Towill, S., *Carlisle*, Phillimore, 1991
Watson, W.J., *The Celtic Place-Names of Scotland*, Birlinn, 1993
Wilmott, A., *Birdoswald Roman Fort*, Heritage Services, 1995

Index

Note: Material enclosed in a box is indicated by '*box*' after the page number. *Passim* indicates scattered non-continuous references over a page range. Roman names are generally indexed under the second element (*nomen*) followed by the third element. The elements are explained in the boxed text on page 27 and the list of Governors on page 259 follows this pattern. Emperors and well-known classical authors are indexed under the name by which they are commonly known. Book titles beginning with 'The' and places beginning with 'St' are indexed as spelt but Christian saints are found under their names.